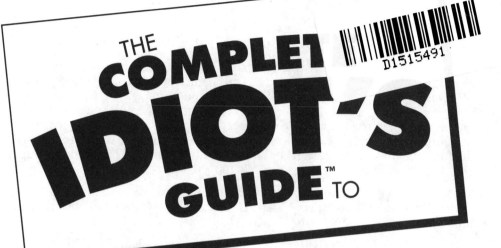

THE COMPLETE IDIOT'S GUIDE™ TO

Changing Careers

by William Charland

alpha books

A Division of Macmillan General Reference
A Simon & Schuster Macmillan Company
1633 Broadway, New York, NY 10019

To Phoebe.

Copyright © 1998 Alpha Books

Macmillan Publishing books may be purchased for business or sales promotional use. For information please write: Special Markets Department, Macmillan Publishing USA, 1633 Broadway, New York, NY 10019.

THE COMPLETE IDIOT'S GUIDE name and design are trademarks of Macmillan, Inc.

International Standard Book Number: 0-02-861977-3
Library of Congress Catalog Card Number: A catalogue record is available from the Library of Congress.

00 99 98   8 7 6 5 4 3 2 1

Interpretation of the printing code: the rightmost number of the first series of numbers is the year of the book's printing; the rightmost number of the second series of numbers is the number of the book's printing. For example, a printing code of 98-1 shows that the first printing occurred in 1998.

Printed in the United States of America

The Complete Idiot's Reference Card

Career Change Checklist:

➤ Keep your cool. The instinct to move quickly to find another job similar to your last one can lead to long-term career dissatisfaction.

➤ Remember: Unemployment, misemployment, and mismanagement are the primary causes of career dissatisfaction. Which category best describes your situation?

➤ Know what kind of group you work best in. Work groups are social groups; if your values mirror the values of the group where you work, you'll be much more likely to be happy and productive on the job.

➤ If it's appropriate to your situation, consider part-time work that's just plain fun. It lends some order to the day, keeps money coming in, and leaves you some energy at the end of your shift to focus on career issues.

➤ Ask yourself: "Where are the markets? What needs doing? Where am I? What can I do? How can I connect with the markets?"

➤ When analyzing the latest "hot new career fields," ask yourself: "How important are the problems those jobs are intended to solve?"

➤ Get a better handle on your current aptitudes by practicing explaining to others what you do.

➤ Take the time to reflect on exhilarating "peak experiences" on the job. Identify what you've done and how you did it.

➤ Identify your core competencies—the fundamental, underlying skills you use to solve problems and develop income.

➤ Conduct a "trial search" in an employment field that interests you.

➤ Check out temporary employment services. They may offer notable opportunities in the field you're exploring.

➤ Put your time and energy into direct contact and networking activities. Be skeptical of any career-change strategy that stalls when other people don't take action.

➤ Decision-makers within today's new-style "diamond-shaped" organizations may react more positively to a proposal for a project than an application for a job.

alpha
books

➤ Identify the value you've delivered on the job by thinking of people who benefited from working with you.

➤ Engage in "professional recycling"—the act of taking what you've learned and using it to learn something new.

➤ Remember: For adults, the first option to consider is always self-managed learning.

➤ Make your own, thoughtful decision when it comes to an advanced degree. Don't be misled by the rhetoric of a specific educational institution.

➤ If you try to get a job within a big corporation, don't try to do so as a full-time manager.

➤ The best maxim to follow in organizations of any size is probably the time-less "Find a need and fill it."

➤ Don't bury yourself in the help wanted ads.

➤ Don't fall prey to tunnel vision—remember that you need many job leads, not just one.

➤ Develop an effective phone presentation.

➤ Do the research! The biggest branch of a major metropolitan library system is an excellent place to track down information about your target companies.

➤ Remember that you may turn off some contacts by giving them a resume early on in your discussions. Don't distribute resumes randomly, and don't mistake a flurry of resumes for a job search.

➤ Be prepared to ask intelligent questions.

➤ When you can, make a detailed written offer specifying the details of a contract-based assignment you'd take on for the target company.

➤ Remember: Even a post-interview rejection can lead to opportunity—so follow up on those "no" answers and stay on the prospective employer's radar screen.

Alpha Development Team

Brand Manager
Kathy Nebenhaus

Executive Editor
Gary M. Krebs

Managing Editor
Bob Shuman

Senior Editor
Nancy Mikhail

Development Editors
Nader Mikhail
Jennifer Perillo

Production Editors
Jessica Ford
Christy Wagner

Technical Editor
Rich Seller

Editorial Assistant
Maureen Horn

Cover Designer
Kevin Spear

Illustrator
Judd Winick

Designer
Glenn Larsen

Indexer
Nadia Ibrahim

Production Team
Aleata Howard, Mary Hunt, Kristy Nash, Angela Perry,
Laure Robinson, Lisa Stumpf

Contents at a Glance

Part 1: Changes   **1**

  1 Welcome Back to the Jungle   3

  2 Working It Out: Career Change Survival Strategies   11

  3 Ask Questions Now or Forever Hold Your Peace   21

  4 Good News, Houston. We Have a Problem!   27

  5 The Most Important Sale You'll Ever Make   33

  6 Hey, Buddy. Learn This!   45

  7 Welcome to Act I of "Your Career Change"   57

  8 Phone Calls, Resumes, and More Rules Not to Live By   71

  9 Networking 101   81

Part 2: Directions   **91**

  10 Diamonds in the Rough   93

  11 New Jobs for Generalists   101

  12 Thinking Like an Employer   111

  13 Recycling Skills   119

  14 A Matter of Degrees   125

  15 Big Employers, Small Employers   137

  16 Goals 101   147

Part 3: Connections   **157**

  17 How Not to Conduct a Job Search in Today's Economy   159

  18 Getting the Information You Need   167

  19 Letting the World Know on Paper   179

  20 Letting the World Know in Person   193

  21 Following Up   203

Part 4: Challenges   213

22 Advice for Older Workers   215

23 Advice for Younger Workers   225

24 When You're New to the Field   223

25 Overcoming Problems in Your Background   241

26 So You're Not a "Computer Person"   249

27 Call It a Comeback!   257

A Online Resources   271

B The Current Hot Employment Industries   273

C Associations and Advocacy Groups   279

D Employment Letters for the Career Changer   285

E Sample Resumes for the Career Changer   297

F Glossary   311

Index   317

Contents

Part 1: Changes   **1**

1 Welcome Back to the Jungle   **3**

Working in the Best and Worst of Times 4
Jobs and the People Who Hate Them 5
When the Job Is Just Not You 5
Good Morning. You're Fired! 6
Love the Job, but Everything Else Stinks 7
A Career Is a Terrible Thing to Waste 9
The Least You Need to Know 10

2 Working It Out: Career Change Survival Strategies   **11**

Job, Adventure, or Both? 11
Consider Some Alternative Thinking 14
Dollars and Sense 15
Don't Wing It! 15
If You Fall, Can You Still Afford to Get Up? 15
Check Your Retirement Funds 15
Cancel the Yacht and the Trip Around the World 16
Look Before You Leap! 16
Warning: Clock Watching Can Be
  Hazardous to Your Career 16
In Praise of Odd Jobs 18
The Least You Need to Know 18

3 Ask Questions Now or Forever Hold Your Peace   **21**

You're the Boss 21
Rule 1: There Are No Rules 22
Skills! Skills! My Kingdom for Some Skills! 22
Time to Pop the Big Questions 23
Where Are the Markets? 23
Relationships 24
Where Are You? 24
How Can You Connect with the Markets? 25
Big Questions! 25
The Least You Need to Know 26

4 Good News, Houston. We Have a Problem!   **27**

Your Job, Should You Accept It, Doesn't Exist Yet 27
    Banker Gives Birth to Financial Planner 28
    Help Wanted: Telling People Where to Drill 29
What the World Needs Now Is More New Problems 30
To Retrain or Not to Retrain 31
The Least You Need to Know 32

5 The Most Important Sale You'll Ever Make   **33**

The Toughest Sell of All 33
Defining Yourself 34
    What Field Do You Play In? 34
    The Title/Degree Thing 35
    So Whaddya Do? 35
Testing, Testing… 36
Cop an Aptitude 36
Hey, Wait a Minute! 37
Twin Peaks 37
    Step One 38
    Step Two 38
Prove It! 39
Hard Skills versus Soft Skills 40
    How Not to Get a Job Offer 40
Time to Try on Your Strong Suits 40
    Projecting 41
    Producing 41
    Promoting 41
    Balancing the Three Ps 41
You'll Need More Than That! 42
    The Good and the I Can't Stand It 42
Tracking Down What Works 42
    Staying in Balance 43
The Least You Need to Know 43

6 Hey, Buddy. Learn This!   **45**

Is a Skill Ever Really Obsolete? 45
    Reality Check 46
    Plans for Lifelong Learning 46

Skills as Building Blocks 46
Branching Out but Staying Rooted 47
    Tracking 'Em Down 47
Where Do They Come From? 48
Everyody's Got Something Special 49
    Tinkering, Refining, Expanding 49
    Looking at Yourself 50
Changing Lanes 50
Another Line Down the Middle of the Page 51
    What It Might Look Like 52
Peak Experiences Part Two 53
    Peak Experiences in School? You're Kidding! 53
    The ABCs of Learning 53
    The Three Senses 54
    Uh, Teacher—Is This Going to Help Me Right Now? 54
Go for It! 55
The Least You Need to Know 55

7 Welcome to Act I of "Your Career Change"   57

Testing the Waters 58
A Friend of a Friend 58
Help Wanted Ads 59
    Downers, Downers, Everywhere 60
    Yeah, but Look at This Opening! 60
Don't Call 'Em "Headhunters" 61
    Now for the Bad News 61
    They Want to Hire You! Quick, Get Out of Town! 61
For Members Only 62
    Beware the Gloomy Group! 62
Back to School 63
    Learn, Learn, Learn 63
    Or Teach, Teach, Teach 63
Hanging Out with the Insiders 64
    What to Look for 64
    Meet and Greet 64
Just Passing Through 65
    The Way We Were 65
    Invasion of the Temp Snatchers 66
Paging Uncle Sam 67

Private Matters 67
  Should You Seek Professional Help? 68
  The Benefit of Experience (Maybe) 68
What's Next? 68
The Least You Need to Know 69

8 Phone Calls, Resumes, and More Rules Not to Live By   71

3-2-1: Direct Contact 71
This Ain't Your Father's Workplace! 73
  Just Tell Me What to Do! 73
  It's Not My Job 74
  It's All Down in Black and White 74
  I Solemnly Swear… 74
  It's Not What You Know, It's Who You Know 74
  Hello? Personnel Office? 74
  I Don't Make Calls 75
  No, Thanks. I'm Looking for a Real Job! 75
  Thank God That's Done! 75
  Can You See a Pattern Emerging? 75
Hi! I'm Already Working! 76
  The Independent Contractor 76
  Managing Change 77
Same as It Ever Was 77
What Do You Do? 78
  Three Familiar Steps 78
  Covering All the Bases 78
  Anyone Can Network 79
The Least You Need to Know 79

9 Networking 101   81

Call It What You Will 82
  Identify the People Who Matter 82
  Make Friends with Strangers 82
  Good Opening Lines 84
  Take Notes 85
  Keep It Up! 86
Introverts and Extroverts 86
Enough About Me. Let's Talk About Me! 87
So, When Can We Get Together? 88
Let's Review 89
The Least You Need to Know 89

Part 2: Directions   **91**

10 Diamonds in the Rough   **93**

What Kinds of Employers Are Out There? 94
   Climbing the Corporate Pyramid 94
   Diamonds Are a Career Changer's Best Friend 95
Working with Diamonds 96
Mixed Messages 98
Adapting to the Shape of Things to Come 99
   Another Option 100
The Least You Need to Know 100

11 New Jobs for Generalists   **101**

Anybody Seen My Career Ladder Lately? 102
Life, Liberty, and the Pursuit of Change 102
Three Paths to Career Change 103
   The Advanced Slope 103
   The Beginner Slope 103
   The Intermediate Slope 104
Exploring a Middle-of-the-Road Strategy 104
   Looking Beyond Job Titles 104
   Looking Beyond Industry Stereotypes 105
   Looking Beyond Industry "Downturns" 106
Jobs versus Skills 107
How to Build a Bridge 108
He Who Snoozes, Loses 108
   Adapt and You Shall Survive 108
   If It's Good Enough for Big Companies,
    It's Good Enough for You 109
   A Balancing Act 109
   The Least You Need to Know 110

12 Thinking Like an Employer   **111**

A Brief Refresher 111
Results Are the Name of the Game 112
   Of People and Products 113
   Try It Yourself! 114

Toward the Informed Interview 114
Questions Employers Like to Hear 114
   Value Means...Producing in Chaos 115
   Value Means...Carrying the Ball over the Goal
     Line Yourself 116
   Value Means...Asking About What You're Up
     Against 116
Two-Way Streets 117
The Least You Need to Know 118

13 Recycling Skills   **119**

Learning "Inside Out" 120
   Turning On to Inside Out 121
   How It May Work 121
Outside-In Learning 122
   The Power of "Need to Know" 122
   Hands On! 122
Inside Out or Outside In? 123
On-the-Job Training (You Hope) 124
Course Matters 124
The Least You Need to Know 124

14 A Matter of Degrees   **125**

Questions and More Questions 125
The Power of "What?" 126
   How Much Knowledge? 126
   What Needs Strengthening? 126
   What Kind of Sheepskin? 127
The Power of "How?" 127
   On Your Own 127
   Help Me Get My Feet Back on the Ground... 128
   Pomp and Circumstance 129
The Sad Truth About Higher Learning 130
   Degree-Mania 130
   Two Years and Out 130
   Beyond Narrow Skills 131
   Don't Buy the Okey-Doke! 132

And Don't Forget… 133
    Logging On 133
    Want to Learn? Watch TV! 133
    Get Involved! 134
It Never Ends! 134
The Least You Need to Know 135

15 Big Employers, Small Employers   **137**

The Lunch Date 137
Mismatched Mindsets 138
Questions Revisited 139
Brand Management for Yourself 140
The Vanishing Manager? 141
Big Company, Small Company 142
    Issues, Anyone? 142
    Pink Slip? Who Cares? 143
    The Power of the "Dead-End Job" 143
Could You Do That? 144
    Words, Words, Words 144
    Information, Please 144
Drum Roll, Please… 145
The Least You Need to Know 145

16 Goals 101   **147**

Taking the Initiative 147
But I Don't Know Enough About the Industry! 148
Questions About Your Career Goals 149
Two Alternatives 154
    Situation One: You Don't Fit in 154
    Situation Two: You Know Where You Belong 155
What Now? 155
The Least You Need to Know 156

Part 3: Connections — 157

17 How Not to Conduct a Job Search in Today's Economy — 159

Emphasize Solutions, Not Positions! 160
What Doesn't Work 160
   Burying Yourself in the Want Ads 160
   Falling Prey to Tunnel Vision 161
   Getting too Casual 161
   Getting too Weird for the Market 162
   Terrifying or Infuriating the Decision-Maker 163
   Sounding Like You're Desperate 163
   Dos and Don'ts 165
Words to the Wise 165
The Least You Need to Know 166

18 Getting the Information You Need — 167

What About the Internet? 168
Your Primary Resource Is (Gasp!) Human 168
   Business Directories 169
   Company Information 170
   Printed Indexes 170
   Business Information Handbooks 171
   Directories for Market Analysis/Demographics 171
   Career Development and Job Search Directories 172
   Print Guides to Electronic Databases 173
   Online Electronic Databases 173
   CD-ROM Databases 174
Data Overload? Naaah… 174
   Does Anyone Get Hired via the Internet? 175
   Who Are You, Anyway? 175
   Handle with Care! 176
   Pluses and Minuses 176
So Is the Internet Bad? 176
   DO Start Big 176
   DO Focus on Highly Relevant Newsgroups 177

DO Use the Internet for Specific Company Research ... 177
DON'T Waste Time with Virtual Job Fairs 177
DON'T Think the Internet Is the Only Place for a
Job Search 177
The Least You Need to Know 178

19 Letting the World Know on Paper 179

Culture Connections 179
Use It, Don't Abuse It 180
Surprise: You're the Expert! 180
Length 181
Layout 181
Opening Paragraph 181
Professional Experience 182
Education 182
Accomplishments 183
Closing Paragraph 183
And Whatever You Do... 183
So How Do You Use It? 184
And the $64,000 Question Is... 188
DO Develop a "Basic Resume" that Only You See 188
DO Use Your Resume as a Visual Aid 188
DO Forward Targeted Resumes to Networking Allies ... 189
DON'T Distribute Resumes Randomly 189
DON'T Mail Resumes... 189
DON'T Send Electronic Gobbledygook 190
DON'T Mistake a Resume for a Career Search 190
The Least You Need to Know 191

20 Letting the World Know in Person 193

This Is for Real! 193
Two Models 194
The Stakes Are High! 194
That's a Lot of Work! 195
So What Do I Do? 195
Do the Research! 196
How to Shine When the Spotlight Is on You 196
Don't Let This Happen to You 197
The Right Life Story 197

Any Questions? 198
   Turning the Tables 198
   So What Do You Ask? 198
Interviewers Who Need a Clue 198
What You're Trying to Get Across 199
Intriguing Variations 200
The Least You Need to Know 201

21 Following Up   **203**

Immediately After the Interview 203
Now What? 204
What's in the Letter? 205
Mixed Signals 206
What If They Say "No"? 207
Yeah! They Made an Offer! 208
Check It Out 209
The Least You Need to Know 211

Part 4: Challenges   **213**

22 Advice for Older Workers   **215**

Why Work? 215
What You're Up Against 216
   It Doesn't Have to Be Obvious 216
   Block That Stereotype! 217
The Road You'll Be Traveling 217
Creative Employment in Later Years 218
   Presidents, Anyone? 218
   ACE It! 218
   Computer Power 219
What's the Right Kind of Job for Older Workers? 219
   Co-Created 219
   Customized 219
   Composite 220
   Caring 220
Where Do You Fit In? 220
Surprise! 222
A Strategy You May Not Have Expected 223
The Least You Need to Know 223

23 Advice for Younger Workers   **225**

Ain't Gonna Work on Maggie's Farm No More 225
Changes? Cool! 226
Your Reputation Precedes You 226
    The "Slacker" Thing 227
    The "Changing Jobs" Thing 227
    The "On the Clock" Thing 228
Are You the Signpost for a Generation? 228
Giving Yourself the Third Degree 229
Make the Most of Internships 229
Who's the Boss? 230
Keep the Package Complete 230
Keep the Package Up-to-Date 230
Be True to Yourself 230
The Least You Need to Know 231

24 When You're New to the Field   **233**

Can It Be Done? 233
A Step at a Time 234
A Career Changer Who Came Out on Top 234
Branching and Transplanting 235
    Fishing for Leads 235
    Back to the Source 236
How Inventive Do You Want to Get? 237
Play It Straight 238
    How Did You Get Started? 238
    What Should You Do Next? 239
The Least You Need to Know 239

25 Overcoming Problems in Your Background   **241**

Bad Breaks 241
Take It Easy 242
What to Do? 242
    Resume Rewrites 242
    Application Blues 243
    Face to Face 243
    No Cover-Ups! 244

Be Prepared! 244
If It Was (at Least Partly) Your Fault 245
If It Really Wasn't Your Fault 246
Some Parting Thoughts 247
Common Ground 247
There Are Problems and Then There Are Problems 247
The Least You Need to Know 248

26 So You're Not a "Computer Person"   249

"I'm Not Getting All This…" 249
A Different World 250
Clinging to Low-Tech 250
What Will You Do? 251
Techniques for Technopeasants 251
Touting Your Current Skills 251
Back to Basics 252
Boot Up! 253
Author! Author! 253
Turn, Turn, Turn 254
Mix and Match! 254
What Works? 255
The Least You Need to Know 255

27 Call It a Comeback!   257

Asking Questions (Again!) 258
The Biggie: Where Am I? 258
How Much to Give? 259
What's Next? 259
Finding Your Phoenix 260
"Where Am I?": Overcoming Obstacles 260
"Where Am I?": Beyond the "Bone Heap" 261
"Where Am I?": The Bottom Line 262
The Other Side of the Page 262
"Where's the Market?": The "What" Factor 262
"Where's the Market?": The "How" Factor 263
"Where's the Market?": The "Who" Factor 263
"Where's the Market?": The "Where" Factor 264

Where Lone Eagles Soar 264
    Tracking the Flocks Further 264
    The Death of the Daily Commute 265
"Where's the Market?": The "Why" Factor 268
The Fateful Question 268
Toward "Hey! This Matters!" 268
The Least You Need to Know 269

A Online Resources   **271**

B The Current Hot Employment Industries   **273**
    On the Decline 275
    Regional Growth Industries 276

C Associations and Advocacy Groups   **279**

D Employment Letters for the Career Changer   **285**

E Sample Resumes for the Career Changer   **297**

F Glossary   **311**

Index   **317**

Foreword

You're certainly no idiot—because you were smart enough to pick up this book!

If you are facing a career change today and need solid direction, or if you are just exploring a new career path, you've come to the right place. Bill Charland will help you put it all into focus and set your priorities. He'll help you identify what you want to do for a living—because work should, after all, be rewarding, fulfilling, and, yes, fun.

Bill helped me a number of years ago. I had been in television news for about 15 years, and all the imagined glamour of the business had pretty much disappeared for me. I wanted something with more challenge and a sense of personal accomplishment at the end of the day. I also wanted something that was not too far afield from journalism, where I could use my writing and creative-strategy skills.

Speaking with Bill, I've found, is like meeting with a "career sage"—an old soul who's out to impart insight and direction to as many of us as possible. As this book will demonstrate, he shows you when—and how—to listen to your own intuition. Bill helps you to find a unique career direction to follow, one that truly makes sense for you.

For me, the right career path turned out to be in the field of public relations, and the direction I got from Bill during our conversations back in the early '80s have served as guideposts to this day. I've refined his guidance into a philosophy I think about each morning and openly express to my colleagues. It goes like this—try to do good work for clients, make a reasonable profit, and have some fun in the process. Today, I am vice president of a major Washington D.C. public relations firm. Along the way, thanks to Bill, I've learned that regardless of any unsatisfactory work experiences in the past, none of us are idiots as long as we seek out good counsel—the kind that helps us to follow our own best instincts.

If you're looking for help in making a career transition, you've come to the right place; Bill Charland's guidance is the best you can get.

David E. Henderson
Vice President
Edelman Public Relations Worldwide

Introduction

There's a reason you've picked up this volume—something in your working life has prompted you to look for a new and rewarding career. As you look through the book, I'd like you to know that I've been thinking of you as I've been writing it. I've been trying to envision who you are and trying to imagine the kinds of questions that you're experiencing right now.

You might like to know one or two things about me. I've spent many years working with people in mid-career who were trying to get a handle on their working lives. Part of the time, I've worked in colleges—developing and directing programs for adults who were returning to school. At other times, I've led workshops and done counseling in public and privately funded career centers. Sometimes I've worked as a consultant on employment and training for corporations and government agencies and schools, including a college in Kenya.

So I have a good deal of hands-on experience in career management. Career issues are not just something I've thought about. I've wrestled with these issues with many clients, and I believe you'll sense that background of experience in this book.

I'm also a writer. I've written reams of newspaper and magazine articles, and this is my fifth book. Writing is my way of trying to make sense of things, and I've done it for as long as I can remember.

The book you're holding in your hands has been written with the help of many people. My editors and I have had a good time sharing some different perspectives as we've worked on this project; for one thing, everyone who's been involved in reviewing the text has been on the east coast, and I'm in Denver. So we assembled the book by e-mail, fax, and telephone—something I really couldn't have imagined a decade ago. Plus, there's the perspective of different generations. Some of the people I relied on a great deal for input and feedback during this project are just a year or two older than my daughter and my son. That fact didn't really impress me until—in a development I still find astonishing—I turned 60 while writing this book! So if you think you're in transition, believe me, you're not the only one.

How to Use This Book

This book is arranged in four sections.

The first section, "Changes," offers an overview of the kinds of shifts you are likely to face in today's often-unpredictable employment world, and puts a spotlight on some of the most important questions you'll be focusing on during your career change-campaign.

The next part of the book, "Directions," shows you how to evaluate your current skill sets—in other words, how to figure out what matches up with the demands of likely groups of employers, what doesn't match up, and what to do about the gaps you may discover. (By the end of this second section, you'll be in a position to establish a career goal that makes sense for you.)

In the third section, "Connections," you'll learn about the best—and worst—ways to identify and develop employment opportunities in your field of choice.

And in the final section, "Challenges," you'll get some insight on overcoming some of the most daunting obstacles to a successful career change.

Extras

As if that weren't enough, the book also offers other types of information that will make your career-change campaign go even smoother. Here's how you can spot these elements:

Job Jargon
"What's that mean?" This is where I explain unfamiliar terminology and ideas related to career assessment.

Work Alert!
Watch out— things can get tricky when you're charting a new career path. These warnings will help you avoid potentially hazardous wrong turns.

Career Counsel
Use these tips and advice to keep your career-change efforts on track.

> ## Bet You Didn't Know
>
> "Bet You Didn't Know" sidebars will provide helpful background data that will let you get up to speed quickly on a particular topic. You won't want to skip these informative summaries.

Acknowledgments

I'm grateful to the Center for the New West and its President, Phil Burgess, for the administrative and moral support I received while writing the book. I'm also grateful to the many other colleagues in the career field whom I've mentioned in the text. I know they all join me in hoping that this book is a helpful resource for the next chapter in your life's work.

Special Thanks from the Publisher to the Technical Reviewer

The Complete Idiot's Guide to Changing Careers was reviewed by an expert who not only checked the technical accuracy of what you'll learn in this book, but also provided invaluable insight and suggestions to ensure that you learn everything you need to know when undertaking a career change. Our special thanks are extended to:

Rich Feller, Professor of Counseling and Career Development at Colorado State University, directs the Clearinghouse on Career, Equity and Labor Market Information. He is co-author of *Career Transitions in Turbulent Times*, and the *CDM Career Video: Tour of Your Tomorrow*. He speaks nationally about the changing workplace and has consulted in 49 states, Japan, Thailand, China, Africa, and Europe.

Part 1
Changes

Are you confused about today's employment world? Take heart—you're not alone. This part of the book will help you understand what's going on in this occasionally unpredictable economy of ours. It will also give you some strategies for reaching out to employers in ways that will help you clarify your own goals.

Chapter 1

Welcome Back to the Jungle

In This Chapter

➤ Handling career ups and downs

➤ Unemployment: learning to deal with pink slip blues

➤ Misemployment: when you realize it's a nice job...for someone else

➤ Mismanagement: seeing how a bad boss can ruin your great career

"Was I pushed? Or did I jump? Or did it really matter, after all?" Believe it or not, that may well be the way you one day come to view the employment-related problems you're experiencing today. Does that mean the concerns you're feeling about your career direction right now somehow don't matter, or aren't valid? Of course not. But it's worthwhile to remember that even the most daunting career obstacles have a way of seeming larger than they really are when you're confronting them, perhaps for the first time, head on.

This book will help you make sense of the career management questions that you're facing now. It will also help you get your bearings in a turbulent economy, take control of the career-planning process, and find a new career that leaves you both satisfied and, yes, compensated fairly. So take heart. You've already gotten the first and most important step out of the way: You've taken action. You've started reading this book. You're one step closer to that "What was I so worried about?" realization that has a way of following life's most challenging and intimidating moments—those "moments of truth" we all get so excited about.

Those moments are exciting, but that doesn't mean they have to be scary. In this chapter, you learn more about the dimensions of those critical times that affect your career—and learn how this book will help you make sense of the career decisions you may be facing as a result.

Working in the Best and Worst of Times

You probably picked this volume up because you're dissatisfied, and perhaps even a little anxious, about the direction your career path is currently taking you. That dissatisfaction, that anxiety you may have with your *job*—these are the precursors to positive change in your work life. Look into the careers of many successful people, and you'll find they're full of stops and starts, reversals, and even some "bottoming-out" moments when they realized that, like it or not, they could no longer count on doing things the old way.

Job Jargon
The word **job** is derived from the same root as *gob*, or the middle English term *gobbe*, which translates to lump, or piece. Some people in England still speak of "a job of work." In our culture, we tend to use this word when we view work as a unit of activity or a means to an end: "It's just a job."

Such challenges are par for the course for modern career-changers, who might live in a supposedly "robust" or "fast-growth" economy, in which high-end, mid-level, salaried jobs are scarce, indeed. What new approaches are in order for such workers?

Consider the (fictional) case of one Benjamin Barnacle—a character whose story illustrates how you can make the most of the challenges you face as you try to develop a *vocation* in a changing economy.

In 1910, our hero Barnacle was on top of the world. At age 30, he'd spent 10 years building a business in the expanding and exciting field of indoor illumination. Barnacle had recognized an opportunity in kerosene, the first commercial product of the brand-new petroleum industry. He had a team of horses and a specially outfitted wagon that he used to deliver barrels of kerosene to the homes of his customers for their lanterns. Barnacle was as regular with his deliveries as the local milkman was with his. He kept his customers very happy—for a while.

Job Jargon
The word **vocation** carries many meanings these days, and encompasses everything from a religious occupation to a course of study. The root is found in Hebrew and Greek words meaning "to call out" or "summon." A vocation is meaningful work that we feel called to do.

Meanwhile, a New Jersey inventor by the name of Thomas Edison had the audacity to invent something he called an electric light bulb. Edison's invention spread like wildfire, and soon the kerosene industry was history. Barnacle went out of business, but not for long. For at the same time Edison was refining the filaments of the light bulb, a mechanical wizard in Michigan was perfecting a commercially viable automobile. Henry Ford's product created vast new markets for the oil and gas industry, and an astonishing new array of occupations. Within a few years, Ben Barnacle had traded in his team of horses for a job with Ford, selling newfangled horseless carriages.

The moral? Change brings losses but also creates opportunities.

Jobs and the People Who Hate Them

First things first. That's the big rule of thumb when it comes to changing careers: Attack the big questions before you do anything else.

So why are you unhappy about your current situation?

I've counseled well over 1,000 adults in mid-career, and my experience leads me to believe that the answer to that difficult question is to be found in the answer to another one:

Is it because you're unemployed, misemployed, or mismanaged?

When people complain about their working lives, it's generally because they find themselves in one or another of these circumstances. To get the most out of this book, figure out which label best describes your situation. Someone who is unemployed is in a declining field, or at best, "between engagements." Someone who is misemployed is working in a job for which he or she is temperamentally unsuited, at least for right now. Someone who is mismanaged is working in the right field, but under the wrong conditions.

When the Job Is Just Not You

Misemployment: This is the career management problem that's hardest to ignore—both for employees and their supervisors. It's the wrong-job/wrong-time, square-peg/round-hole syndrome.

Do you often find yourself thinking, "This is a good job for somebody, but not for me"? It's the same feeling you may harbor for an old flame your mother always wanted you to marry.

What does misemployment look like? One summer in college I did some work in the recreation department of a local veterans' hospital. I helped organize softball games, field trips, and the like.

I'd been on the job about a week when I noticed that the head of the recreation department never left his office. He worked at his desk all day and had absolutely no contact with the patients. I questioned one of my coworkers and he chuckled. "Oh, you've got to understand Irv," he told me. "The man has a Ph.D. in recreation administration from the University of Minnesota. He's a brilliant guy but painfully shy. Irv can't lead a game."

Career Counsel
The person you are today may not be the person you are tomorrow. Misemployment can (and often does) evolve as a result of personal change. Being an introvert today doesn't mean you can't become an extrovert in the future—and vice versa!

That's what it means to be a square peg in the round hole of misemployment. However, misemployment can—and often does—evolve as the result of personal change. The fact that you're an introvert today does not mean you can't be an extrovert tomorrow—and vice versa.

Not long ago, I counseled someone who originally went into accounting because it was "something he could do by himself." (He was, like Irv, painfully shy.) Eventually, however, he found himself enjoying working with people more and more. Today, he uses his accounting background as a consultant, and helps people who own small businesses run their operation. He figured out a way to meet his changing career needs, and is misemployed no longer.

Good Morning. You're Fired!

This is the ultimate gut-wrenching experience everyone fears. It's also a fact of contemporary working life, an experience that nearly everybody will experience at some point or another. I've known very few people who haven't found themselves unemployed at some time in their lives. Why does it happen? These days, it may be because the work you used to do has simply gone away as the result of technological change. You were a carbon-paper manufacturing specialist, and somebody came along and invented a self-correcting typewriter. Or you were a self-correcting typewriter repairperson, and someone came along and introduced the personal computer.

Bet You Didn't Know

"You can quit or be fired." Which should you do? No two situations are identical, of course, but don't be too eager to resign. Sometimes people choose that option in the hope of saving face. Quitting a job will not necessarily get you a good recommendation from a boss who was ready to fire you anyway, and being let go may leave you eligible for unemployment insurance you'll need while exploring new career options. No, being fired isn't exactly good for your resume or your self esteem—but in today's economy, it doesn't carry the same stigma it once did.

Whatever you do, don't resign on the spot if you're given the "quit-or-be-fired" option. Ask for time to think things over. Your transition to a new career field will be much smoother if you're able to make a series of conscious decisions, rather than simply reacting to someone else's action. See Chapter 7 for more advice on dealing with being fired.

When technology convinces your employer to stop paying people to do what they used to get paid to do, those jobs become obsolete. These days, *job obsolescence* is affecting more and more of us, especially in mid-career. In Chapter 13, you'll learn a number of strategies for transferring what you thought were lost skills and experience to other fields.

Have you ever heard the old Fred Astaire song about picking yourself up, dusting yourself off, and starting all over again? There's an art to starting over when that "unemployment" button flashes and your career goes into retrograde. What you have to do is find the reset button.

Ever since her sophomore year in college, Susan Kelley knew that her love in life was journalism. She was accepted into a good school, and her career was off to a rousing start. But then she dropped out of college to get married, and moved to an unfamiliar city. Seven years later, when the marriage ended, Kelley found herself with no degree, and she couldn't find a job in her field.

Undaunted, she applied for an internship with a local T.V. station. She soon discovered that this station awarded all its internships to students at a local college. So she enrolled at the school and stuck around for one term, long enough to win the internship she was after! When I met her several years later, she confessed (somewhat guiltily) that she never had finished her degree. But the internship had served its purpose. She had a job at a TV station with 95 employees. The title on her door read "Managing Editor."

Love the Job, but Everything Else Stinks

Mismanagement is the experience of doing the kind of work you love under conditions you wouldn't wish on the fifth-grade bully who pummeled you on the playground every day at lunch time. Sad-but-true department: Mismanagement is such a common career phenomenon in the United States that the ex-corporate employee who draws the popular comic strip *Dilbert* probably will never run out of material.

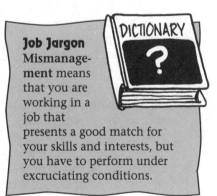

Job Jargon
Job obsolescence is the elimination of a position in which the skills and objectives associated with it often live on.

Work Alert!
The instinct to find another job quickly—preferably one that's essentially identical to your old position—can be a recipe for long-term career dissatisfaction. Don't fall into that trap. Take the time to assess your current situation in depth. And remember that unemployment is sometimes a catalyst to a satisfying career change!

Job Jargon
Mismanagement means that you are working in a job that presents a good match for your skills and interests, but you have to perform under excruciating conditions.

Mismanagement is an all too common career problem. A few years ago, the Wyatt Company, an international human resources consulting firm, conducted a survey of American employees. Seventy-two percent of those surveyed declared that they enjoyed their work, but only 55 percent said that they appreciated the supervision they received. The Wyatt survey was repeated four times over a period of eight years. Each time, those figures came out about the same. As the late novelist Michael Dorris put it, "It's not the working, it's the working for" that gets us down.

What causes feelings of dissatisfaction on jobs we feel we ought to be able to love, or at least enjoy? The same Wyatt Company survey points to some possible answers. Many employees reported serious problems in downward organizational communication. Although management often appears to do a commendable job of conveying messages about overreaching corporate goals, only 34 percent of employees said that management explained the reasons behind corporate decisions that affected them. The percentage of workers who felt involved in making corporate decisions was even lower.

Under the "mismanaged" category, we might list two other conditions: "overworked" and "underemployed." Today, many corporate employees find that they're expected to perform not only their own jobs, but those of others who have left the organization (the casualties of downsizing). Others may find that new technology or staff reorganizations or campaigns to improve efficiency have taken the heart out of jobs they once enjoyed doing. It's been my experience that employees complain more about being underemployed than overworked.

Bet You Didn't Know

These days, worker loyalty is shifting from employers to professions and industries. Research data from the U.S. Department of Labor shows some interesting shifts in the career patterns of Americans. The average length of time an American stays in a job is now only 3.5 years and dropping; the average stint with an employer is down to 4.5 years, and that's also dropping. The average length of time spent in a particular occupation, however, is at 6.5 years and rising. (Peter Capelli, Bureau of Labor Statistics)

I know of a customer service representative who spent all day on the telephone, responding to customer complaints. She was working for one of those overnight delivery companies, tracking packages that went to Poughkeepsie instead of Pasadena. She was good at what she did, and got a significant amount of job satisfaction from the tangled problems she unraveled. Then, one day her company installed a device that measured "talk time"—the average length of time she spent on the phone per customer. Calls that went over a certain period of time had to be referred to her supervisor. Suddenly, all the challenge of the job was gone.

Undaunted, this woman found a way out of her dilemma. She hooked up a second phone in her cubicle. Whenever a thorny problem turned up, she spent a minimal amount of time on the phone as the service representative and then referred the call to her second line, where she took her time resolving it as the "supervisor."

I was told this story by the top human resources manager at the company in question. It seems that when the woman's ploy was first discovered, she was threatened with the loss of her job. Eventually, however, company officials had second thoughts, and decided to reward this employee for her initiative. If only every such story had a similarly happy ending!

A Career Is a Terrible Thing to Waste

Unemployment, misemployment, and mismanagement: These are three very tough problems facing contemporary workers. This book will supply you with plenty of strategies for dealing with each situation. Take a look at another success story:

Work Alert! In an uncertain economy, many people choose to exacerbate problems of mismanagement by building walls instead of bridges. Sometimes, people try to hang on to any scrap of data that will make them appear "indispensable" in an effort to lend some security to their positions—a tactic that has a nasty way of backfiring when discovered.

DITCH DIGGER WANTED

I first met Gary Chapman a couple of years ago, while I was doing job-lead development for a group of unemployed aerospace workers. He was running a successful multimedia production studio, turning out CD-ROM programs on subjects ranging from preschool reading readiness to sales presentations. I can't recall ever meeting anyone who seemed to be having as much fun on the job as Chapman. But it wasn't always like that.

Three years earlier, Chapman was a corporate vice president with a $2.5 million budget and staff of 75. Unfortunately, his career was in the doldrums. The last few proposals he'd submitted to top management had been turned down flat. There was talk that he might be transferred to an unappealing outpost in the firm's corporate empire. Things didn't look good.

One day, a brochure came across Chapman's desk for a conference on multimedia technology. He didn't know much about the field, except that it was growing. But the meeting was being held on the other side of the country, in Boston, a city he'd never even visited. He made plans to take a vacation trip to Boston and Cape Cod, planning to poke his head in for a couple of hours at the conference.

As fortune would have it, however, Chapman was completely smitten by the technology he saw. He stayed at the conference for four days. When he returned home, he enrolled in a course in multimedia software development. He did so well in the course that, the following semester, he found himself teaching it! Not long afterward, he quit his job and started his own company, hiring his best students.

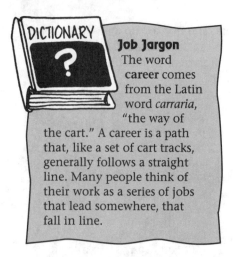

Job Jargon
The word **career** comes from the Latin word *carraria*, "the way of the cart." A career is a path that, like a set of cart tracks, generally follows a straight line. Many people think of their work as a series of jobs that lead somewhere, that fall in line.

Chapman showed me an animated 3-D corporate logo he'd designed for a client's sales presentation. Even a layman like me could tell that it was state-of-the-art work. The soundtrack soared and zapped; the logo expanded, tumbled, did some fancy end-over-end maneuvers, and then came to rest in the middle of the screen. Chapman sat back and beamed at his creation.

He'd made a very good trade: a corporate *career* that had become stale and unsatisfying for a workplace that meant something to him. That's the kind of transition I'd like to help you make, as well.

So read on, and I'll try to help you make sense of some potentially intimidating problems. In the next chapter, you'll discover some survival strategies you should become familiar with during this exciting time in your life—the time you grant yourself to explore your career options.

The Least You Need to Know

➤ Even though unpredictable times can be scary, they may also present significant career opportunity.

➤ The instinct to find another job quickly—preferably one that's essentially identical to your old position—can be a recipe for long-term career dissatisfaction.

➤ Unemployment, misemployment, and mismanagement are the primary causes of career dissatisfaction. It's important to know which problem you're trying to solve.

➤ You can make the transition from an unsatisfying career situation to a satisfying one—so keep reading!

Chapter 2

Working It Out: Career Change Survival Strategies

In This Chapter

➤ Identifying what's important to you

➤ Going through paycheck withdrawal

➤ Time can really be on your side

Time, money, and sanity—all three of these resources are likely to be at a premium when you take on the "job" of changing from one career to another. In this part of the book, you learn about some financial and time-management strategies that will help you make the most of your resources during this critical time—and about the power of values to support you during this important time of your life.

Job, Adventure, or Both?

At first glance, the process of values clarification may not appear to have much to do with changing careers. After all, if we're bent on getting out of a bad situation and into a better one, we probably don't want to waste time with too much philosophical analysis—especially when we're worried about making next month's rent or allocating the appropriate amount of time to our career-change campaign.

But identifying what you want from a job is fundamental to getting all of your needs met. It may be surprising, but career counselors will tell you that most of their clients who are unhappily employed have difficulty defining exactly what it is that would make them happy on the job—be it salary, or status, or some other source of personal satisfaction. No matter what your current situation is (in other words, whether you're dissatisfied with your current career because of unemployment, misemployment, or mismanagement), you owe it to yourself to take a few moments now for self-assessment. By clarifying your needs and values, you'll be able to determine exactly what it is that is likely to drive you, and what types of rewards make the most difference to you emotionally. These will be important factors in your later career-planning decisions.

Bet You Didn't Know

Many people are apt to base their careers on financial rewards at the cost of other values that could bring them greater satisfaction. This is not to say that a low initial income can't eventually lead to significant success in a new field. The other day, I noticed this list in the morning paper:

First professional earnings:

Ray Bradbury (the famed science fiction writer)—$27.50 for first story.

W. C. Fields—30 cents for first juggling act.

Judy Garland—$100 per week, first MGM contract.

Cary Grant—$150 for first film.

(Source: World Features Syndicate)

To take a quick reading of your personal work-related values and needs—the ones you may have to get along without during a period of career transition—try this simple exercise:

VALUES AND NEEDS MET AT WORK	ALTERNATIVES
_____	_____
_____	_____
_____	_____
_____	_____
_____	_____
_____	_____

The idea is to list in the left column every sort of financial, personal, and psychological gap you've ever tried to fill by working. Complete that column first, before going on to the right side (we'll get to that later). Try it now. Take some time to open up and brainstorm. Don't assume that the needs and values are all monetary. What about status? Are you the kind of person who needs to pass around business cards that bear an impressive title? Plenty of us value that highly. That's probably why we meet so many self-employed people who've given themselves the title of president and even CEO when there's no one else in their office but the family dog. In many cases, the fact that these people are working out of a back bedroom doesn't diminish the importance they assign to job-related status.

Speaking of home offices, what about social interaction? I believe that one of the most basic needs most of us bring to the workplace is the search for a good, congenial place to hang out. When people are unemployed for any length of time, usually the first thing they complain about is their lack of social interaction.

By the same token, of course, some of us are driven to change jobs (and even careers) by the need to get away from incompatible coworkers. I once did an audit of employee concerns at a small company whose owner was trying to put the place on an even keel so he could retire. One of the questions on the form I used was: "What is your greatest challenge on the job?" A fellow in the accounting department wrote, "Sitting next to Cindy."

Some years ago, a psychologist by the name of E. K. Strong set out to interview individuals who were veterans of various career fields in order to learn their basic values and preferences—not just in work, but in life per se. His research data formed the basis for the Strong-Campbell Vocational Interest Inventory, today one of the most popular instruments in the vocational testing field.

Strong's instrument is based on the premise that occupational groups are primarily social groups. I believe he was right on target. It's been my experience that groups of people who enjoy spending time together will find a way to do so on the job. Once organized into a profession, they will welcome to their midst people who share their interests and enjoy interacting as they do. And they'll exclude those who like to spend time in a different way.

Career Counsel
Work groups are social groups. If your values mirror the values of the group within which you work, you'll be that much more likely to be both happy and productive. That's why network interviewing is vital when considering a new field. It's important to find out who's working in a field and how they like to function before jumping in to join the group. Find a way to attend one of their cocktail parties!

Work Alert!
In establishing values, don't place all your emphasis on issues like salary or the potential for visibility within your industry. Remember the day-in, day-out social component. Occupational groups are primarily social groups. You need to find the tribe that fits you.

Sometimes two occupational groups with similar titles are anything but alike in the way they like to function. Consider secondary-school teachers and college teachers, for example. As research with the Myers Briggs Type Indicator (another popular test instrument) shows, elementary and secondary teachers tend to be much more extroverted than their college counterparts. Walk into a convention of one and then the other. Measure the sound volume at cocktail hour, and you'll know which bunch you're visiting.

The same basic principle goes for broadcast journalists and print journalists. For my part, I enjoy interacting with the latter much more than with the former. Print journalists (such as newspaper reporters and book editors) are much more like me. They're my tribe.

I once had a client who spent years selling steel before he decided to pursue another career. I asked him why he wanted to change. "It's my liver," he told me. I invited him to explain what he meant.

It seems that at that time, the business of steel was so standardized that every sales rep's product was basically the same. People cut deals over cocktails, usually far into the night. If you weren't up for "social drinking" during sales calls, you were in trouble, because your product certainly wasn't going to stand out on its own. That's the kind of data one needs to know before considering a change into a new field.

Consider Some Alternative Thinking

Have you developed the left side of your list? In addition to items like "income," "social fulfillment," "social status," "personal challenge," "intellectual growth," and "potential for advancement," you may also have found yourself writing things like "family acceptance and approval" or "emotional support I now receive from such-and-such colleague." Get it all down. Write down everything you have received or are receiving from the world of work. If it's important, and if you've ever gotten it as a result of working, it should be on your list.

Now comes the interesting part. Look at each item on your list. Suppose you couldn't meet that need or value in your work for a while? What would you do? Could you get along without it? Would you even want to think about getting along without it? Play out the best- and worst-case scenarios in each instance. Then brainstorm some possible alternatives for each value you've listed.

Take at least 10 minutes to review your list and develop alternatives now.

If you listed the value, "$3,000 in monthly after-tax income," an alternative for you might be found in supplementing current savings with appropriate part-time work during the transition period.

If you listed the value, "social fulfillment I enjoy by interacting with other writers," an alternative for you might be found in joining a local writers' group.

If you listed the value, "emotional support I now receive from my colleagues," an alternative to that value might be found in expanding your social network and developing more close friendships.

You'll find this exercise of identifying values—and thinking about the potential alternatives you may need to develop—a useful preliminary to any career transition campaign. Devote some time to this self-review before you proceed with the rest of the ideas in this book.

Dollars and Sense

The full implications of a career transition period on your bank account are likely to be many and varied. As you make your way through this book, you'll find advice on selecting part-time and freelance employment that supports you emotionally, professionally, and, most of all, financially. For now, though, you should take a brief look at some basic principles of financial management that will serve you well during this time in your life.

Don't Wing It!

Robert Tull, a certified financial planner in Norfolk, Virginia, has worked with a number of clients who were in the process of career transition. His sound advice is worth reviewing closely.

If at all possible, try to plan every aspect of your transition, including its financial aspects. You say you've got a little bit of lead time before you leave a major income source? That's great. Begin to set aside funds in some form of investment that doesn't fluctuate. Whether or not you have a great deal of time before you separate yourself from a paycheck, avoid the temptation to improvise a brighter short-term financial future by piling your resources into high-risk investments. At this stage of your life, you're probably not looking for an instant primer on the perils of reckless investing!

> **Work Alert!**
> Save yourself some trauma. If you're drawing on reserve funds while unemployed, you don't want them in the stock market. Put them in a high-yield mutual fund instead.

If You Fall, Can You Still Afford to Get Up?

Investigate your current health and life insurance policies as part of your career transition process. Check to see if any work-related benefits you have now can be continued when you leave your present job. Federal law requires your employer to allow you to pay for premiums for 18 months on the same coverage you had while you were working. Take out special, short-term policies if you need them.

Check Your Retirement Funds

Many people have retirement funds in either an Individual Retirement Account (IRA), which one can't borrow against, or a 401K account, which can be used as collateral. If you have borrowed against your 401K plan with your current employer, be aware that the amount of your loan will immediately come due when you terminate employment. You also may be assessed a penalty. However, it is possible to roll that debt over to a new employer.

Cancel the Yacht and the Trip Around the World

Finally, Tull recommends being prepared to adjust your budget downward—that's certainly sound advice. Tull adds, though, that you should also make some plans that will allow you to (gasp!) enjoy your period of transition. If you can plan ahead and budget for it, take a good vacation while you're between jobs. Your transition period may be your last chance to relax before you begin working again. And a "battery-recharging" period—even if it takes the frugal form of, say, a week-long camping trip to a nearby national park—can end up doing your career a world of good.

Career Counsel
For referrals to recognized financial advisors in eyour area, contact the Institute of Certified Financial Planners at (303) 759-4900.

Other important steps to take include:

➤ Applying for unemployment insurance if you've been terminated rather than resigned

➤ Analyzing the severance package with the help of a qualified professional

➤ Examining your cash flow position closely

➤ Postponing major purchases

➤ Continuing your health insurance package (Federal law requires that, for 18 months, your employer allow you to pay for premiums on the same coverage you had while working)

➤ Scheduling regular reviews of your financial situation

Look Before You Leap!

Ed Morrow, a certified financial planner in Middleton, Ohio (Cincinnati), offers some important words of advice to those who are considering a career change that involves starting a business: "Don't put yourself in the position of borrowing capital. The amount you need will vary, depending on the business you're in. For a trained and certified financial planner, for instance, you're probably talking about $20,000 to get started. But startup costs are just the beginning. After spending three or four months investing capital in your business, you can probably expect to spend another three months foregoing income." So on average, it will be seven months before you realize any profit. The alternative is to look for a paid internship in someone else's company. That's one way to limit startup expenses."

Warning: Clock Watching Can Be Hazardous to Your Career

Did you ever see that bumper sticker that reads, "Work is for people who don't know how to fish"? Every time I spot one on the car ahead of me, I seem to be locked in an early-morning traffic jam with an overheating radiator. I find myself wondering, "Why are we all living like this? Aren't there other ways we could be spending our time?"

But, working is a vital part of life. Whether we like to admit it during rush hour or not, work adds structure to the day; it's a way of structuring time. Getting up to go to the office, meeting people at lunch time, traveling home at the end of the day—all of these are rituals that add structure to our lives. Talk with people who've been out of work for any length of time, and you'll find that they almost always complain about time—about having too much of it! (I once came across a book on the hazards of retirement. One chapter had a bone-chilling title: "A Lifetime of Saturdays.")

The lack of daily structure is an important concern for most people who leave a full-time job and find themselves in career transition; they have the same concerns and face the same hazards that usually arise for those workers who are entering retirement. One possible exception: factory workers. My experience is that most of these people are pretty well equipped for retirement, because their jobs are often so boring that they've already cooked up an interesting set of after-hours hobbies. "The main thing is to keep active," one assembly-line worker advised me. "You've got to do something to make the beer taste good!"

Sound advice. But how do you pull it off? How do you stay active, and remain goal-oriented, when you're between jobs or in the process of career transition? Here are some dos and don'ts to try on for size.

If you're not working:

➤ *Don't panic.* Don't rush out and blindly attempt to track down any job. (You'd be surprised at the kinds of career mistakes people make when they start asking themselves, "What do I do after my second cup of coffee?")

➤ *Don't try to impose a time structure immediately.* Give yourself some space and time for constructive floundering (known as reflection not too long ago). If, at the end of two weeks, you still find that the morning talk shows are the highlight of your day, you can begin to be concerned.

➤ *Do look for part-time activities that lend some structure (and some income!) to your day, but won't intrude on your career quest over the long haul.* You'll be looking at part-time employment strategies in greater detail later in the book.

➤ *Do commit to activities that expose you to other people and situations.* Ushering base-ball games is one such example. While the pay may be low, you may find the atmosphere stimulating.

Don't push yourself too hard for tangible "results" immediately after you leave your old job. The Canadian educator John B. McLeish once observed that "creativity has everything to do with making the most of time—not in the sense of frantic pacing, but in the sense of a kind of private peace in which one is quietly making time come alive."

In Praise of Odd Jobs

Remember: Not everything you do for pay has to go on the top line of your resume.

I once took a weekend job driving an airport van for the summer when a course I'd been scheduled to teach was canceled suddenly. It was a great experience. Something about airports has always fascinated me; when one of my students mentioned that he'd driven a van, I took him to lunch and grilled him about what to look for—and what to avoid. He cautioned me not to drive an unscheduled van for one of the airport hotels. The stress level, he warned, was too high: "People are always jumping on those vans because they're late for a plane. They'll try to get you to do 75 miles an hour down the parkway. Drive a scheduled van instead."

Career Counsel
Taking a part-time job that's just plain fun can re-energize your whole approach to the world of work, lend structure to your day, and help you establish important values.

Armed with his advice, I applied for—and got—a job driving a scheduled van. It was quite an adventure. One fellow who rode in my van was a psychologist with a firm that specialized in helping people adjust to working night shifts; I later interviewed him and his boss, and wrote a magazine article on the subject.

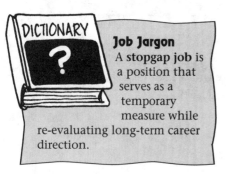

Job Jargon
A **stopgap job** is a position that serves as a temporary measure while re-evaluating long-term career direction.

Plenty of professional people are taking this tack and stepping into *stopgap jobs* while they re-evaluate their long-term career direction. One of my fellow drivers that summer was a former IBM manager who was winding down for a bit after a demanding project. A friend of mine who's leaving a career as a marriage and family therapist, and looking into health care career planning, just started an interim job as a bus driver. It makes perfect sense for her now, because it lends some order to the day, keeps money coming in, and actually leaves her some energy at the end of her shift to focus on career issues.

The Least You Need to Know

➤ Clarifying what you want from work is basic to getting all of your needs met.

➤ Work groups are social groups; if your values mirror the values of the group within which you work, you'll be much more likely to be both happy and productive on the job.

➤ Review the basic principles of financial management discussed in this chapter; they'll serve you well during the coming weeks and months.

➤ Take the time to identify your needs and values and establish alternatives. This will help you clarify your goals.

➤ Don't rush out and blindly attempt to track down any job.

➤ Taking a part-time job that's just plain fun lends some order to the day, keeps money coming in, and leaves you some energy at the end of your shift to focus on career issues.

Chapter 3

Ask Questions Now or Forever Hold Your Peace

In This Chapter

➤ The who, what, where, and why of starting a career change

➤ Rules? Who needs 'em?

➤ Connecting with the marketplace

Old Ukrainian saying: "If you don't know where you're going, any road will take you there."

If that observation rings true for you, congratulations. You understand the importance of planning, which is the first step toward bringing about successful career change. In this chapter, you learn how to address the most important questions relating to career planning.

You're the Boss

If you've made it this far in the book, that's a good indication that you are in the process of developing a take-charge approach to career matters. The premise of the system you'll be learning in this and subsequent chapters is pretty simple: Set a course of action—decide where you're going and what you aim to do. This makes more sense than letting someone else plan your career for you. Twenty years ago, this was not necessarily the case in the world of career management. If you had a stable job with Huge Multinational

Outfit, Inc., there was probably a certain strategic advantage to following the dictates of the top brass and marching down the well-trodden career paths of that more or less unchanging organization. The rewards for doing so, at any rate, were likely to be significant: security, continued good pay and benefits, an important and ongoing series of social relationships in the workplace.

In the '50s, '60s, and '70s in the United States, those who had good jobs with major employers were, as a general rule, repaid handsomely for their unquestioning loyalty to their companies. Today, unquestioning loyalty often doesn't get you much of anything—and it may do you a world of harm. That's important to remember. For many of us, the rules of the career game have changed at halftime. The images and expectations some workers held when they began working simply don't fit the way the labor market works today. The game is played in an entirely different way as changing technology and market conditions have made long-term plans an unaffordable luxury.

Rule 1: There Are No Rules

The situation many workers face today is not unlike some historic revolutions in the world of sports. One of these took place on a fateful day in 1823, when William Webb Ellis, an English schoolboy, took it into his head to catch what we would call a soccer ball and run with it, instead of giving it a kick as the rules prescribed. Ellis unwittingly invented a new game that would immortalize his alma mater. (He was playing for the boarding school of Rugby.)

Or consider the football game between Army and Notre Dame in 1913. The Cadets were heavy favorites, but during the game Notre Dame quarterback Gus Dorais broke out a brand new play—the forward pass. As Dorais started sailing passes across the line of scrimmage to a speedy end named Knute Rockne, the stunned Army players realized they were in for a very long, very bad day. Dorais's innovation (which was not technically illegal, but simply hadn't been tried much before) led the Irish to a stunning 35-13 upset.

Imagine what it felt like to play in one of those games, when it seemed as though the rules had been arbitrarily changed in the middle of the contest. For a good many workers, that's exactly what work feels like today. Someone has changed the rules at halftime.

Skills! Skills! My Kingdom for Some Skills!

A quarter-century ago, a graduate of a good liberal arts college who had majored in medieval musicology could go out into the working world with no marketable skills and, usually, no real career worries. There were always management training programs in large, established institutions (such as banks and insurance companies). Employers could be counted on to provide exposure to every aspect of the industry in question, with hands-on training in *hard skills* provided all along the way.

Today, on-the-job programs of that kind are almost impossible to find. A little later on in the book, you'll look at some alternative ways to get started in an industry or profession you target. For now, simply note that the rules and assumptions that held sway some years back may have changed and, for many workers, they've changed right in the middle of the game.

Job Jargon
A **hard skill** comes from training in a certain discipline, experience in a related industry, or knowledge of technical tools.

Time to Pop the Big Questions

The first thing you need to do in planning any sort of career change is to begin asking questions—the kinds of questions that generate different answers from different people in different situations.

I've met with people in all kinds of career transitions over the years. My experience is that people need to learn to ask two sets of questions during this phase of their lives. Here they are in parallel form.

What needs doing?	Where are the markets?
What can you do?	Where are you?
What have you been learning that can make a difference?	How can you connect with those markets?

Ultimately, you'll need to address all of these, but it doesn't much matter which question you start with. Which question or set of questions make you feel like responding? You can take your pick, and even mix and match the questions in the two sets. Notice, though, that the questions on the left side are really subtle restatements of the questions on the right and that the right set of questions sounds a bit more practical, more market-driven. Because the open-ended questions are likely to help you brainstorm, start with the question in the upper right corner and go from there.

Where Are the Markets?

The first step in getting our bearings is to look outward. What's out there? Where are the markets? What needs doing? (That last question, by the way, comes from the late John Crystal, one of the career field's true pioneers. I think it's a great one.)

Many career counseling books ignore this vital question in favor of more introspective strategies. Study your navel, find your passion, follow your fantasies. Those can all be very worthy pursuits, but they represent a less-than-sturdy foundation for your career. As any good entrepreneur will tell you, one's passion and one's dreams eventually have to interact with, and solve problems for, other people.

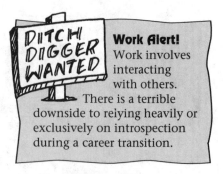

Work Alert!
Work involves interacting with others. There is a terrible downside to relying heavily or exclusively on introspection during a career transition.

It's not that I don't believe in meaningful work; I do. (Some of the most unhappy workers I've ever met were people who picked a field because it offered plenty of jobs that paid well, then realized, after 20 years as an insurance broker/financial analyst/whatever, that they were counting the minutes until retirement.) Finding meaningful work is vitally important, but the meaning we find in work is seldom found solely within our own aspirations and beliefs.

Relationships

I believe that the meaning of work is most often found in the kinds of relationships it creates, the interaction it promotes, and the way your work puts you in contact with others. Ask a lifelong elementary-school teacher what he likes about his work, and you'll often hear something like this: "There's a certain way of looking at the world that I pick up from the kids—sort of seeing it wide-eyed."

Where Are You?

Or, if you prefer a more purposeful form of the question: What can you do?

Have you ever found yourself in the presence of an exciting new trend—maybe a terrific new technology or an overwhelming social need—and found yourself thinking, "Maybe I could do something there"? Many people my age who entered the workforce in the 1960s had that feeling about the civil rights movement. The whole reason I got involved in college teaching and spent 20 years of my career in higher education was that, back in the early '60s, at a time when I felt a deep need to do some kind of work to promote social change in the South, a certain college teaching program provided me with the best opportunity to do that.

Today, I see many younger people turning to the Internet for similar reasons. They have interests in business, or graphic arts, or publishing, and the Internet offers them a venue to do something new. Once again, I think it's the intersection between the out-there and the in-here where the meaning of life and work resides.

Sometimes, the direction we seek is not so much a matter of what we do as who we are. I can remember going through a set of vocational preference tests with a young nurse who had carved out a successful career as a pharmaceutical representative, but found the work held little meaning for her.

We were reviewing the results of her tests when I noticed she was staring off into space. "I know how I want to be," she said, "but not what I'll be doing when I'm that way." After that, I found she was much more focused. Somehow she used this observation to connect with some important personal values. If you can follow that young woman's lead into exploring specific fields, you'll be making use of one of the best tools for career-oriented self-questioning I've ever heard—your own values.

How Can You Connect with the Markets?

Or, what have you been learning? What skills can you pick up to close the gap between "out-there" and "in-here"? Once you identify the work that you care about, how can you make connection with it? You'll find that it's simply not just a matter of hanging out with the right people in the right places. It involves learning what it takes to get where you want to be and ultimately make the connection.

Ten years ago, I knew that I wanted to do some different kinds of writing. I'd written mostly for academic journals and wasn't satisfied with my first two books. I thought my style was very stodgy—crammed with multisyllabic words. Sometimes it seemed to me that reading what I wrote was like wading through wet cement.

So I began looking for ways to break into journalism—a brand new career at age 50, and one that would force me to learn to communicate more clearly. I became a newspaper columnist. Then I tried my hand at sportswriting. Today, one of my favorite activities is to go out and cover a football, basketball, or baseball game. I love sitting up in the press box, interviewing players in the locker room, and hobnobbing with professional sportswriters (who are, by the way, some of the most talented and happily employed people I've ever met).

In order to open that door to sportswriting, I had to make direct connection with people in publications that used *freelance* writers (like me). But I also had to learn certain techniques and "rules of the game." (One of them is "Never cheer in a press box." They'll throw you out bodily if you do. That was one of the more painful lessons in my new career.)

Job Jargon
Freelancing is pursuing a profession without a long-term commitment to a single employer.

Big Questions!

These are big questions. You'll be coming back to them again and again as you work your way through the book. You may want to revise them slightly to suit your own needs and special circumstances. That's fine. The point is that, in today's economy, we all need to frame some set of directions for the roadmap of our working lives. Because if you don't set a destination, someone else will do it for you—and you may not like where they send you.

The Least You Need to Know

➤ Unquestioning loyalty to an employer doesn't get you much these days—and it may do you a world of damage if it causes you not to learn.

➤ Realize that the "rules of the game" have changed in today's job world and that these changes, such as reduced or nonexistent loyalty to employees, will affect your career-change plans.

➤ Ask yourself market-driven questions that focus on a career field you care about and explore your answers in depth.

➤ Ask: Where are the markets? What needs doing?

➤ Ask: What can I do?

➤ Ask: How can I connect with the markets where those needed skills are?

Chapter 4

Good News, Houston. We Have a Problem!

In This Chapter

➤ Finding out how problems and market changes can create new opportunities and careers

➤ Learning why bad economic news isn't bad for everyone

➤ Determining the worth of retraining

Now that you have an idea of the questions you need to ask yourself about your career change, you'll want to get a better sense of some of the forces behind the economic shifts that may affect your livelihood. In this chapter, you'll find out a little about how change affects the job market and you'll begin to see how you can make that change work for you.

Your Job, Should You Accept It, Doesn't Exist Yet

Some years ago, former Colorado Governor Dick Lamm made the comment that one-third of all the jobs likely to be important in the future had not, as of yet, been invented.

It was a catchy statistic, not unlike the startling U.S. Department of Labor estimate that young adults now entering the workforce will, on average, have careers in seven—count 'em, seven—different fields before they walk away with the gold watch. Lamm's eye-catching remark was widely quoted in the media.

I wanted to use the stat in my own writing, and I called Lamm up to ask him where he'd heard it. He thought for a moment, then left the phone to look in his files. "Sorry, Bill," he said when he returned. "I have no idea where that came from."

Mysterious as its origin may be, I think the one-in-three figure is as good as any. There's just no question that occupational roles are evolving at an ever-increasing pace. At the same time, however, I have found that there's nothing more difficult to predict than the future of a specific job title. Take a look at two growing fields (one considerably larger than the other) and you'll see what I mean.

Banker Gives Birth to Financial Planner

Is it a paradox or does it just look like one? At the same time that the ranks of old-fashioned bankers are shrinking, the need for professional financial planning help appears to be ready for explosive growth.

Career Counsel

Even stable and conservative industries can undergo major periods of realignment. No matter how "tried and true" your current industry is, you owe it to yourself to explore the new developments likely to affect it in the future.

Talk with bankers who've been in the field a while and they'll tell you about the long-lost days when there was such a thing as a career path in their industry. At one time, banks had clearly defined career succession ladders based on sequences of skills. Start out as a credit analyst and you could become a loan officer, then head of a loan department.

But those days are history. Banking careers have been battered by two powerful trends: automation and deregulation. If you're like most of us, perhaps eight or nine of your last ten encounters with your bank took place via an automatic teller machine or a personal computer. And when deregulation carried the day in the mid-1980s under the Reagan administration, banks suddenly found themselves in an unfamiliar position—competing fiercely for customers.

Within today's banking industry, staffs and budgets are lean, and management jobs have changed radically. Rather than supervising large staffs, most managers now oversee projects...and are often rewarded for flexibility and creativity, rather than for a conservative, predictable approach to a narrow set of problems.

The banking industry has been downsizing. Now take a look at the financial planning industry. Twenty-five years ago, it didn't even exist—at least, not in sufficient numbers to attract the interest of regulatory agencies and educational institutions. Today, some 27,000 individuals have been designated as certified financial planners, and their ranks are growing. (And more operate without official designation as a C.F.P.) These people are out to save America's 37 million Baby Boomers from impending financial disaster, and from the looks of things, they're going to have plenty of problems to work on.

For decades, the boomers have overspent and undersaved, which leaves them vulnerable during tough times, because many of them will live quite a long time. (Current actuarial charts now run up to age 115!) A lot of them are reaching out to financial planners as the result of the career shock that accompanies being the victim of downsizing. For good measure, the average boomer has also deferred having children until a later-than-average age, so they'll be paying college tuition later than their parents did. Add it all up, and you've got a huge demographic bump, a massive group of people who are likely to continue to need lots of help making sense of financial matters, even if they don't need to meet with bankers as often as they once did.

Work Alert! Think carefully before you commit to a career as an independent consultant or analyst. The skills required for independent success in your field may extend far beyond simple technical competence.

So all a dislocated banker has to do is hang out a shingle and set up shop as an independent financial planner, right? Well…

Granted, the need for financial advice is evident. But how many opportunities will there be for people to operate an independent professional practice? Many of the skills necessary to do so involve sales and marketing expertise, and if these are in short supply, the banker-turned-entrepreneur may have a hard go of it. The truth is that the skills associated with successful self-employment are very different from the skills many banking professionals have traditionally brought to the table. Most of these people are used to analyzing financial data and listening sensitively to clients' needs rather than selling the client something. Yet, as a general rule, self-employed people can count on spending about 40 percent of their time in marketing and sales activities. The skills they use are more like those of insurance salespeople, which is one reason why so many independent financial planners come from that field.

However, there is good news for those with experience in the banking industry who are eager to move into financial management. Huge investment management organizations are creating large numbers of routinized jobs in this field, jobs that don't require the same level of sales and marketing skills an independent planner would need to succeed. But there is bad news too. These jobs don't begin to match the annual income of the most successful financial planners.

To make the most of the current demand for financial planning services, someone whose entire working life has been defined by the rigid, bureaucratic corporate culture we used to associate with banks is going to do more than pick up new skills. He or she is going to have to pick up a new working style, as well.

Help Wanted: Telling People Where to Drill

Seismic data brokers market the information geophysicists need to track potential oil deposits. Geologists produce their data by taking mile-by-mile soundings across large stretches of countryside. It's an intricate—and expensive—process. The big oil companies used to handle all the data acquisition themselves. These days, cost-conscious energy companies are more likely to buy or license data from independent contractors. Today there are 50 seismic data brokering companies in the United States, with about 1,000 total employees.

The most successful companies are highly market-driven. And what do these companies really sell? It's not, as one might expect, geological advice. (Most of the brokers have no background in geology.) What they're actually selling is lower finding costs. Horrific "bust" years in the oil industry can yield significant opportunities for a seismic data brokerage firm that knows how to add value to a customer's bottom line: As one industry leader told me, "The best opportunities often turn up in the worst of times."

What the World Needs Now Is More New Problems

The important point to note in each of the two occupational fields we've just examined is that jobs evolve from unmet needs. As career specialist Tom Jackson has observed, "A job is a problem to be solved."

The rise of seismic date brokerage firms is an example of a newly emerging occupation that arose from a declining industry. As any number of labor economists and investment analysts will attest, the best time for innovation is when things aren't really going all that well.

Bad times create new problems. New problems create new jobs. Seismic data brokers add value not by drilling more and bigger oil wells, but by providing additional information, information that enables organizations to operate more effectively.

Sometimes, as in the case of financial planning, the new problems require entirely new approaches. Displaced bankers need more than just new skills to succeed as independent financial planners; they need new working styles as well. There are countless new career opportunities. If America's Baby Boomers have both the lowest savings rate in history (which they do) and are likely to receive an unprecedented $6.5 trillion in inheritance funds within the next dozen years or so (which they are), and if they are likely to live longer than any generation on record, then the problem to be solved is clear. Someone's going to have to help these people figure out how and when to make important financial decisions.

Career Counsel

If the problem is evaporating, thanks to changes in technology or the influence of new market forces, the job may not be one you want to cling to indefinitely.

Can you develop the aptitudes and the attitudes necessary for success within any given emerging field? Are you likely to enjoy doing so?

When you ask "What's the problem to be solved by this job?" you're really asking a variation on John Crystal's question: "What needs doing?" An important implication of Crystal's question is: "Do I care about the problem enough to help solve it?" Follow the process through. Ask more variations on that question. Does the resolution of the problem you're looking at really mean anything to you? Does it "float your boat"? Is this a problem you would find it meaningful to become involved in? These are especially important questions to ask if the problem to be solved requires retraining. Education requires motivation!

To Retrain or Not to Retrain

Not long ago, I walked into a school in California where unemployed people were being retrained in the use of multimedia software. The school was nothing but a Quonset hut crammed with about 100 computer workstations. It looked like a supply shed for a shipyard. The students sat hunched over their keyboards and terminals, working through a self-paced curriculum, holding up their hands to call an instructor when they had problems. This was a full-time program that lasted for three months! I couldn't imagine trying to learn in those conditions for even a day, but a good many people resurrected their careers in that dungeon!

Listen to your own intuition when it comes to retraining. If the material you're supposed to be learning is inherently uninteresting to you, the likelihood that it will yield positive results for you is slim. As a recent article in the *Harvard Business Journal* suggests, "know-how" is never enough. "Know-how," "know-why," and "care-why" are all important elements of any successful career. When in doubt, ask yourself: "Do I care about the process of seeing this problem solved?"

Bet You Didn't Know

In the early 1980s, as the first word processing software programs became available, the Sunday papers were filled with help wanted ads for word processors—people who could use the technology full time. These days, however, those ads are much harder to find.

What happened? The need that was met by word processing programs continued to grow; there is an ever greater need to process information efficiently. But the need was so pervasive that word processing skills became a part of many other jobs rather than a stand-alone occupation. By and large, it's easier to predict the future course of needs and skills than occupations.

And the next time some news magazine runs an article about the "hot new job titles" ("knowledge engineer," say, or "electronic data processing auditor"), ask the questions you learned about in the previous chapter. How important are the problems those jobs are intended to solve? The depth of those needs will determine the outlook for the occupation...not some number-crunching analysis from a forecaster. Do your own information gathering and come up with your own answers before you leap into something new.

The Least You Need to Know

➤ Occupational roles are evolving at an ever-increasing pace, and there's nothing more difficult to predict than the future of a specific job title.

➤ What may seem like a bad time in one industry can mean a windfall for another, which may mean new job openings and career opportunities to explore.

➤ When analyzing the latest "hot new career fields," ask yourself how important are the problems those jobs are intended to solve.

Chapter 5

The Most Important Sale You'll Ever Make

In This Chapter

➤ Marketing yourself effectively

➤ Using work and personal experiences to your advantage

➤ Finding out your strongest skills

Self-promotion is an art, but as any struggling salesperson will tell you, it's an art that can sometimes take a while to master. In this chapter, you'll learn how to figure out what you have to offer that is likely to catch the interest of potential employers. You'll also define your *strong suits* and how they should (or shouldn't!) be guiding your career change decisions.

The Toughest Sell of All

We'd rather go to the dentist than give a sales presentation—especially when the "product" is ourselves. People who are highly creative or possessed of an artistic temperament probably have the toughest time of all "selling themselves." I know a fellow who worked as a concert promoter. One day he received a phone call from a performer he'd booked in previous years, asking if he could appear in an upcoming program. The fellow seemed to be struggling with his sales pitch, stumbling over his presentation.

Job Jargon
Your **strong suits** are something in which you excel, or your *forte*.

Job Jargon
Marketing is the process of promoting, selling, and distributing a product or service.

Finally, the promoter interrupted. "Why are you so nervous, Art? You know, every time you and Lou have performed here, the concerts have been a smashing success."

The artist paused for a moment. "Well, you know, we let our booking agent go. We thought we could do as good a job ourselves. But now we're paying the price—it's harder than it seems to promote yourself."

Who were the artists who found themselves in such a bind? None other than Ferrante and Teicher—the most popular piano duo in history!

How do we get around this fear of self-promotion? The best strategy is to think about the process less as "sales" and more as *marketing*. One-on-one sales work can be a part of marketing, of course, but the marketing label implies a more strategic, less hit-and-miss approach. As you'll learn in a later chapter, it's the approach I favor when it comes time to contacting prospective employers directly. It's also the approach I'd recommend you take as a preliminary to that contact, while you're in "research mode."

There are three parts to the process of identifying and evaluating your strong suits from a marketing perspective:

➤ Defining yourself as a product

➤ Establishing where the market is (and is not) for your services

➤ Identifying the appropriate media for making the connection

If you take those tasks one step at a time, you'll find that emphasizing your own strong suits becomes a much less intimidating—and, occasionally, even enjoyable—process.

Defining Yourself

This is an important task, and for some people it can be learned only with difficulty. You need to figure out not just who you are, but who others perceive you to be, and whether or not that perception furthers your goals.

What Field Do You Play In?

Take Deion Sanders, the phenomenally talented athlete known for playing both football and baseball at the professional level. Sanders is a flamboyant figure on the football field—"Neon Deion," master of end-zone celebrations, and all that. When he entered major league baseball, Sanders tried to play the same outlandish character with the media, and he got a poor response. Baseball people were not primed for his brand of flamboyance.

But watching Deion Sanders play center field for the Cincinnati Reds today, you'll see a completely different personality. He's subdued, subordinating his media image to that of the team. Sanders now knows that the two sports have different cultures and recognizes that he's more accomplished on the gridiron than on the baseball diamond. So he reserves his "prime-time" persona for football.

Not all of us have quite that range of talents to contend with—the ability to make contact with a 90-mile-per-hour fastball in one job and a 220-pound fullback in the other. But if we have any sort of variety in our work history, we do face the challenge of presenting ourselves selectively. It's important that we show prospective employers only one those skills that pertain to their needs.

The Title/Degree Thing

I happen to have a doctorate. When I'm in an academic environment or some other setting where folks are identifying themselves by their titles, I'll follow suit and introduce myself as "doctor." But in other environments, such as newspapers or career-counseling centers, I never use the title. It would only serve to distance me from people I want to feel comfortable with. And I'm not alone. At the newspaper where I spent years as a columnist, the one-time restaurant critic had a Ph.D. in theology from the University of Chicago. And yet, except when he was on special assignment covering a religious event, he never used the title. A doctorate didn't have much to do with evaluating the barbecue sauce at a rib shack!

So, who do you want to be in the next phase of your career? You can learn a lot about your own strong suits by playing a simple role-playing game I call "So Whaddya Do?" This is an exercise in strategic small talk.

So Whaddya Do?

Find a partner and pretend you're at a social event: a cocktail party, or a coffee hour between church services. Your friend walks up and asks that daunting question, "So whaddya do?" You have to improvise your way through three possible response styles:

Option one: You present your current or most recent job title and describe it in depth. (Hey—your partner asked for this, right?) Use imposing acronyms and multisyllabic words whenever possible. And once they're thoroughly befuddled, explain that you're looking for work in a similar field. Then, fix 'em with a stare and ask if the person has a close friend or relative who's hiring.

Work Alert!
Your current or former title may make perfect sense to you, but may leave people outside of your organization glassy-eyed. One woman I read about won a job as "Senior Diversity Planning Analyst for the Office of the Vice Provost for Educational Equity" at a big university. Not exactly a conversational icebreaker.

Option two: Skip the talk about job titles and tell your partner what you've been doing in terms of what, how, and who. Summarize the service you've provided (the what), the skills you've employed (the how) and the clientele you've served (the who). Tell your partner you're beginning to explore new fields where this type of work goes on.

Option three: Describe the kind of work you'd like to do in terms of the benefits you can offer. Paul and Sarah Edwards, the home-based business experts, call this the "ya-know-how?" approach to marketing. ("You know how most people dread going to the dentist? Well, I'm a painless dentist, and I'm setting up a practice.")

Try each of these approaches with your partner. Which encourages the most positive response?

Testing, Testing...

If the process of charting (and discussing) your own general career direction seems too daunting, or if you find you're getting lost in the lint of your own navel-gazing, you might consider taking part in some vocational testing. Tests will never tell you all you need to know to make a good career decision, but they may offer a fresh breeze of objectivity—some data from outside your own skin.

There are two vocational tests that most career counselors like to use: the Strong Campbell Interest Inventory and the Myers-Briggs Type Indicator. Both are fun tests, not the sort of testing you can fail. They're generally available at a modest fee from local community colleges or universities. The value of the interpretation often varies with the training of the test administrator, so it's important to ask about the credentials of personnel at various centers. Someone with a master's degree in a counseling-related field generally is well-qualified to do this kind of test interpretation.

Both of the above tests should offer insights into the kinds of occupations where people like you are to be found, as well as some hints about why your current career may not thrill you.

Cop an Aptitude

For a small minority of individuals who seem to have difficulty pinning down their abilities, a program of *aptitude* testing may be worthwhile. Most people of this sort have serious problems focusing their energies on a single path—often because they're skilled in areas that don't fit well in a single job.

A friend of mine who has a Ph.D. in American literature has spent most of his career working as an engineer. His father was an engineer and his mother an English teacher. My friend acquired some strong abilities from both sets of genes. Currently, he works at a college directing an information technology telecommunications program. It's a unique way to combine those gifts.

Over the years, I've met many other individuals with mixed aptitudes who've not been so fortunate. They'll get an undergraduate degree in engineering and then train to be a lawyer. That sets up an either-or dilemma where, no matter what happens, half of the person feels frustrated. Testing experts call these people TMAs, for "Too Many Aptitudes."

Job Jargon
An **aptitude** is an innate ability to learn something.

> **Bet You Didn't Know**
>
> The best aptitude testing program I know of is offered by the Johnson O'Connor Foundation. These tests are useful for people who sense they might be TMAs and who want some help in prioritizing their aptitudes; they also may be helpful to young adults who are stymied by the prospect of choosing a career. The organization is founded on the work of a pioneering American industrial psychologist, and has offices in major cities. For information, call (800) 452-1539.

Hey, Wait a Minute!

Do you really need a test to tell your strengths? In most cases, the answer is no. Unless you're feeling down in the dumps because of an overlong stay in a bad job, a few simple exercises (along the lines of "So Whaddya Do?") may be all you need to zero in on the strong points of your working life.

Here's an approach you can follow to put you in a more reflective frame of mind.

Find a setting where you can think in depth, and without interruption, about what you do well, how you've done it well in the past, and how you'd like to do it well in the future. Where can you most easily close your eyes and take a good deep breath? Maybe out in your back yard early in the morning. I've been known to come up with some illuminating insights during the seventh-inning stretch of an afternoon baseball game.

The idea is to find some sense of freedom to think about fresh directions in your life. That's not easy, considering how close we all are to our own experiences. As the saying goes, "Whoever it was discovered water, it probably wasn't a fish." A change of scenery can do you a world of good.

Twin Peaks

Here's a two-step exercise that can get you off to a running start. It will help you reconsider the course of your career, and make it easier for you to get a fix on your own strong suits.

Step One

Take out three sheets of paper. At the top of each page, draw a horizontal line and write down a title for some *peak experience* in your life thus far.

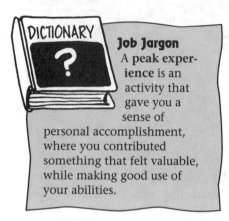

Job Jargon
A peak exper-ience is an activity that gave you a sense of personal accomplishment, where you contributed something that felt valuable, while making good use of your abilities.

Peak experiences may come from any era of your life. They might have been long or short time periods. And they need not have been monumentally successful. What counts is how they felt inside. One of my peak experiences was the year I spent as editor of my small college newspaper. That experience probably was as challenging and rewarding as anything I've done, even though I've taken on far larger assignments since then.

Take time to reflect on these experiences. Talk over your choices with a spouse, a current or ex-coworker, or some other friend. It's good to reflect on the times of our lives. (And there's no reason to restrict yourself to just three items. If you find yourself getting into the exercise, by all means, keep on writing down peak experiences!)

Step Two

Under your heading on each sheet, draw a vertical line down the middle of the page. That will give you two columns to work with. On the top of the left column, write "What I Did." On the right column, write "How I Did It."

On the left side, list everything you can remember doing in the course of the peak experience at the top of the sheet. Fill in the column as completely as you possibly can. Don't worry about leaving some word or detail out. You can always go back and fill in.

Then, on the right side, try to come up with a word or two that describes the skills and traits you used in completing each task.

Here's what it might look like:

DESIGNED SUCCESSFUL MAILING TO NONPROFIT ORGANIZATIONS

What I Did	*How I Did It*
Interviewed librarians and senior center personnel	Establishing rapport, interpersonal skills
Summarized findings and recommendations for superior	Analysis, composition, and verbal communication skills
Designed mail piece	Composition, editing, word processing skills

---

What I Did	How I Did It
Selected print vendor	Analysis, negotiation skills
Oversaw mailing process	Management, supervisory skills

Don't worry about listing every item in the correct column. Right now, it doesn't matter if you list a *skill* as a *trait*, or vice versa. But do try to get all your hard skills down in black and white. When you produced the newsletter for the Society of Bluetail Fly Watchers, did you use Pagemaker or some other software program? When you took over the management of that pancake house that was about to go defunct, did you demonstrate some skills in cost accounting, as well as a supple wrist for flipping flapjacks?

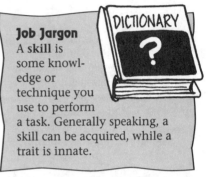

Job Jargon
A **skill** is some knowledge or technique you use to perform a task. Generally speaking, a skill can be acquired, while a trait is innate.

What we're trying to do here is answer the one basic question of evaluating the peak experiences of your career: "What were you doing when you did that?"

Take time to note the results of your good work. That's what future employers and colleagues will want to know. If you performed seven surgeries and six patients died, that may not be the best material for your cover letters. Look for skills you have used that produced tangible positive results.

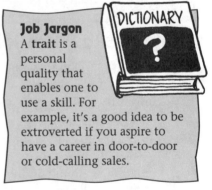

Job Jargon
A **trait** is a personal quality that enables one to use a skill. For example, it's a good idea to be extroverted if you aspire to have a career in door-to-door or cold-calling sales.

Prove It!

Not long ago, my coworkers and I had a meeting with the human resource managers of a large corporation. We were trying to sell them on the idea of forming a cooperative alliance with other local companies in their industry. The idea was to collaborate in enlarging the pool of candidates for the jobs they were trying to fill, rather than cannibalizing by stealing one another's employees. Like many other industries, companies in this field are short of qualified candidates; they have jobs they can't fill.

The H.R. managers thought ours was an interesting idea, but they had some preconditions. "There are two things we need," one of them pronounced as our meeting ended. "We want a line-item budget tied to the products you'll provide us. And, we need information on someplace where your approach has been tried before. What difference did your program make? We want to see some hard data on the outcome."

Employers are like that. So are lending institutions. Like Cuba Gooding, Jr.'s character in the film, *Jerry Maguire*, they want to see outcomes from expenditures. "Show me the money!" Or, at least, "Show me some tangible results that I can tie to the services for which you want to bill me."

Hard Skills versus Soft Skills

Working with career changers over the years, I've learned to draw a clear line between hard skills and soft skills. Soft skills are abilities like sharing leadership or team-building. They're vitally important, especially in technical fields where many people have rather narrow outlooks. But soft skills alone ("I'm a people person") will never get anyone hired.

Career Counsel

If you can demonstrate a good combination of hard and soft skills—say, the ability to work efficiently with both software and subordinates—you'll find that the doors will swing open in other fields.

Most employers I've interviewed follow a simple rule of thumb when screening job candidates. They'll begin by looking for hard skills—training in a certain discipline, experience in a related industry, knowledge of the technical tools they're using. Then, they'll evaluate personal or cultural factors such as "people skills"—say, the ability to work as part of an engineering team.

How Not to Get a Job Offer

To be sure, candidates can get knocked out of the running in that soft-skill phase. I was talking with a colleague of mine who teaches in the geography department of a local university. Geography is a field that has suddenly come alive due to the impact of a new technology. In this case, it's something called GIS (Geographic Information Systems).

"We're having a hard time filling a couple of positions," my friend said. "The last person we brought in to interview had great GIS skills. A real techno wizard. But he started ordering us around during the interview! That guy may have been the most incorrigible human being I've ever met."

Guess who didn't get the job.

Time to Try on Your Strong Suits

Today, most good jobs require a mix of skills, both hard and soft. Project management is a good example.

Project managers in technical fields follow a problem-solving process that I've found in many different fields.

It's a three-phase process that's similar to the cycle of business operation: *projecting*, *producing*, and *promoting*. Here's an example from a client who's a software manager.

Projecting

Software developers begin by seeing and solving problems. They need to perceive the problem their new product is intended to solve, and then project the steps they'll take to resolve it. What kinds of programmers will be needed? How many? For how long?

This phase is essential to any job in which people are required to be creative. It's comparable to the product-development stage of business operations.

Producing

A technical project manager must have a good, working knowledge of the tools his or her employees are using. It's also important to be aware of emerging technologies that might benefit the project. Programming in C++ and UNIX are examples of producing skills.

Promoting

This has to do with leadership functions such as team building. "Software development is always one step from chaos," claims my client. "It's like 30 people writing the same book." The final phase, promoting, is where the rubber meets the road in terms of people skills.

Together, these three types of skills—projecting, producing, and promoting—form a kind of sequence. They're three phases of a cycle. One step leads to the next in the course of problem-solving. And solving problems is the whole reason people hire other people.

Balancing the Three Ps

For most of us, rounding out these skills is always a challenge. David Kolb, an organizational psychologist from whom I learned to see jobs this way, has pointed out that many people flounder in their careers because of *overspecialization*. He cites a phrase in French, "déformation professional" to describe what happens to those who get very good at just one thing.

> **Job Jargon**
> Overspecialization is to limit oneself or to concentrate too much in an activity, field, or practice.

I once had a client who was such an introverted software developer that he was almost totally oblivious to his work environment. One morning he came to work and found the door locked. His company had gone bankrupt overnight, but he'd no idea they were in financial trouble. That's professional déformation at work.

You'll Need More Than That!

In today's changing economy, many people are frustrated—not because they have no skills, but because their skills are too narrow. Some of the most troubled people I know are managers who have lost touch with the core skills of their fields. I know software development managers who've become specialists in one facet of project management such as leadership skills, but have let their own programming skills go stale. One of them said when he lost his job, "I'm an expert in team building, but where the hell's my team?"

In one high-tech industry center, a group of unemployed specialists has formed a professional association to market their narrow skills to employers. They fund their organization by charging dues, and the members are expected to fork over a share of their fees when they get a consulting assignment. That's one approach to the problem of overspecialization, although it still leaves people stuck in their specialties. I think it's better to broaden one's skills.

The Good and the I Can't Stand It

Jobs come in two basic forms: the good and the insufferable. The latter variety generally involves a narrow range of duties and a solitary skill. Many telephone-based customer service jobs are like that. If the service rep who can't tell you why your credit card bill has just become larger than your annual income says something like, "I only know what's on my screen," you know you're dealing with a person who's stuck in the kind of job you want to avoid.

Good jobs call for *skill sets*, or combinations of skills. Rather than the one-kerchunk rhythm of a repetitive job, good jobs require you to draw on more than one kind of skill and both sides of your brain. Often, some of the skills are unfamiliar, and not part of your original training. (I've had to learn a few new tricks about e-mail as part of this book-writing project, and I can tell you, technology is not one of my strengths! But good jobs are like that—they force us to diversify our skills.)

Tracking Down What Works

If you can A) learn to recognize the skill sets you have developed thus far in your career, and B) learn to look for the skill sets that new jobs require, you will have made great strides toward connecting with the good jobs on this planet. For you'll have gotten beneath the titles of these jobs down to the substance of them—the skills they actually require.

To do that, just apply the line down the middle of the legal pad exercise to the work you've done and the work you want to do. Separate the work from the skills.

Staying in Balance

For most people who find they're overspecialized in mid-career, the best solution is to round out their skills in other sectors of the spectrum. If all you have is soft skills in management, it's generally better to learn the current software package in your field, rather than picking up another degree in management.

Today, in many of America's 1,200 two-year community colleges, some 25 percent of the entering students already have four-year degrees. They're back in school for a limited time, to pick up a few skills from other parts of the spectrum. In the next chapter, you'll look at some strategies for continuing your education. You'll also get an idea of the importance of learning styles in that process.

The Least You Need to Know

➤ You can get a better handle on your current aptitudes by practicing explaining to others what you do.

➤ Informal (or formal) aptitude testing is another great way to get a fix on your existing skills.

➤ You should take time to reflect on past peak experiences: Identify what you did and how you did it.

➤ You should apply the same peak-experience exercise to the work you're doing now and the work you'd like to do.

➤ Remember: Your focus should be on skill sets—not job titles.

Chapter 6

Hey, Buddy. Learn This!

In This Chapter

➤ Identifying your core competencies

➤ Finding out how you like to learn

➤ Preparing yourself for Peak Experiences, The Sequel

Skills obsolescence is what training specialists call a condition that many people suffer from nowadays. It's the sense that what you know how to do is no longer in demand, that new skills are in vogue. In this part of the book, you're going to learn about how you can best bridge the gap between obsolescent skills and competitive skills by making the most of your own interests and learning style.

Is a Skill Ever Really Obsolete?

It's not that the skills we have are useless. Even a skill nobody else expresses much of an interest in can serve you quite well.

I happen to be writing this book in WordStar. WordStar is a software program I know so well it's second nature to me. I can zap out the commands in my sleep. The only problem is that for some time now, WordStar has been off the market. And skills in WordStar have been unmarketable for longer than that.

Reality Check

A few years ago, I decided to write a newspaper column about new trends in temporary employment services. As part of my research for the story, I put on my business duds and

Job Jargon
Skills obsolescence refers to skills that generally are no longer in use.

began knocking on doors of some temp services in town. I filled out their forms and then took some office skills exams. It was a humbling experience. The only test I was even qualified to take was word processing and the only word processing program I knew was WordStar. But I did manage to pass the WordStar exam by five words a minute. Then I waited for the phone to ring—waited for an employer to place an order for an office worker who was fully qualified in using WordStar.

Can you guess how many calls I got? Nada. Zero. Zilch. My WordStar skills were worth nothing on the market.

Plans for Lifelong Learning

Perhaps you've had a similar experience. It's quite common. I remember a conversation with a college physics professor who was struggling in mid-career. "No one wants to know what I have to teach," he sighed.

He reminded me of a Catholic priest I'd spoken to about the same time. "I have all the answers," the priest lamented, "but nobody's asking the questions." What do we do when that happens? One solution is to develop a personal, strategic plan for lifelong learning—a plan that helps us scan the environment to see how the skills in fields we care about are changing, and one that helps us upgrade our skills by building on our natural strengths and styles as learners.

The way to do all that is to concentrate on *core competencies*—the skills you can build on.

Skills as Building Blocks

Job Jargon
Core competencies are the underlying skills you use to solve problems and develop income. As a rule, they're what you do best in the field you know best.

Two specialists in corporate strategic planning, C. K. Prahalad and Gary Hamel, coined the term in a *Harvard Business School Review* article a few years ago. The basic idea was that corporations ought to concentrate their energies on the skills they use to create new products, rather than the products themselves.

My favorite story about core competencies comes from the early days of Minnesota Mining and Manufacturing, known as the 3M Corporation. It seems the original product of 3M was sandpaper. The corporation dominated the industry, selling tons and tons of sandpaper and outshining every competitor in that area. But eventually, they exhausted the market. There was only so much demand for that product.

That's when one of their prime inventors stepped to the plate—a fellow named Francis G. Okie. One morning, he came up with the idea of shaving with sandpaper. It was a cheaper, if somewhat uncomfortable, alternative to razor blades.

Okie never lost faith in his inspiration. He shaved his face with sandpaper every day. (I imagine he was readily identifiable around 3M by his ruddy complexion.) But fortunately, other views prevailed at corporate headquarters. 3M executives decided to shift their attention from their leading product to the skills that enabled them to produce it in the first place: the development of abrasives, adhesives, and coating/bonding products.

As a result, 3M has gone on to turn out 56 major product lines in the course of their 75-year history—everything from Scotch Tape to Post-Its. It beats trimming your sideburns with sandpaper, right?

Branching Out but Staying Rooted

Today there are all sorts of published histories of *corporations* and their core competencies. Procter and Gamble has built several generations of products from its knowledge of fats and oils, emulsifiers, and skin chemistry—everything from bar soap to acne drugs. Canon has based its product lines of copiers and cameras on competencies in precision mechanics, fiber optics, and microelectronics. Sony has specialized in miniaturization of electronic devices. The list could go on and on.

Job Jargon
Core competencies are the basic abilities that help us generate marketable products and job-specific skills.

For individuals, the point is that each of us ought to pay attention to the competencies that have been driving our careers. Building on core competencies—that which you've already learned and shown an aptitude for learning—makes just as much sense at the individual level as in the life of a corporation. Core competencies can be found in every profession.

Tracking 'Em Down

An executive at a meat-packing plant once confided to me that he didn't know much about livestock. He'd built his career around his experience as an accountant. He said, "I spent so much time in cost accounting, reviewing travel expenditures and the like, that now I can take those skills into any area of a business. I pride myself on knowing what's reasonable."

I once asked a writer and consultant friend who was trained as an attorney what he'd gotten from law school. He said, simply, "The ability to advocate a cause." That's a core competency—a transferable skill I've seen in many lawyers.

So what are your core competencies? One place to start is with the roster you've begun of peak experiences in your work life. Take a look at those lists you developed in Chapter 4. What are the skills that show up repeatedly in those mountaintop moments of your working life?

Another approach is to look for core competencies in your professional training. Here are a few examples.

Typical core competencies of:

Lawyers

➤ The ability to think critically and test the validity of arguments (or the application of rules)

➤ Verbal skills and the ability to think on one's feet

➤ The ability to write, research, and conduct electronic database searches

➤ The ability to manage work in a stressful, unpredictable environment

➤ The ability to resolve conflicts and deal with people who are in crisis

Bankers

➤ Knowledge of financial products and services

➤ Accounting skills

➤ Knowledge of external and regulatory reporting

➤ Customer service skills

Writers

➤ Outlining, organizing, and summarization skills

➤ The ability to determine what will be of interest to others

➤ The ability to construct a logical argument

➤ The ability to engage a reader's interest

➤ The ability to review, edit, and rewrite material

Where Do They Come From?

What are the origins of core competencies? Some of them are acquired; some are inborn. They "come with the product."

People who develop extensive perceiving skills, such as artists and psychologists, often point to experiences that led them to pay close attention to their surroundings. Many acclaimed Southern novelists (Truman Capote and Reynolds Price, for instance) have said that their education as writers began with the rich, regional language they learned as children as their relatives swapped stories around the Sunday dinner table.

Career Counsel
Good news department: Competencies can evolve for both people and institutions, carrying over into new industries.

Bet You Didn't Know

In an interview, Duke Ellington once described his basic skill as a composer as the ability to listen. He'd just returned from a tour in West Africa, and had spent much of his time there simply listening to birds in the jungle. Those exotic sounds were woven into the melodies of his next composition.

In *Accidental Empires*, a book on the history of the computer industry, Robert Cringely cites an article by Harvard psychologist George A. Miller, "The Magical Number Seven, Plus or Minus Two." Miller observed that the average person can remember about seven digits in a series of numbers. (That was the rationale AT&T used to standardize seven-digit telephone numbers.) However, Miller found that about three individuals in a thousand can remember fewer than five or more than nine numbers in a row. It's the plus-nines, the people at the high end of the memory scale, who are likely to become computer programmers, according to Cringely!

In contrast, listen to the way E. Annie Proulx describes a journalist in her novel, *The Shipping News*: "Partridge saw beyond the present, got quick shots of coming events as though loose brain wires briefly connected." Isn't that a great line? It reminds me of many a scatter-brained, creative writer I've known.

Everyody's Got Something Special

We all have certain core competencies that weave their way in and out of our careers and our lives. Some competencies are genetic. They're gifts we inherit from our forebears, like brown eyes or red hair. Others are cultivated in our formal education, or our early years on the job.

Tinkering, Refining, Expanding

Johnny Mathis once told of his tutelage by Mitch Miller, that impresario of popular music. When he first heard Mathis, Miller knew he'd found an exceptional talent. But he thought the singer's style was too ornate. So he gave Mathis these instructions. "Sing every one of your songs in such a simple way that the person listening will feel that he himself could sing it just as well."

"I did that," Mathis said later. "I sang as simply as possible. But a few slight embellishments did come out, and that became the style that people associate with Johnny Mathis." By learning to look for our core competencies, you can decide how best to take advantage of them. And you can also pay attention to the ways they may limit you in certain situations. A lawyer trained to argue relentlessly, for instance, may find that competency is unappreciated in another profession.

At the most fundamental level, core competencies are essential to survival. The question isn't whether or not you have any core competencies—you do, or you wouldn't be breathing. The question is, are you getting the very most from your campaign to expand and refine your core competencies?

Looking at Yourself

One of my core competencies comes from being educated for the ministry. I have a couple of seminary degrees. For some time, I didn't think much about that training as I began to work in other fields. Then I became aware of my ability to "look at the big picture." People with theological training tend to adopt an overview of the work they're involved in, and that can be beneficial.

But as I watched the struggles that some of my ex-ministerial friends and I have had in our careers, I became aware of another trait we had in common. Whatever field we entered, we had a tendency to try to reform it. This is something I have to keep an eye on in my own work life to this day.

What tendencies in your own life should you be monitoring? What new ways of thinking would be healthy for you to develop?

Tom Toch, an education editor for *U.S. News and World Report*, notes that the reason John Dewey introduced a course in woodworking to his laboratory school students at the University of Chicago was not to train woodworkers, but to teach them to think in a medium other than words.

Work Alert! As essential as they are, core competencies can blind you to other ways of looking at the world. Sometimes it's important to compensate for our professional training or existing predispositions.

Changing Lanes

Today, we live in an age when many people are bridging skills and training from one field to another. Part of the reason is that many of the most popular professions in America have become remarkably overcrowded.

An estimated 50 percent of all the people in the United States who have law degrees are not practicing law. They're like my friends, Paul and Sarah Edwards, who are leading authorities on home-based businesses. Paul is a lawyer and Sarah is a clinical social worker.

How far should you bend your competencies if you're trying to change careers? Once you identify a core competency that really motivates you and gets your juices flowing, you should think twice before embarking on a course of study or career change that ignores that competency entirely.

I once counseled a lawyer who had an undergraduate degree in engineering. (Remember the too-many-aptitudes type? This fellow was a perfect example.) Having always struggled with the fact that his technical interests never seemed to get fed in the practice of law, he became enamored of his Macintosh computer after spending days cooking up programs for it, and eventually concocted a special case-management program. He looked into marketing the program to other lawyers. In the end, it didn't sell. There was too much competition in the legal computer applications field, and the Macintosh began to suffer a serious loss of market share. His passion was still unfulfilled.

The last time I spoke with him, though, he'd found an apparent solution to the problem. He has become a specialist in medical-product liability law. By trying cases where health technology is at stake, he has found a way to integrate the two core competencies—in engineering and law. The moral: It may take you some time to find the setting where you can satisfy your learning style and competencies, but the overall feelings of balance and satisfaction that will result are likely to be worth it.

So, what are your core competencies, and how do they match up with the skills required in particular career fields?

Another Line Down the Middle of the Page

Let's go back to a basic exercise format you were first introduced to in Chapter 5 of this book. Draw a line down the middle of a page in a legal pad. Label the left column "My Skills" and the right column "Others' Needs." Under the "My Skills" heading, summarize some of the skills you've acquired—and under what circumstances you acquired them.

Remember the "What," "Who," and "How" components of the "So Whaddya Do?" exercise in Chapter 5? Those are good categories to begin with—they'll help you get a handle on how you've acquired your core competencies thus far. What kinds of products and services have you offered? How have you done your work? What tools have you learned to use? Who are the clients you've served? What new skills did you have to acquire to meet their needs? How did you pick up those skills?

Skill sets

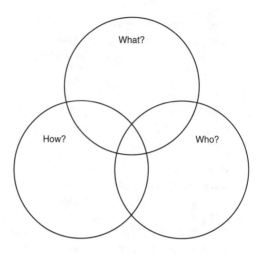

What It Might Look Like

On the left side of your paper, summarize your skills and the way you acquired them. On the right side, note the basic skill sets you may know about already in a variety of work environments or industries that interest you. (You don't have to limit yourself to a single field yet.) For example, a job as a trust officer in a bank probably will require skills in finance, probate law, and accounting, along with some ability in human relations (since many of its clients will be in bereavement).

An airline ticket counter service representative will need strong skills in data entry and retrieval, verbal communication and conflict management, and the ability to lift 75 pounds (the maximum weight of checked luggage). The skill sets will vary with the field you're exploring, so the process of matching what you can do with what others feel needs doing is an ongoing challenge. But that's the way good career connections are made.

MANAGING A PAPER ROUTE

Tasks	*Skills*
Pick up, fold, and deliver alotted number of newspapers to customers on route	Resilience to rain, wind, sleet and snow; ability to ride a bike
Cultivate and maintain good customer relations	Social skills, ability to relate to people of various age groups and personality types, as well as those with special needs
Manage finances systematically	Collect monthly payments at a time when majority of customers are at home; keep accurate records and pay bills on time; deal with deadbeats

---

In the next chapter, we'll learn some techniques for matching your skills while making contact with colleagues and employers in new fields. For now, we want to focus on the principle of matching your core competencies with the needs in the marketplace—and how you should expand those competencies when it becomes clear that you should. That's Career Changing 101, whatever the profession or industry.

Peak Experiences Part Two

Whenever we set out to change course in a part of our lives, our own experience generally provides the best guidance. If you can identify the life experiences that called forth your best efforts, and if you put your finger on the factors that made those experiences feel like "prime time," then you've gone a long way toward putting yourself in a position to repeat them.

That's especially true when it comes to learning.

Peak Experiences in School? You're Kidding!

If you're like me, you've had learning experiences—in and out of school—that have ranged from the "that was fun" to "that wasn't so hot." Somethings about those experiences made them successful or unsuccessful, satisfying or frustrating. But most of us have no sense of what factors made the difference.

That's too bad—if we don't understand our needs and strengths as learners, there's no way we can negotiate for the condition under which we'll learn best. Sometimes those conditions are as basic as class size. If I look back upon my own checkered academic career, I note that I've always done best in small classes. That was true in grade school, in college (undergraduate), and in my doctoral program. By the same token, the times I struggled and disliked school (junior high and in my master's degree program), I was lost in large classes.

If you can sort out the key components of your peak learning experiences, you might well be able to find similar settings in the future—and avoid the kinds of educational programs where you don't do well at all.

The ABCs of Learning

Try the old, reliable "line down the middle of the legal pad" test again. On the left side, write the label "Peak Learning." Write down a few experiences that describe times when you felt you were clicking on all cylinders in your learning. (They needn't be in school.) Perhaps you were trying to teach some subject to a new employee and found yourself growing a lot in the bargain. That certainly qualifies as a peak learning experience.

On the right side, list the "Key Factors" that seemed to contribute to your learning. In my case, I realized that I do better in small classes. You might find some other factor in your successes. Maybe the opportunity to study as an individual, outside a class altogether, so you could learn at your own pace.

Career Counsel
The *Learning-Style Inventory* by David Kolb is available from McBer & Company Training Resources Group, 137 Newbury St., Boston, MA 02116. (617) 437-7080.

If you have the opportunity to test your learning style, there are some good instruments available. One of my favorites is the *Learning-Style Inventory* by David Kolb. Another is by Gloria Frender in her book, *Learning to Learn* (Incentive Publications, Inc.; Nashville, Tennessee).

Here are some of the key factors that the Kolb test explores when it comes to the ways people learn best. I'll frame them as questions so you can explore your own peak learning experiences.

➤ Do you do best as an active or passive learner? (Some people thrive as a member of a large group where they can take notes and there's little danger they'll ever be called on. Others do best in an active role.)

➤ Are you at your best with abstract or concrete material? (Maybe you're the kind of person who enjoys science labs.)

The Three Senses

Frender's instrument helps people consider whether they learn best in an auditory, visual, or kinesthetic mode—hearing, seeing, or touching the material. With her help, I've learned to watch people closely whenever I'm trying to get them to understand new material. Does the person receive information best by listening, reading, or manipulating the material? Nothing is more frustrating than trying to tell a person something he'd rather be reading, or vice versa.

Many people are well into adulthood before they realize that education does not have to be (and indeed, shouldn't be) a one-size-fits-all experience. As adults, we have choices about when and where to learn, although as children we may not have been offered them. That's especially true in large cities where there may be a great variety of educational programs. Fortunately, today most adult learners have options.

Uh, Teacher—Is This Going to Help Me Right Now?

If people have differences in learning styles, there are nevertheless two striking similarities. Adult learning is present-oriented and project-oriented.

Adults learn best in practice, and that's especially true in their weak areas. I've noticed that in my own work with computers. The only time I learn a new software program is when I need it to complete a project. Most adults have little tolerance for subjects that have no bearing on their current work.

Adult learning is also very present-oriented. People in mid-life have little use for "some-day-you'll-thank-me-for-this" tutelage in subjects that may benefit them at some point in the great beyond. They want to see an immediate payoff from their education. For adult learners, the future is now.

Of course, that's not to say adults are unwilling to put forth energy in their learning. Quite the contrary! Most college professors I know would much rather teach a class of people in their late 30s than in their early 20s—the traditional age for undergrads. There's a sense of reality and dedication about adults who've been around the block a few times that enriches education.

> ### Bet You Didn't Know
>
> According to former Labor Secretary Robert Reich, college graduates are 50 percent more likely to receive employer-sponsored training than are high school grads. And in high-tech companies, those with Ph.D.s are twice as likely to receive further training than employees with lesser degrees.

Go for It!

Some important principles about skills and learning to bear in mind:

➤ Job-specific skills go out of date. Given (sometimes very little) time, they all lose market value. Remember my attempt to market my WordStar skills?

➤ All the same, there are core competencies underneath those skills. Keyboard typing and English composition are core competencies for most American writers, and these often undergird specific software skills.

➤ One way to identify your core competencies is to consider the kind of work in which you were originally trained. Look for the core competencies in a law degree, for example. What does your degree enable you to do? Employers in other fields will want to know that.

➤ Another way is to use the line-down-the-middle-of-the-page and look for the skills you have drawn on to do the work you've done.

Use the exercises in this chapter to figure out what you do well, how you've learned about it most effectively in the past, and how you'd be likely to learn more about it in the future. Then go for it! You'll learn more about how to do that in the next chapter.

The Least You Need to Know

➤ Core competencies are the fundamental, underlying skills you use to solve problems and develop income.

➤ Job-specific skills, on the other hand, go out of date; given (sometimes very little) time, they all lose market value.

➤ Testing your own learning style (as briefly outlined in this chapter) can help you get a fix on the approaches to learning that will benefit you the most.

➤ Adults learn best in practice, and that's especially true in their weak areas.

➤ You should take the time to evaluate the skills you have drawn on to do the work you've done so far in your career.

Chapter 7

Welcome to Act I of "Your Career Change"

In This Chapter

➤ Taking the first steps to career change

➤ Finding out why it helps to have a friend in the industry

➤ A insider's approach to want ads, headhunters, and temp agencies

Suppose I were to tell you something like this: "Well, it's time to set sail. Time to call a halt to all this analysis of you and the workplace, or at least set it aside for the time being. Now it's time for you to go out and make some contacts."

If you're like many of the people I've worked with, you might say, "What? You can't expect me to do that. What kind of program is this? I'm only part of the way through your system!" I'd say, "Hey, I understand." I once had a swimming instructor do that to me once, and I nearly drowned in the deep end of the pool. But a crash course is not what I have in mind.

In this chapter and those that follow, you'll take the information you've put together in previous chapters and test the waters of the job market. For there's an art to venturing out beyond the boundaries of past history, and it's best learned in practice.

Testing the Waters

So let's try to put together a strategy to help you explore some field in which you have an interest. This field doesn't have to represent your final choice of a new career, but it does have to be something that is compatible with your core competencies and your emerging sense of the employment market. Let's call this campaign your Working Hypothesis.

Let's assume that, based on the conclusions you reached in the previous chapter, you've got a good idea of at least one career direction that makes sense for you. Now you need to ask yourself: "What do I need to do to get some practice at contacting employers in such-and-such an area?"

You're going to be conducting what we might call a "trial search"—a set of "rehearsal" contacts with prospective employers that will support your career change process as a whole and help you to bring things into focus. Where's the best place to begin?

There are some typical points of contact with the *labor market*—what economists call "labor market intermediaries"—that you should know about. In this chapter, you'll find a quick rundown on each of these sources, some of the pros and cons of dealing with them, and some idea of the best ways to use them to make contact.

A Friend of a Friend

Employers have a strong preference for hiring new employees from their own networks. By that I mean that employers like to hire people who are either known to them or are known to those they know. This may, at a distance, seem unfair, but there's a very good reason employers act the way they do.

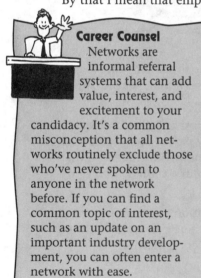

Career Counsel
Networks are informal referral systems that can add value, interest, and excitement to your candidacy. It's a common misconception that all networks routinely exclude those who've never spoken to anyone in the network before. If you can find a common topic of interest, such as an update on an important industry development, you can often enter a network with ease.

Years ago, I put out a job notice for a staff position in a university program I was directing. After a long process of reviewing resumes and conducting interviews, one candidate seemed to lead all the rest. But I found I had a couple of unanswered questions, and they nagged at me. No one in my community had ever heard of this fellow. That was one problem. And when I called his three references, I found that each of them was out of the country. Hmmm…

I placed another call to an administrator I knew at the college where my job applicant had worked previously. "What can you tell me about this guy?" I asked. Because he was a friend, he leveled with me confidentially: "He's bright and well-educated, and a fine person to hire…if you're looking for a rabble-rousing Maoist. The last year he was here he organized a strike of students and faculty over some bogus issue. They almost shut down the school. You can bet he'll do the same to you." Guess who didn't get the job.

For every story of near-disaster like that, seasoned personnel and human resource people can pass along at least two or three others that resulted in actual disaster. The best employers hire through networks—out of self-protection. So your best strategy, no matter what message you're trying to send to a prospective employer, is to work your way through networks—groups of people who know each other or have some common affiliation.

Let's take a look at those other "labor market intermediaries" mentioned earlier.

Help Wanted Ads

Help wanted ads are likeliest to point you toward jobs that can be found in high volume, where the pay is low and the turnover high.

Help wanted ads are the meat market of the American workplace—the employment equivalent of a singles bar. If you're smart, you'll put meaningful long-term relationships higher on the priority list than disappointing short-term affairs. That means that you won't make the classifieds your primary means of contacting employers.

But the classifieds are good for something other than short-term employment in turnover jobs. They can tell you a lot about the hiring patterns of particular companies. And if you want to know more about the duties and qualifications of a particular occupation, the classified ads are a good bet. Note the titles of jobs. They change over time. (What are they calling janitors these days? For a while it was "Sanitation Engineers.") And yes, for a few lucky seekers, the want ads also can provide leads to good jobs in specific fields, usually in the Sunday edition and sometimes in the business section of major metro papers. I know an economist who turned up an $80,000 a year job with a brewery, managing its alcohol education program. He found the job through a help wanted ad.

But my friend's story is the rare exception. The sad truth is that there are hordes of people out there who just read the same paper and noticed the same good job that you did. And guess what? They're applying, too. It's typical for 300 to 400 applicants to apply for a single promising position. Only 4 to 5 percent of quality jobs are found through the want ads.

Many of these notices advertise positions that aren't even open. I know a college professor who's been in a temporarily funded position for three or four years. Now his college has received approval to make the position permanent, so they're advertising his job nationally, as their policy requires. Dozens of people will apply, but who do you think will get the job if he wants it? My money's on the incumbent, the fellow who's sitting in the chair.

Work Alert!
There are some major downsides to responding to help wanted ads. The most serious problem is that answering an ad puts you in a passive position. You'll spend too much time doing nothing if you conduct your entire job search—or even a significant chunk of it—by waiting for an answer to mail you've sent out.

A lot of help wanted ads are like that. They're postings of jobs that often aren't really "open." And, only 4 to 5 percent of quality jobs are found through the want ads.

Downers, Downers, Everywhere

Finally, help wanted ads are bad for your morale. The vast majority of the answers you receive will be negative. When you wait six weeks to get a form rejection letter, it really casts a pall over the whole process. How many of those negative messages can you handle? As Lou Tice, who runs the Pacific Institute in Seattle, puts it: "The basic threat [in dealing with difficult problems] is selective perception. Everyone is susceptible to it. Once you get hold of three dysfunctional ideas at one time, you're in a downward spiral. You begin to experience the self as worthless, the world as hostile, and the future as hopeless."

Work Alert! Studies have shown that the typical unemployed person spends only 10 or 12 hours a month looking for work. A large percentage of these people are simply supremely demoti-vated, thanks to neg-ative experiences with the want ads! Don't let that kind of catastrophic time-management approach sabotage your career-management campaign.

So what is the solution? Tice believes that it's important to focus on your own aspirations. When up against a problem such as unemployment, he advises, "we should keep asking ourselves, 'Is it bigger than me or am I bigger than it?' Keep your aspirations out there, and you'll become bigger than your problem."

I agree, and would like to add this bit of advice: Whenever we venture into strange territory, as in exploring new career directions, it is critical to keep going forward, to stay on the move. That's why I recommend that people make answering ads a secondary strategy (at best), and that they put most of their energies into doing something active.

Yeah, but Look at This Opening!

If you do decide to act on an opportunity you read about in the classified section, use the following guidelines:

➤ Note the three or four key areas of responsibility listed in the ad. Call up the company that has placed the ad and find out the department head to whom the position listed in the ad will report. (That's the person who will make the hiring decision. But you still need to write directly to the personnel clerk whose name appears in the ad. Don't threaten her livelihood.)

➤ Draft a letter to the personnel clerk and send a copy of it to the department head. In your letter, summarize your skills and experience under each of the skill headings listed in the ad. Include a resume that's tailored to the position. At the very least, list the job for which you're applying as your resume objective.

➤ Put your application out of mind, and go on to the next task on your list. Keep a record of the advertised jobs for which you've applied, and follow up by phone in a couple of weeks if you like. But don't keep waiting for a response. Move forward.

Don't Call 'Em "Headhunters"

Executive search firms, also known as "recruiters" and "headhunters" (a term they don't apply to themselves), are a great resource if you're a square peg in search of a square hole.

Search firms are paid large fees (typically 15 percent of a candidate's annual salary) to find job candidates whose skills and experience exactly fit the client's vacant position. Given that mission, recruiters are generally not inclined to assist career changers (although most of them are called on repeatedly for that kind of assistance).

If you're interested in a job that's closely related to your current work and want to find a recruiter, ask colleagues and friends in your field for the names of search firms that may have contacted them.

Bet You Didn't Know

The *Directory of Executive Recruiters* is a very useful book produced annually by Kennedy Publications of Fitzwilliam, New Hampshire. You can contact Kennedy at (603) 585-2200. This resource classifies search firms both geographically and by industry and has extensive advice on the protocol of dealing with these firms.

Now for the Bad News

The downside of this strategy, even for those who fit the position being filled, is that waiting to be recruited is a lot like sitting on a folding chair at the edge of the ballroom, hoping to be asked to dance. It puts you in a passive position. Registering with recruiters, like pursuing the classifieds, should always be a secondary strategy to some other approach that lets you initiate the dance. We'll take a more extensive look at what should be your primary strategies in upcoming chapters of this book.

They Want to Hire You! Quick, Get Out of Town!

One other word of caution: Remember what I said about the importance of networks in hiring? Networks are the employer's safety net, but they can also be a safety net for the applicant. If you receive a call from a recruiter who is being paid handsomely to fill a position with a firm you know nothing about, you should always ask three basic questions:

➤ Why is this job being filled by a recruiter?

➤ Why can't the prospective employer find a good pool of candidates through his or her own network of professional contacts?

➤ Why does he or she have to hire a search firm?

There may well be good answers to these questions. Perhaps the job requires a specific set of hard-to-find skills. Maybe they need a COBOL programmer to fix their mainframe computer so it doesn't crash at one second past midnight on the first day of the year 2000. Or it may be there are a zillion positions to be filled and no one has time to deal with them all. Those are perfectly valid (and, broadly speaking, quite common) reasons for hiring a recruiter.

But the other possibility is that the employer is an ogre in waiting—the kind of individual to whom no one with a shred of decency would refer his worst enemy. So do your own networking and find out about the place that's interested in you. Track down other people in the industry (preferably former employees) and see what they have to say. Don't work without a net!

For Members Only

Job Jargon
A **job club** is a group for unemployed workers in a certain field in which job briefings and leads are passed out.

Job clubs for the unemployed are a good resource, if they take the form of job briefings where leads are passed out within specific fields, or to benefit a particular group, such as alumni of a certain college or university.

But if someone asks you to pay for the privilege of joining a lead-sharing club, think long and hard before you agree to fork over the required dues. The potential for abuse and exploitation is just too great.

Beware the Gloomy Group!

One problem I've found with networking groups for the unemployed (no matter what their motivation) is that they tend to breed dependence and depression. I've seen people become mired in groups like that for years. I once ran a career services program for a university that had a lot of alumni who lived in the same city as the school. One of the approaches I tried was sponsoring a coffee and doughnut support group for career-changers and job-seekers, assuming they could form a network and provide one another with good leads.

But I found that the same people kept coming back week after week, with the same story. "I'm Joe Schmoe, and I'm still unemployed." The group became a terrible downer. I gave up the program and set up a computer-based one-on-one networking system. As individuals signed up for career services, I invited them to fill out a card indicating their willingness to meet with others in the program who might like to know more about the fields in which they had experience. By joining the referral network, they could ask the same kind of assistance from others. Then I made selective referrals based on individual interests and needs. That approach worked very well because it put people in an active role. If you can find a group that offers a similar service, consider joining.

Back to School

Continuing education courses are another good way to go. The benefits are twofold.

Learn, Learn, Learn

Of course, there's the content to consider. If the whole world is firing up the latest release of Windows Whatever, and you're still figuring out how to turn on a 1986-era personal computer system, a continuing ed course may be just the ticket. (But remember what you discovered about the ways adults learn in Chapter 5! In my own experience, software courses are useful only if I'm using the program in my own work. Otherwise, the instruction is like water off a duck's back.)

In addition to the subject matter you might learn, the networking contacts in continuing education can be incredibly valuable. That's true not only for the students in these programs but also the faculty. I know of professional groups whose officers all teach in a degree program at a certain college. The college is their network, and taking their courses is tantamount to being interviewed by their companies!

Or Teach, Teach, Teach

I've also seen instances of part-time faculty networking with one another successfully.

While teaching part-time is not a way to get wealthy (stipends of $2,000 per course are common), the contacts one can make across professions are invaluable. Programs such as the University of Phoenix, which caters exclusively to working adult students and employs nothing but part-time faculty, may be especially good options. Generally, the qualifications required are a graduate degree, some good professional experience, and a willingness to learn some teaching skills.

Recently, I took on a project where I needed a specialist in a particular scientific field. Where did I find my contractor? On the faculty of a department at the school where I'm a part-timer.

Hanging Out with the Insiders

Professional or trade associations offer even more focused opportunities for networking as well as training. One of the most pervasive trends in today's changing economy is the shift of loyalty and power that has been occurring away from employers and toward professional organizations. More and more, the watering hole where workers gather to trade leads and upgrade skills is not the office water cooler but the bar in a hotel where their professional association holds monthly meetings.

This is part of a movement I call *reorganized labor*—almost a new form of unionism, where people are organizing once again on the basis of their craft or trade. At its worst, this movement toward professional networking takes the form of vacations at ski resorts that masquerade as continuing education conferences. (Physicians are notorious for getting together at Waikiki to discuss important new issues in medicine in between visits to the beach.)

Job Jargon
Reorganized labor is a movement toward the organization of people based on a craft or trade.

But I've seen many people ground their careers in professional organizations that offer genuine opportunities to learn new skills. The numbers of these associations have been increasing at a rate of 10 percent per year for the past couple of decades.

The best source of information on professional organizations is *The Encyclopedia of Associations*, a multi-volume compendium put out by Gale Research, Inc. of Detroit. The encyclopedia is available in the reference section of most major libraries, and a reference librarian can show you how to use it.

What to Look for

When trying to find information on a new field, use the encyclopedia to look up the headquarters of the largest association in the industry (the associations are usually listed with the size of their staffs and annual budgets). Then call the main office and ask for the name of the chapter president in your area. Call that individual and ask for the date, time, and location of their meetings. Invariably, you'll find yourself welcomed as a guest. That's because the typical association is always on the lookout for new members.

Meet and Greet

Then simply go and mingle. Look up the officers of the group. Tell them you're interested in learning more about their field, and ask them to introduce you to someone who could meet you over breakfast.

It's as simple—and as challenging—as that. Networking in associations is an untapped, overlooked resource in an economy where loyalty to profession is replacing the ties that once bound people to employers.

Just Passing Through

Temporary employment services are the fastest-growing sector in America's labor market. Today, that fact is no longer news. But is it good news or bad?

That's the tough question career-changers need to consider. The fact is, temp services are changing radically. No matter how you feel about them, the opportunities many firms present to career changers today are truly remarkable.

If you were guided by the stereotypes of a few years ago, you might conclude that temporary employees are folks who fill in answering the phone and making coffee. But today's reality is something very different. The outfit that used to call itself "Kelly Girls" now goes by "Kelly Services," and the change in moniker says a lot about recent changes in the industry.

Bet You Didn't Know

People in the field are careful to use the term temporary *services*—not *agency*. They note that an agent is someone who acts on behalf of someone else. But a temp service takes on all the functions of an employer. The service becomes the employer of record when it comes to tax reporting and all the rest. That's part of the value they add to the process.

The Way We Were

Although "contract work"—that is, hiring staff as needed, rather than employing people for a lifetime—has deep roots in American history, many of us were raised to think of the single-employer career model as the norm. What would today be called *contingency hiring* was common practice in the 19th century. At one point, half of all workers earned their living on a temporary basis. Around the time of World War I, the move toward corporate growth took hold and the ranks of career employees grew steadily. By 1970, the percentage of American workers who spent their entire careers with one firm was about the same as that in Japan; at that time the ranks of self-employed shrank to 7 percent of the American workforce.

Job Jargon
Contingency hiring is the practice of employing workers on a temporary or as-needed basis.

Today, the pendulum has swung back. Conservative estimates of the self-employed begin at 15 percent of the workforce. Some analysts believe the current percentage is much higher, and all agree that the numbers of entrepreneurs are rising. Recent research indicates that more than a third of all workers who start out as temps are offered full-time jobs as a result of their assignments.

So is the trend toward contract employment. In a 1995 article in the *Wall Street Journal*, Peter Drucker wrote, "In the U.S., the number of temporary agencies doubled to 7,000 in 1994 from 3,500 five years earlier. Perhaps half if not more of this growth is in agencies providing professionals—all the way up to senior managers." Drucker is off the mark on one point—using the expression "temporary agencies."

Invasion of the Temp Snatchers

Temp services are growing like kudzu vines in south Georgia. As Peter Schaub, a specialist in the temp field, writes in Denver's *Rocky Mountain News*, "The contract staffing industry encompasses almost every skill set, including accountants, programmers, lawyers, doctors…as well as office professionals." A typical professional, niche market service is Accountants On Call. Founded in 1979, the company has 60 offices in the U.S. and several foreign countries. It specializes in placing accountants and management information professionals in temporary assignments, but also doubles as a recruiter for companies seeking full-time employees.

The temp/headhunter combination is common today because it's a way of working both sides of the street in the employment business. That trend benefits job candidates because many employees get hired into full-time, staff positions after starting as temps. The downside of temp services is that they skim off a hefty share of their employees' wages in return for the service they provide.

But a temp service may just be able to point you toward a new industry or skill application you hadn't thought of previously.

There are three employment groups that are most likely to benefit by hooking up with temp services:

➤ People who are just starting out, such as recent college grads or those trying to establish themselves in new fields.

➤ Mid-career workers, such as those who have relocated with a spouse to a new city and have no local contacts.

➤ Unretiring retiree types who want to keep active (and maintain an income source). *The Registry of Interim College and University Presidents*, for instance, developed as a service that hooks retired college presidents up with educational institutions that need experienced administrators on a short-term basis.

Paging Uncle Sam

Federally-funded employment programs, usually billed as Job Service Centers, offer potential access to some excellent resources for people in career change. Unfortunately, the operative word in that statement is "potential."

The sad reality is that these federal programs are largely ignored by employers. Manpower, Inc., America's largest temporary employment service—and also the nation's highest-volume employer—has the distinction of placing far more job applicants than all of the Job Service Centers combined.

But there's a problem with the federally funded programs—bureaucratization. When Robert Reich became Secretary of Labor under the Clinton Administration, he set out to consolidate an unwieldy number of 163 federal employment and training programs into something like a consumer-oriented system. His efforts became known as One-Stop Career Centers, a format that is now taking shape around the country.

While the new one-stop centers will likely simplify matters for clients, rearranging the data and the existing staff (who are for the most part employed on the basis of seniority) will not do much to change the perception of the people who count the most in the employment game—the employers.

Bet You Didn't Know

Some local employment and training centers have developed special services for *dislocated workers*, which is federal-bureaucratese for those whose jobs have been eliminated as a result of changes in the economy. For eligible career changers, those services often offer funding for retraining and other specialized assistance. In approaching federal employment services, find out if you qualify for services as a dislocated worker. Those are the services worth looking for.

Private Matters

Private career counseling services are advertised every day in the classified section of major newspapers. The companies that offer these services represent an industry that is less than 50 years old...and one that may not enjoy a long history. My instinct is to trust these organizations with a healthy skepticism—and ask to talk to satisfied customers before forking over any dollars.

Should You Seek Professional Help?

Career companies appeared after World War II and the Korean War to help returning veterans reconnect with the labor market. Periodically, these companies have been the object of class action lawsuits owing to the occasional disparity between their extravagant claims and their paucity of actual services.

Some of the grievances seem well-founded. I know of cases where individuals paid five-figure sums to "career specialists" who basically coached them in interviewing and reworked their resumes. Some of the more unscrupulous practitioners in this field advertise themselves as executive search firms and collect resumes of professionals who are looking for work. They then re-contact the same individuals in the role of career counselors, completing a gambit that deserves a spot in the Bait-and-Switch Hall of Fame.

The Benefit of Experience (Maybe)

There is one feature of private career counseling firms that has merit: Many of the individuals who operate these outfits corporate career veterans who understand the ins and outs of business. In that regard, they have a clear advantage over a psychologist offering career services from a college placement center who has never worked outside a college.

If you decide to explore a private career counseling company that advertises in the classified ads, there are a few rules of thumb: First, read the contract very carefully. Be sure that you are not being charged a higher hourly fee than you would pay for other professional services (such as seeing a psychotherapist or a lawyer). Be sure that you understand the nature of the services. Will the company provide you with job leads? Perhaps most important of all, does it have a network of former clients who are now well-employed and eager to help others in the system? Ask to talk to these people!

Finally, ask to meet with the individuals who will provide you with career services. Be sure that you feel comfortable with them, not just with the person who sells you on the service.

With those guidelines in mind, if you're a careful consumer, you may find a private service that can benefit your career search.

What's Next?

As you've no doubt gathered, I feel more positive about some of these resources than others. You may be asking yourself, "Which of these options should be my primary means of contacting employers?" The truth is, none of them should be. Each of the intermediaries you've just read about represents a secondary resource for your trial search. In the next chapters, you'll learn about the tactics worthy of the lion's share of the time you spend developing contacts within a given field.

The Least You Need to Know

➤ Resources likely to benefit you include: temporary services, professional associations, and continuing education courses.

➤ Temporary services, in particular, may offer notable opportunity in the field you are exploring; one-third of all who are employed in this way are reported to receive full-time job offers.

➤ Resources likely to leave you leadless, disappointed, or a combination of the two include classified advertisements and private career counseling firms. Federal job assistance programs may be helpful if you qualify for retraining.

Chapter 8

DID YOU GET MY FAX? OK, I'LL RESEND.

Phone Calls, Resumes, and More Rules Not to Live By

In This Chapter

➤ The power of one: why the only person you can count on when changing careers is yourself

➤ Common misconceptions about changing careers

➤ Networking as an independent contractor

In the last chapter, you learned about some resources that may help you as backup methods for connecting with potential employers during your "trial search." In this chapter, you'll learn about the methods that should occupy most of your time as you conduct this search. You'll also learn how to look beyond some of the most popular misconceptions connected with career changing.

3-2-1: Direct Contact

Perhaps the first and most potentially damaging misconception about changing careers is that someone else can do it for you.

The mode of contact you'll be using as your primary tool during your "trial search" is blissfully simple. You'll be acting as your own CEO—and your own executive recruiter— by setting your own course and making direct contact with important players in the

Work Alert! Any career change campaign that relies primarily on strategies that stall when other people don't take action is likely to disappoint you. Taking personal responsibility for outcomes is an essential talent in today's employment marketplace.

employment marketplace. No intermediaries, no one else in charge of the game, no one to commiserate with about whether or not what's happening is fair. Just you, on the phone, at meetings, at industry events, and writing letters. That's your first line of attack—the strategy you should be using for 70 to 80 percent of the time you devote to this "trial search."

Does that prospect make you a bit nervous, a little bit uneasy? Good! The butterflies you feel in your stomach are the essential beginning point in any career change campaign for which you take personal responsibility. And that's the kind of campaign that's likeliest to land you in a job—and a career—that makes sense to you.

So, yes, you read correctly. You'll be acting as your own president and chief executive officer. That means you've taken a careful look at current market conditions, made some preliminary decisions about your direction, and are now ready to oversee a "test marketing" scenario. This will allow you to make an informed decision about whether or not a greater investment of your time, effort, and energy is warranted in the career area you've identified.

Being your own chief executive officer means:

➤ Setting important goals

➤ Taking a proactive, self-directed approach

➤ Understanding the needs of the industry you've selected on a provisional basis

➤ Changing course when what you're doing isn't bringing you closer to the goal

And, yes, you'll also be acting as your own executive recruiter. That is, you'll take personal responsibility for asking yourself the most important questions about the type of employer and career that will bring you satisfaction. You'll also be taking personal responsibility for contacting the people who can make your career change a reality.

Being your own executive recruiter means:

➤ *Sourcing*—defining your own needs, understanding the requirements of the position, and knowing when you fit the bill

➤ *Recruiting*—making the necessary contacts, and testing to confirm a match with your own skill levels

➤ *Handling offers intelligently*—finding out what you're worth in the marketplace and in the industry

➤ *Increasing the chance of retention*—by arranging, on your own, for continued education, and by developing opportunities for recognition and career growth

That's a lot of work—a lot of responsibility on your end. For people who want to change careers successfully in today's economy, however, those responsibilities are part of the package.

Bet You Didn't Know

The S.R.A. Corporation has conducted surveys of American employees since the 1950s—a half million workers in all. They found that ratings of job satisfaction were more or less stable until the early 1980s when they began to slide. Then, in the mid-1980s, the job satisfaction scores went into free fall.

"I believe that management is looking out for my interests" was a typical item on the questionnaire. In the 1980s, the percentage of workers who agreed with that statement fell by half. (Peter Capelli, *Change at Work*)

This Ain't Your Father's Workplace!

You may remember that I spoke earlier about some "changes in the rules" that affect today's career changers. Now it's time to look in-depth at rule changes that directly affect the job search. There are nine major career rule shifts that can stop you from connecting with interested parties during your "trial search" for meaningful employment within a new field. Here they are, complete with their modern-day corollaries. Failing to adhere to these rule changes may leave you in the uncomfortable position of playing soccer while your prospective employer has moved on to playing rugby!

Just Tell Me What to Do!

Old Rule: By emphasizing loyalty, diligence, and the ability to carry out commands carefully, you'll be well positioned to impress most of the prospective employers out there today.

New Rule: Today's organizations are looking less for rule-followers than for internal entrepreneurs. They're looking for people who can naturally bring creativity, perseverance, and personal commitment to bear on new challenges.

Career Counsel
Make no mistake. A newcomer who projects energy, a sense of direction, and the willingness to assume personal responsibility is a good match for the new economy.

It's Not My Job

Old Rule: Ultimately, it's your past job titles that will determine how employers will evaluate what you ought to do next.

New Rule: A self-employed person knows that he or she *is* the graphics department, the accounting department, the operations department, and any and every other department on the chart. Employers in rapid-growth industries are likelier to be impressed by this outlook than by one that fixates on particular titles, titles that may not be of relevance six months from now.

It's All Down in Black and White

Old Rule: The content of your resume is one of the most important factors determining whether or not you'll find employment in a new field.

New Rule: Your resume's ultimate purpose is to serve as a visual aid in the interviewing process. Don't think of it as a mass-mailing piece. Customize it and deliver it in person once you land the interview. Resumes can't be the only tool you use to navigate a career change (and the truth is, they never could).

Career Counsel

Your resume will be most effective if it includes only pertinent information about your work history rather than a litany of facts and figures likely to make sense only to a past employer.

I Solemnly Swear...

Old Rule: Your resume has to spell out, in accurate, honest detail, all the specifics of your past work experience, including terminations.

New Rule: It's not an affidavit...it's an advertisement. You should be honest in handling direct queries about past terminations, but there's no need to broadcast them on your resume.

It's Not What You Know, It's Who You Know

Old Rule: Insiders have all the advantages—you've got to "know someone" already in order to make any headway in a new field.

New Rule: You do have to "know someone" in order to make progress on the career front...but what you really need to know about is that person's needs! These days, not even the "old boy (or girl) network" will convince an employer to continue a relationship that isn't addressing core problems.

Hello? Personnel Office?

Old Rule: You have to go through the "proper channels" to pursue employment opportunities, and that means contacting the personnel office.

New Rule: Personnel staff rarely make hiring decisions, but they can present a barrier to the people who you really want to see. The best approach is to communicate directly with the person who is your prospective boss (that's the person who will decide who to hire) while sending a copy of your correspondence to the personnel clerk. Remember that processing paper is that person's livelihood, so don't ignore him. But don't count on personnel clerks to hire you, either.

I Don't Make Calls

Old Rule: People who aren't seasoned phone professionals may face a serious—and perhaps insurmountable—obstacle when it comes to one-on-one networking.

New Rule: If you can use the phone to order pizza or ask for a carpentry estimate, you can use the phone to help turn your career change into a reality. (You'll learn a lot more about improving your phone technique in the next chapter.)

No, Thanks. I'm Looking for a Real Job!

Old Rule: If there's no full-time opening, there's no opening.

New Rule: Finding a good part-time opportunity is a perfectly acceptable way to gain experience with— and access to—a potential employer. These days, full-time opportunities often emerge from projects. That "project work" may be the perfect staging arena for meaningful full-time employment.

Career Counsel
A short-term project (say, designing a newsletter) may often turn into a long-term employment commitment in today's economy (heading up the production department when the newsletter turns into a magazine).

Thank God That's Done!

Old Rule: Once you've successfully made your transition to a new career in a hot growth industry, you won't have to worry about career management issues again—at least, not for a long while.

New Rule: Regular *career audits* are the name of the game in today's economy. The more you know about how your skills match the requirements of your industry, the better off you'll be.

Can You See a Pattern Emerging?

What do all nine of the "old rules" have in common? They put the responsibility for developing and maintaining your career on someone else.

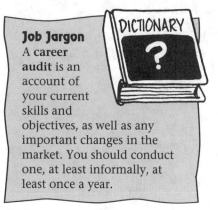

Job Jargon
A **career audit** is an account of your current skills and objectives, as well as any important changes in the market. You should conduct one, at least informally, at least once a year.

What do all nine of the "new rules" have in common? They put you in the driver's seat, and encourage you to act as though you were already self-employed, regardless of your current work status.

Career Counsel
Between jobs? Don't think of yourself as unemployed. Think of yourself as *self*-employed. Your current assignment is in marketing. Your current product is yourself. Treat this job with every bit of care, diligence, and commitment you'd devote to the job you want to land in your target industry.

Hi! I'm Already Working!

"Think like an employer." That's typical advice for anyone who's facing the tongue-twisting trials of a job interview. It's also a good approach for making contacts within your target industry during your "trial search."

Whenever we're trying to communicate with another person, it's a good idea to adopt her perspective—to try to take her point of view, and look at things as she does. That's especially true in the case of someone whose support we need, such as an employer.

But I'd go even further. In addition to trying to understand the needs of an employer, we should view ourselves as employers, and progress through our careers on the assumption that we're essentially self-employed.

The Independent Contractor

The term I like to use is *independent contractor*. For, whether we're currently on someone else's payroll or off, the only true employer we can count on over the long term is the one who stares back at us from the mirror each morning. That's the way our society has changed in the course of our lifetimes. We grew up under one system. Now, another system has taken hold. Today, all workers are either self-employed (CEOs of their own careers) or temporarily employed. We're all either owners or temps.

Studies of the workforce show that many Americans are having difficulty accepting and adjusting to the new conditions. Surveys of employers during the past few decades have found that 40 to 50 percent of American firms have been downsizing. Other studies show that the percentage of men in their mid-30s to mid-50s who permanently lost their jobs—men in their prime working years—basically doubled between the 1970s and the early 1990s. That's the key difference in today's world of work compared to 20 or 30 years ago. Traditionally, some 44 percent of workers who were laid off from their jobs could expect to be called back to their jobs. But in the most recent waves of downsizing, during the late 1980s and early 1990s, only 15 percent have been re-hired. (Peter Capelli, *Change at Work*)

Job Jargon
An independent contractor is a person who is responsible for his or her own livelihood, and who works "by the assignment" (as opposed to being kept on indefinitely).

! Bet You Didn't Know

"It has been very difficult for displaced workers to find new jobs since the 1980s," one labor market analyst has written. "Displaced workers had seven times the unemployment rate of others as long as two years after their job loss. [They] were more likely to be working only part-time, and on average their wages were about 15 percent less than those of equivalent workers." (Peter Cappelli, *Change at Work*)

Managing Change

What does all this mean? Well, if you are contemplating a career change and are still employed in a job that pays the mortgage, you ought to think a half dozen times about quitting in a huff. Maybe you should execute a plan to pursue your career change after hours, rather than setting off on your own tomorrow morning with no income source in sight.

But the other side of the coin is that the new economy has a vision and a language all its own. Lots of opportunities are out there—and the way to look for openings in today's new workplace is to view it through the eyes of self-employment.

We need to see ourselves not as prospective employees who are trying to impress an employer and win a job, but as independent contractors who are trying to negotiate a good assignment.

Career Counsel
Approaching career change issues as an independent contractor, rather than an "applicant," means seeing yourself in an active, rather than in a passive role.

Same as It Ever Was

Finally, another good reason to approach our careers as though we're all self-employed is that the American economy is essentially organized that way. Historically, this is a country with deep roots in self-employment. We're basically a nation of entrepreneurs. As we've seen, around the turn of the century, about one-third of all American workers were self-employed. Even as late as World War I, half the workforce consisted of contract labor—like the "contingent workforce" the media laments today.

We need to recognize that lifetime employment was a brief interlude in the history of the American economy. It wasn't until the 1970s that U.S. corporations began to emulate the Japanese in the job security game. The historic, traditional American way to work is as an entrepreneur.

> ## ! Bet You Didn't Know
>
> "A recent study of displaced workers in the 1980s and 1990s found that half of those who found new jobs changed industries in order to do so." (Peter Cappelli, *Change at Work*)

What Do You Do?

So, what does all of this mean in practical terms?

Here's the first premise. Whatever you do to make a living in this economy—whatever you do to make direct contact with employers during your "trial search," you need to assume you are a business. That means you have to address three basic steps in running a business: 1) product development, 2) production, and 3) promotion.

Three Familiar Steps

Or, if you're not into MBA-speak and prefer a more general view, think of the process this way. In any enterprise, the first thing you have to do is prepare what you're going to offer. You perceive unmet needs in the world around you and you process some sort of solution. You end up with a *product design*.

Second, you go into your *production* phase. You produce that product you've conceived. You set up a plant and whip out those widgets.

And, third, instead of letting your goods gather dust in the warehouse, you go out and *promote* what you've created. Business experts estimate that no less than 40 percent of an entrepreneur's time goes into marketing. Think of your skills as the products you are marketing and promoting.

Covering All the Bases

Whatever path we pursue in our careers, be it pottery or poetry, plastic prostheses or patent leather shoes—the basic steps of being in business are pretty much the same. If we find ourselves employed in a large organization, we may become specialized in one phase of that process or another. Maybe we're specialists in promotion—marketing lava lamps to aging Baby Boomers. Other employees are designing and producing the lamps.

But, if we're independent contractors in charge of our own careers, we need to do everything possible to take on all these phases of the cycle for ourselves. Not that we won't find ourselves in a large organization from time to time. But it's no good relying on an employer to cover the bases for us.

These days, you have to be ready to handle all three elements. You have to be ready to project, produce, and promote.

Anyone Can Network

For an independent contractor, covering all the bases means developing the skills we want to use in our work, producing some goods and services that we can demonstrate to other people, and, yes, finding an effective way to get our message across—some method of promotion that fits us and feels comfortable.

This final promoting phase is, of course, especially vital during your "trial search"—and it's the subject of special attention in the next chapter. Even if you've always shied away from the dreaded job of "networking," the strategies you're about to discover will help you develop a personal marketing style that makes perfect sense for you.

The Least You Need to Know

➤ Most of your "trial search" time and energy should go into direct contact and networking activities.

➤ Any career change campaign that relies primarily on strategies that stall when other people don't take action is likely to disappoint you.

➤ Be prepared to act as your own CEO and also as your own recruiter.

➤ Networking as an independent contractor reflects the "promoting" portion of the project/produce/promote cycle.

Chapter 9

Networking 101

In This Chapter

➤ Marketing yourself during your "trial search"

➤ Finding out how to make contact calls work better for you

➤ Getting contacts to want to talk to you

➤ Using your strengths as an extrovert or introvert

In the last chapter, you looked in depth at the new rules of the employment game, and you saw why it was necessary to think like a self-employed person during your "trial search" in your industry of choice. In this chapter, you learn more about acting as your own CEO and recruiter by putting your networking skills to work. Even if you're uncomfortable with the whole idea of networking, this chapter will help you develop a networking style that will yield tangible results—and fit your personal style.

As the title of this chapter suggests, networking has to do with promoting yourself, that is, acting on the third "P" in the projecting/producing/promoting scheme you examined earlier. But "promoting" doesn't mean changing the way you approach work, life, and relationships. As you'll see in this chapter, "promoting" really means being yourself, but simply doing so in front of more people than usual.

Call It What You Will

Some people get very nervous when they're confronted with the word *networking*. They think it means assaulting complete strangers and putting on some kind of hard-sell salesperson act. If it helps you in removing such negative stereotypes, feel free to call "networking" something else entirely (and I don't mean "schmoozing!"). Try using "needs assessing" or "information interviewing."

Job Jargon
Networking means taking action to expand your current contact network to benefit both you and the people to whom you're reaching out.

Think of this whole process—taking initiative on your own behalf to expand the quality and quantity of your professional acquaintances—as upsizing. That's what you need to do as an independent contractor in this economy, in order to offset the effects of downsizing in large organizations. You need to upsize and increase the range of your self-management skills. You need to incorporate your skills in the sense of bringing them together in a single whole—and letting other people know about them.

So, how do we do this in the marketplace?

Identify the People Who Matter

The first step is pretty simple. Identify at least a dozen people who know something about your (provisional) target industry. You might identify these folks by means of an industry trade magazine or a directory you find at the local library, or via the Internet, or through some other information resource. Let's assume, for the sake of argument, that you don't know any of these people. Who can you contact about an industry, a profession, or even (yes!) a job opening?

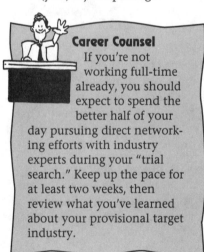

Career Counsel
If you're not working full-time already, you should expect to spend the better half of your day pursuing direct networking efforts with industry experts during your "trial search." Keep up the pace for at least two weeks, then review what you've learned about your provisional target industry.

Make Friends with Strangers

When it comes to establishing new professional contacts, some people are more comfortable talking. Other people are more comfortable writing. If you fall into the latter category, here's a strategy that will make networking calls a little easier.

Consider developing a short, one-page letter that you can use as an intermediary step. Your letter should highlight your current knowledge of the industry based on some preliminary library research. It might look something like the letter below. Note how the tantalizing opening paragraph doesn't use the words "I," "me," or "mine."

[Date]

Mr. Jake Bigshot
Vice President of Operations
WidgetCo
555 Smith St.
Anytown, CA 99999

Dear Mr. Bigshot:

Greeley and Company's recent analysis of the widget industry suggests that 60 percent of domestic production will be relocated to overseas facilities by the middle of the next decade. (*Widget Monthly*, June 30, 19XX, page 17). Identifying the best sites for foreign expansion is likely to be one of the most critical challenges facing decision makers in the industry over the next six to eight years.

As an operations professional with 14 years of overseas site selection experience, I've got some strategies to discuss in this area. I'm very interested in learning more about how your company plans to address this challenge—and about the widget industry in general. I'm taking the liberty of assuming that you won't mind a telephone call so we can discuss these matters.

I look forward to speaking to you.

Sincerely,

Brian Relocator

617/555-1212

P.S. I'm planning to call your office this coming Friday, July 17th, at 8:00 a.m.

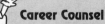

Career Counsel
Don't get distracted by the "no" answers you receive from your calls; focus on the attitudes of the people with whom you speak. If you're both pleasant and persistent, positive conversations with networking candidates who don't have leads or information for you today can turn into opportunity tomorrow.

A letter such as this prepares the contact for your call. Perhaps more important, though, a letter like this one helps you feel a little more confident when the time comes to contact the person on the phone. You can say, "Did you receive my letter?" Since the letter is substantive and customized, a good percentage of the people you talk to will say "yes."

Lots of people love talking on the phone, and don't feel the need for a preparatory letter like the one above. Whichever category best describes you, you should accept that it could take several "thanks-but-no-thanks" calls before you reach someone who's interested in speaking to you in depth.

Good Opening Lines

What do you say to that person when you make your call? Just outline your interest in the company—the more specific the interest, the better. Then say why you want to see the person. Typically, you'll be requesting an in-person meeting:

"Hi, Mr. Smith, thanks for taking my call. This is Brian Newcomer; I'm a financial analyst who's very interested in finding out more about your company's widget operations. Do you have a moment to talk?"

Most of us feel a bit apprehensive when we reach out this way, and that's natural. But the payoff you receive after you overcome that initial shyness can be significant. I recently had a meeting with the author of a well-known series of crime novels about a novel manuscript I've just completed. I wanted his advice about finding an editor to help me refine it. When I left him a voice message, I'm sure I stumbled over my words somewhat. But I told him how much I'd appreciated a workshop he'd conducted. "You gave me an impetus to get this far," I told him. "Now I'd like to ask your advice as I try to go farther." He called back that afternoon and agreed to see me within a few days.

That's the type of message you should be prepared to send over the phone. Be honest. Don't pretend to be someone you aren't. Be ready to ask for exactly what you want. Keep trying—and give yourself plenty of breaks so you can retain your composure after tough calls. Here's a sampling of what contact calls might sound like:

"I've learned a lot about your company from reading *Widgets Monthly*—and I'd like to find out more about what you're doing in X area. Can we get together?"

"I've followed your work in X area with a great deal of interest. I'm wondering if we could get together over lunch—I'd be very interested in getting your feedback on my resume."

"I learned a lot from your recent article about so-and-so. I thought perhaps you could tell me about what types of people you're looking to hire in the future in that area."

"I'd love to get together with you for lunch to discuss your company's expansion plans."

"My research indicates that you're the person who handles hiring in X area, and I was wondering if we could get together to talk about any current openings you're trying to fill."

Don't repeat the previous sentences simply because they appear in this book. Customize them. Make them yours. Practice your own message over and over again, before you make any calls. When it sounds natural and unscripted, you'll be ready to start calling.

Four Commandments for Phone Networking:

➤ Be yourself.

➤ Be honest. Say that you're asking about employment opportunities if what you're interested in is employment opportunities.

➤ Say you're asking about information on the industry if what you're interested in is information on the industry.

➤ Don't agree to interviews over the phone or referrals to the personnel department. Ask for enough time before the interview to conduct appropriate research on the company in question.

Take Notes

Some of your calls will go well. Others will conclude quickly. Most of your calls will tell you something interesting about the organization in question.

Your aim is to get a sense of the lay of the land in the new field—say, whether anyone works at a company who is not a blood relative of the owner. And if so, what department the outsiders are in. Is the research and development group dominated by electrical engineers? Did they get rid of all the mechanical engineers (your field of specialty) during the last layoff? Can your contact tell you anything about plans for expansion?

Respect people's time, but ask questions. Keep records on every company you contact. A call log is a helpful tool in record keeping. Here's an example of what one might look like:

Career Counsel
Some people will react supportively to over-the-phone requests about career opportunities, but the majority will get anxious or "shut down" because they don't know enough about openings in a particular area to talk about them with you. Save specific requests about meeting and job openings for the people who give "green light" signals or ask you pointed questions about your background.

```
                              CALL LOG

Company       Industry      Contact/      Date          Date Call     Outcome
                            Title         Called        Returned

_____      _____      _____      _____      _____      _____

_____      _____      _____      _____      _____      _____

_____      _____      _____      _____      _____      _____
```

Keep It Up!

If you pursue your networking persistently enough, efficiently enough, and long enough, then one way or another, at some stage of the game, something will click. You'll establish some point of connection with your skills. And, equally important, you'll find some group of professionals who feel comfortable talking to you—someone, or some group of someones, who approach work, and life in general, in roughly the same way you do.

A lot of these calls will make you feel less at ease, less sure of yourself, than you were when you started dialing. When you conclude a call with someone that makes you feel more like you're talking to "one of your own," put a star by that company and that contact. It will probably be worth pursuing later on.

Introverts and Extroverts

Are you an introvert or an extrovert?

Cheryl Card, a Denver-based counselor and consultant, emphasizes the importance of determining which of these two groups best describes your style. Card is a born-again introvert who says her life was changed when she learned to honor that trait. She's written a book, *Discover the Power of Introversion*, in which she tells her story.

"I'd majored in international studies and found myself doing office work in international trade," she recalls, "but something didn't fit. I remember often bowing out of office get-togethers, even Christmas parties. At the time, I didn't know exactly why—I just knew I didn't want to go. I simply needed to be alone for some 'down-time.'"

As Card began to understand herself better, she realized that introversion and extroversion are not a matter of being outgoing or shy. It's a matter of where one gets energy. Extroverts receive energy from other people. Introverts gain it by being alone. Introverts might choose to spend New Year's Eve reading a book. Extroverts would rather party.

The introvert/extrovert difference has all sorts of consequences for work environments—and your networking efforts. Cheryl Card writes, "Introverts usually prefer jobs where they work alone or with a few people, where they can utilize their powers of concentration. Extroverts, on the other hand, are curious about all aspects of the organization and often enjoy talking on the phone." Although extroverts may not represent everyone's ideal working model, they often make superb networking contacts.

Card says introverts in America may grow up thinking there's something wrong with them. "All their lives, introverts have heard things like, 'Why do you have your door closed? Come out of your room and meet our guests.'"

Bet You Didn't Know

An estimated 75 percent of Americans are extroverts. In other countries, such as England, for example, introversion is much more the norm.

I've seen plenty of people change careers in order to spend more time with people like themselves. And generally, you have to get very close to a profession to get that kind of data. For example, high school teachers are extroverted in a way that college teachers are not. Public relations people at the upper echelons of their profession are apt to be introverted. Maybe that's because so many of them have come from print journalism, where introversion is the norm.

Enough About Me. Let's Talk About Me!

As part of your networking efforts—and any meetings that result from it—you'll want to prepare a brief summary of your background. You should have a 30-second summary for those people who say "Tell me about yourself" over the phone. (A two-minute summary is a good rule of thumb for in-person meetings.) Summarize your background in the light of the work you're hoping to discuss. Here's an example of a 30-second summary for phone interviews:

Career Counsel
It's vitally important to get close enough to a prospective profession to know if you'll feel comfortable there. Otherwise, you may jump from the proverbial frying pan into the fire. Use your networking time to make sure the culture fits as well as the skills.

I'm a freelance writer with 10 years of experience as a public relations director and four years as an independent corporate copywriter and speechwriter. I've developed promotional copy and internal manuals for companies like FreeLand Outdoor Clothing, American Eastern Communications, and Northern Sales Seminars, and I've also written speeches for Bert Cummings, who's the president of Bert Cummings International, in New York City. Those are some of the high points."

Now here's an example of a two-minute summary for face-to-face interviews:

"I'm committed to developing superior written materials for use in corporate training and promotional and public presentation settings. My early career was in public relations—I spent 10 years at Love Canal Communications, working primarily on corporate P.R. work there for over 50 different clients. In the winter of 1993, I decided it was time to strike out on my own—and I took it as a measure of my effectiveness that my boss offered me a hefty raise as an enticement to stay on at Love Canal. I've been developing my own client base since then, and have branched out into developing ad and catalog copy, speeches, instructional manuals, as well as material designed for appeals to the press.

My clients include FreeLand Outdoor Clothing, American Eastern Communications, and Northern Sales Seminars. I've also written speeches for Bert Cummings, who's the president of Bert Cummings International in New York City, and Ellen Benjamin, who owns PaintBall Unlimited in Denver, Colorado. I'm proficient in Microsoft Office, ACT!, and WordPerfect. Throughout my career, my focus has been on the development of compelling written documents that inform, entertain, and inspire."

Always be selective in presenting your background. Concentrate on the skills you have that are needed in the environment you're in.

Most of us are not accustomed to summarizing the pertinent details of our lives. That means we need practice. It's hard to overemphasize the importance of practicing a sharp, succinct summary of one's life-work history during telephone encounters. It takes practice. Be sure you're up for the task before you pick up the phone!

So, When Can We Get Together?

It may take you a few calls to get comfortable with the process of calling people in your industry (and to get used to the fact that professional folks tend to be pretty busy, and may issue some fairly curt brush-offs). Stick with the process. Remember, you're out to gather information, as well as "hot leads." Learn as much as you can. Don't pretend to be someone you're not. Don't get frustrated.

When you finally hook up with someone who responds positively to your queries—and believe me, you will—you're likely to hear something like this:

"Well, why don't you come down so we can talk about this in detail?"

If what you're going to be "talking about" is a professional job opening, congratulations! Your "trial search" within the industry in question has begun to pay off. You'll need time to find out more about this organization—make sure your conversational partner schedules a date and time that allows you to conduct sufficient library research (and review Chapter 20 of this book, which deals with the subject of interviewing in depth). You'll also want to get a specific answer to some variation on the following question:

"What's the biggest problem your organization is facing in such-and-such an area (your area of expertise) over the next month/quarter/year?"

The answer you get should help you focus your networking efforts even more efficiently.

The objectives of your "trial search" are a) to learn what kind of match there is between your skills and the problems faced by prospective employers in a particular target industry, and b) to find out how happy you would be working within that industry. When you schedule an interview, prepare for it properly—and don't be surprised if you identify areas where matches are lacking!

Let's Review

After two weeks of conducting your "trial search" along the lines discussed in this chapter, you'll be in one of three situations:

a) You'll be convinced that a significant gap exists between what you have to offer and what employers are looking for in your provisional target industry.

b) You'll be convinced that there are professional opportunities for you within this industry, but that they entail tradeoffs you're not willing to make (such as making significantly less money than you'd anticipated, relocating, or working with a bunch of extroverts when you're an introvert).

c) You'll be convinced that the possibility for a satisfying career does exist for you within this industry.

Sad-but-true department: Situations a) and b) mean you need to do some more digging. You need to find out more about a different group of employers, one that can benefit from what you have to offer. It's time to track down another provisional industry! The beauty of the "trial search," is that you haven't kept this entry campaign up for three or four under-researched months by pursuing classified ads and talking to recruiters (as a great many career changers do).

If you find yourself in situation c), you're ready to put your career change campaign into overdrive. You'll learn how to do that in the next part of the book.

The Least You Need to Know

➤ The process of networking is really a process of marketing yourself to people who can help you get to where you want to be.

➤ A strong, well-constructed introductory letter is a good way to make yourself known to a contact. It will make your initial phone call to that person more impactful.

➤ Always be up front about what you want. If you want to know about openings, ask. If you want industry info, ask. Respect people's time and be honest.

➤ Remember that you are a problem solver. If there are no present problem-solving opportunities uncovered during your trial search, dig deeper or track down other related industries.

Part 2
Directions

So, what do you want to do? By the time you finish this part of the book, you'll have a clear idea of the direction you want your career to go. You'll also have a better understanding of the best ways to expand your skills. Finally, we'll explore the different types of employing organizations that are out there to uncover the best possible fit for you.

Chapter 10

Diamonds in the Rough

> ### In This Chapter
>
> ➤ Finding out how the shape of the workplace is changing
>
> ➤ Learning key differences between a pyramid- and a diamond-shaped company
>
> ➤ Exploring a winning strategy to overcoming stereotypes and preconceptions that can keep you from a job with a diamond-shaped organization

Congratulations! If you've made it this far in the book, and followed the advice on conducting the "trial search" discussed in earlier chapters, you have a good initial fix on the industry in which you now want to work. If you've decided to hold off on conducting your "trial search" until later in the process, that's your choice. But beware! The longer you put off this "trial search," the longer it will take you to clarify your career direction.

To make the very best choices, you need to get an instinctive "feel" for your target industry—not just piles of data. The sooner you interact with real, live decision makers who work in that target industry, the closer you'll be to making sense of where that industry may fit into your life.

So, how do you connect with the employers who can take advantage of your capabilities, and what messages should you be sending them? In this chapter, you'll learn how the activities and organizational structures of many companies have changed forever. The more you know about the way the working world has been altered by economic forces in recent years, the better off your campaign to change careers will be.

What Kinds of Employers Are Out There?

Many people now in mid-career have grown up under a set of old rules, in an economy that was dominated by large corporations, structured in the form of hierarchies. There were layers and ladders in these organizations. Many of the figures of speech we associate with the world of work reflect this corporate world view:

"Jennifer is climbing the corporate ladder."

"Bill's moving from a blue-collar job to a white-collar position."

"Ellen's hit the glass ceiling."

> ## ! Bet You Didn't Know
>
> Information changes the way we work, and it does so within an astonishingly short time frame. If you're old enough to remember the resolution of the Iranian hostage crisis, you remember a world in which businesses operated entirely without personal computers—a world in which critical data was precious, and reserved for an elite few within the organization.

In each case we have an image that describes a workplace that, in many settings, simply no longer exists.

Climbing the Corporate Pyramid

Pyramid-like corporations, where there were perhaps twice as many blue-collar jobs as white-collar jobs, and where the most talented workers could climb a ladder from the lower group to the higher one, really took hold after World War II. It was the success of the U.S. and its allies in World War II that helped to bring this model of organization—which is reminiscent of a military structure of authority—to the American corporation. This model hit its heyday around 1970.

In many cases, people in large pyramids were able to move "up the ladder" by continuing their education. The higher levels of the corporation were generally occupied by those who had a great deal of specialized education in particular fields (international marketing, for instance, or corporate strategic planning). Today, we find that many of these top-ranking specialists have joined the ranks of the unemployed.

What happened? The biggest nemesis of that type of structure was the personal computer. Suddenly, data was suddenly much more easily disseminated; many more people had access to critical corporate information. Over the last 10 or 15 years—a period when more and more personal computers were landing on more and more desks around the country—the many-layered system of management that was such an obvious feature of the workplace was suddenly no longer needed. A great leveling of the American workforce took place.

There's an old joke about a Ph.D. who learned more and more about less and less—until he finally knew everything there was to know about nothing. That joke is a pretty accurate description of the direction in which old-style corporate careers pointed people. As you ascended the ladder, you usually narrowed your focus.

Work Alert!
These days, if you emphasize one narrow job function or capability, you're going to have a very tough time of it in the job market. During the 1980s, an estimated one-third of middle-management jobs in extremely narrow fields of activity suddenly disappeared because those specialties were largely irrelevant in the job market.

Diamonds Are a Career Changer's Best Friend

One of the great challenges these people have had to undertake has been to come to terms with a new workplace structure, one that's about as far away from the top-down pyramid as you can imagine. This is a world in which employees must be more self-sufficient, and must rely less on help from "support people." This is a world in which employees are, quite frequently, their own support people. They're responsible for their own "grunt work" and they're likely to have a hard time finding ladders to climb.

Many of today's new organizations—the organizations responsible for a good chunk of our economy's current employment growth—are very thin at the top, like the post-World War II corporation with which many of us are familiar. But that's where the similarity ends. These new outfits are also quite thin at the bottom. They're shaped like diamonds, rather than pyramids. It's very hard to find any employees who perform relatively unskilled jobs. There may be a receptionist or two, perhaps a typist, a security person, a janitor—but that's about it.

Another important distinction between the pyramid organization and the diamond organization has to do with the people at the top. These organizations feature very few full-time managers of any kind. That's a sobering development for people who have their hearts set on "climbing the ladder."

So, today's diamond-shaped organizations are thin at the top and thin at the bottom. What's in the middle, where the organization is very thick? As a general rule, the people there are direct service providers.

Career Counsel
Considering an MBA degree? Think long and hard before you commit to a program. One of the ironies of the American higher education system is that its celebrated MBA programs have been grooming tens of thousands of talented people for specialized management jobs that no longer exist.

Working with Diamonds

There's a company called Confertech that employs perhaps 500 people. They supply conference-call technology that allows users to conduct conversations with many callers at a time, with no loss of signal quality. When times are slow, you may be able to spot perhaps a dozen people at Confertech who act more or less like the managers who would have been positioned somewhere in the upper third of the old-style pyramid structure. When things get busy, however, you'll find those same "managers" in front of the company's computer systems like everyone else, setting up calls for customers.

Confertech is an excellent example of the diamond-shaped organization. Just about everyone has the ability to deliver the basic product or service of the organization, and almost everyone draws on a broad skill set in order to get that work done.

This emphasis on broad skills sets is typical of the diamond-shaped organization (and about as far away from the world of the pyramid-shaped organization as you can imagine). Flexibility is a key skill. If you are familiar with the computer software industry, you know that software engineers are a notoriously introverted lot. A high-tech company I know of gave a software engineer a customer service assignment for an important account in Bratislava. After the initial problem was resolved, he started getting calls from prospective customers. The home office then let him become a salesperson for this new territory. There he was in three capacities: engineer/designer, customer service professional, and salesperson. That's a far cry from sitting at his monitor typing out code.

Career Counsel

Narrowly focused jobs, in the diamond-shaped organization, are pretty hard to come by. There's a growing trend in the software industry, for instance, to put software designers on the 800 lines, helping customers with technical problems.

Career Counsel

Be prepared to rethink what it means to work as a manager within a diamond-shaped organization. Typically, these employees look and sound very much like the workers for whose efforts they are responsible—and they pitch in happily, in a hands-on way, when things get busy.

Earlier in this book, we talked about interlocking skill sets—about professionals who must take a balanced approach to the challenges that confront them, day in and day out, rather than focusing on a single set of familiar patterns within a single skill. That's certainly a good description of the few managers who work within a diamond-shaped organization. These are almost universally hands-on managers, people who get in there and rub elbows with everyone else when circumstances demand.

Diamond-shaped organizations are more fluid, more responsive to customer needs, and better at relaying important information from the front than pyramid-shaped organizations. They don't place as much emphasis on status and "pecking order" issues. Many of these companies embrace a high-risk culture in which anyone and everyone—including, in some cases, the president of the organization—is directly accountable for his or her actions.

Diamond-shaped outfits also embrace a culture that celebrates intellectual ability. The people doing the work are accepted as possessing unique insights and skills. In the diamond-shaped organization, what you know and can do on your own is generally far more important than how many people you supervise. See Figure 10.1.

Three Shape Review

A pyramid organization is based on a hierarchy of jobs. At the low end are blue-collar jobs where people are supervised closely and generally work with their hands. Blue-collar workers are production people. The upper echelon consists of white-collar workers who supervise those in blue. These people work with their minds and pencils and they don't produce any marketable goods and services themselves. They rely on support staff for functions such as typing correspondence. That's why many ex-corporate managers can't type.

An A-frame organization is built just like a pyramid, except that the base is hollowed out. That is, the upper echelon of full-time managers has been retained. But this peak of the pyramid rests upon two legs of temporary, contract workers. One leg is made up of professionals such as accountants who may be employed by an outsourcing firm. The other leg consists of more traditional temp workers such as receptionists and assembly workers. An A-frame has the advantage of being very flexible; the managers can let the temps go at any time. But it's also very flimsy; contract workers aren't likely to have deep loyalties to the organization.

A diamond organization is, as I've noted, thick in the middle with workers who 1) provide the essential products and services of the company; who 2) generally rely on a complex of skills to get their work done rather than a single specialty; and 3) generally work without support staff. Unlike the pyramid and A-frame workers, they're generally the most powerful people in the organization.

Bet You Didn't Know

Although the most dramatic employment growth is often associated with diamond-shaped outfits, the pyramid is by no means dead. There are still major employers, such as Merrill Lynch, that adopt this organizational structure, and new pyramid-like organizations are arising as well. Flexibility is high in these settings, but workplace stability and employee loyalty both tend to be pretty low. All the same, contract opportunities at these organizations can be quite lucrative—many skilled workers make in excess of $80,000 annually!

In the U.S., the hierarchical, pyramid-shaped corporate model (top) had its heyday around 1970. The diamond-shaped model (middle) features few full-time managers and virtually no unskilled staff. The A-frame (bottom) limits full-time employment to top managers only, and relies heavily on contract labor (the two lines beneath).

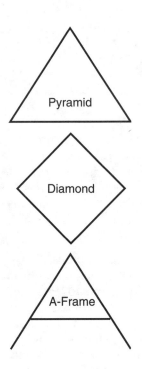

Mixed Messages

Work Alert!
Don't bother contacting a diamond-shaped organization about employment opportunities if you don't have competence in basic personal computer skills. If you need to upgrade your skills in this area, check out these helpful books: *The Complete Idiot's Guide to Windows 95, Second Edition, The Complete Idiot's Guide to WordPerfect for Windows, Second Edition, The Complete Idiot's Guide to Microsoft Word 97,* and *The Complete Idiot's Guide to Microsoft Excel 97.*

Information technology has radically transformed the way we work and has given rise to some new organizational structures. Some of these structures have allowed some successful new companies to emerge—companies that are often on the lookout for skilled employees. That's the good news. Now for the bad news: People in diamond-shaped organizations are, by and large, reluctant to hire a mature worker who has grown up in a pyramid-shaped corporate setting.

It's not that people in these organizations are skeptical of the corporate veterans' skills. It's more that they're afraid that someone who comes out of a pyramid-shaped corporate culture is likely to:

➤ Sit around and write reports or ask for endless meetings to be called.

➤ Find it demeaning to work with his or her hands or perform routine clerical tasks.

➤ Supervise or be supervised, rather than alter or share leadership as the situation demands.

In other words, diamond-organization hiring officials who are evaluating workers with backgrounds in pyramid organizations tend not to believe that workers can make the transition. If you fall into this employee category, and you want to take advantage of the significant employment opportunities in diamond-shaped organizations, you're going to need to develop a strategy that will turn these people around.

➤ Convey your ability to do your own "dirty work" and fill in as the needs of the team demand.

➤ Upgrade and broaden your skills where needed. (If you can't type, learn to!)

➤ Look for project-based assignments, either through a temp service or on your own, to demonstrate your skills.

Adapting to the Shape of Things to Come

Make no mistake. The transition from pyramid culture to diamond culture is immense, and it requires real work from those former residents of the pyramid organization who undertake the project.

In your conversations with people at diamond-shaped organizations, you'll want to make it clear that you are capable of handling the transition, and that you've already grasped some of the most important key points. You'll want to use anecdotes from your own past history to demonstrate, for instance, your familiarity with the following diamond-shaped workplace realities:

➤ Solving problems and keeping customers happy while occupying a position on the "front lines" is something you're comfortable with; you recognize the importance of occasional meetings and reports, but you don't believe they should occupy the majority of the average day.

➤ You are computer-literate and comfortable handling your own word processing and data management tasks.

➤ You work well with teams, and can switch easily and quickly between "supervising" and "being supervised" roles during a single interaction with a single person, if necessary.

Career Counsel
Skeptical officials in diamond-shaped organizations often need to be shown a "bridge." Project-based employment is a great way to establish such a bridge that will help you make the transition from one work culture to another and also help break down any existing stereotypes an employer may have about you.

Another Option

Here's another great way to overcome hesitation on the part of a diamond-shaped hiring official: Propose a "project internship." These are three- to six-month employment slots—an internship for people who've completed an outside program of retraining. You approach the representative of the pyramid organization and say, in essence, "I've gone to the time, effort, and expense of arranging retraining in X area, and I think I could make a significant contribution to your company as a result. I know that, given my background, you may have some doubts about my ability to fit in well in your organization, so let's try employment on a trial basis, for a predetermined period of time, and see what happens."

(Alternatively, you might decide to track down a temporary assignment through an employment agency that works with your target company.)

The very act of proposing such an arrangement will go a long way toward convincing your contact that you have the potential to develop take-charge, quasi-entrepreneurial instincts that outshine those of most "pyramid alumni." A large number of the people I've worked with have benefited from programs similar to the one I'm suggesting you propose here.

Many full-time jobs begin as project-based interim assignments! Don't be shy about suggesting such interim projects, based on your own networking and research. Almost every organization has an important project on the back burner that no one "in-house" has the time to execute.

If your background is in a large, pyramid-shaped outfit, and you want to find a way to land in a diamond-shaped outfit, be prepared to do some research. Then, as part of your networking efforts, propose an interim project that will allow you to gain entry—and visibility—within the diamond-shaped organization.

The Least You Need to Know

➤ The typical organizational structure of American business after World War II was the hierarchical, pyramid-shaped structure. In recent years, a new structure has emerged—thin at the top and the bottom, and thick in the middle, like a diamond.

➤ Within diamond-shaped organizations, most employees interact directly with customers, and do so with less direct supervision, and less "clerical support" than pyramid structures have provided.

➤ Decision makers within diamond-shaped organizations may be best approached by your suggesting a short-term interim project that allows you the chance to prove you can perform (and fit in).

Chapter 11

New Jobs for Generalists

In This Chapter

➤ Identifying how the economy affects your career

➤ Building a bridge between jobs and skills

➤ Why diversifying like the Fortune 500 is right for you

Specialize or generalize? Most of us face that question at some point in our careers. In general, the best advice for most of us is to add more instruments to our tool box, rather than carrying around 20 sets of pliers. In this chapter, you learn how broadening your skills—becoming more of a generalist, and focusing less closely on narrowly defined skills, titles, or duties—can be an appropriate strategy in a rapidly changing economy.

Not long ago, management expert Tom Peters recalled his experience while trying to book a hotel room by telephone.

"I was disconnected, put on hold, etc. Finally I reached a living person at the front desk. He flatly declared he couldn't help me. When I asked why (calmly), he responded (calmly), 'I'm not a reservationist.' Nor is he long for the world of the employed." His point was that any worker who clings to such arbitrary lines in today's economic environment is probably asking for trouble.

Anybody Seen My Career Ladder Lately?

The modern American workplace is, to say the least, a challenging place to make a living.

Perhaps you grew up in a different economy, an economy in which people spent their entire careers working for a single employer. This work universe was an Ozzie-and-Harriet, white-picket-fence sort of place in which careers had continuity and employees knew where they stood.

Usually, they stood on some company's career ladder. Lifelong employers provided both security and opportunities for advancement. In large corporations, employees learned to accept the company's categorizations, and perhaps even wear numbered badges. The hierarchy determined the way workers looked at the world and even interacted with one another. ("Say, check out that number four in marketing by the elevator.")

Rather than a ladder leading upward, today's typical career can feel more like a merry-go-round, where the main idea is simply to grab hold and hang on. It's easy to ask: "Did I do something wrong?" But it's not your fault or mine: The workplace is revolving. Every year in the U.S., about one-third of our job roles are in transition, one-third of our technical skills become obsolete, and one-third of us leave our jobs.

Those are the hard facts about our economic environment today. It's important to acknowledge these facts, for if we don't we may blame ourselves for career-related problems that are not our fault. We live in a spin-cycle economy in which maintaining a career with a single label is pretty tough…and likely to remain so.

In fact, the one-job career is pretty much a thing of the past. Those who prosper in coming years will be those who can adapt, add new skills (often in short order) to the most important existing ones, and develop enough flexible proficiency to get by in a new area without too much trauma.

Life, Liberty, and the Pursuit of Change

For all the uncertainty, there's some good news in this economy, too. For one thing, many workers have discovered that career change—even unplanned career change—is not necessarily a bad thing. A career-driven decision to take a course or two outside your familiar field of activity may enrich your experience and help you see things from some new angles. There's an old saying: "If your only tool is a hammer, all your problems will look like nails."

Today, many people are considering some truly radical changes in career direction. Sometimes the change is of their own making and sometimes it's thrust upon them. These people are getting support from their former employers when they can—and summoning their own inner resources whether past employers are there to help or not. They're charting a new course and following their dreams.

Three Paths to Career Change

Think of the approaches you can take to your career as similar to three ski slopes of varying degrees of difficulty. If you've ever been skiing, you've probably seen the signs: Beginner, Intermediate, and Advanced.

The Advanced Slope

Changing fields in a truly radical way—moving into a completely new career area—is comparable to heading down the Advanced slope. It makes sense only if you have a strong commitment to change and a good grasp of the pitfalls you are likely to encounter in the new field you select.

Consider Eleanor, a laid-off customer service professional who took advantage of her company's tuition reimbursement program to plan a career change into a very different field: massage therapy. Eleanor used the help she got from her former employer to fund retraining, and is now successfully pursuing her new profession on a part-time basis in her own office. She's thinking of getting a second degree in nutrition.

The Beginner Slope

At the other extreme on the ski slope is the Beginner slope. It's a comfortable way for some skiers to make their way downhill, and it offers few (if any) surprises. This is not to say, however that the surprise-free route is always enjoyable!

Some people approach career issues in the same way: The more familiar a new work situation is, the more at ease they are likely to feel. If their company is downsizing—and countless large corporations have—many employees may look for a way to hang on to some kind of job with the company at virtually any cost without having to expand their skills into new and unfamiliar areas.

I know of a public library system that eliminated half of its librarian positions a few years back. Today, you can find a number of former librarians working as clerks and secretaries within this system. They had to accept substantial pay cuts, but they are still working for the employer of choice. These workers chose to stay with their employer (and maintain their benefits), no matter what. That's another way to plan a career: No new skill development or outreach to other organizations whatsoever.

Work Alert!
Making a career move doesn't necessarily mean changing direction completely. Review your plan carefully before you abandon all connection between what you used to do and what you hope to do in the future.

Career Counsel
Sometimes people leave single, long-term employer careers because they want to; sometimes they make a change because they have to. Whichever set of circumstances describes your situation, you should understand the "degree of difficulty" of the career move you're contemplating and its various implications.

The Intermediate Slope

There is, however, a third strategy, one well worth considering in today's economy. That is to change course within the same general area, by building on skills you already possess. You might think of this as a middle path, like the Intermediate slope at a mountain resort.

One variation on this "middle path" would allow you to broaden your employment and compensation opportunities by looking at industries that are closely related to the one in which you've accumulated most of your experience. Another would allow you to stay within the same industry, but to look at ways you can, at your own pace and on terms that make sense for you, make important changes in the kinds of problems you solve on a day-to-day basis.

This middle route makes sense for many workers today. Even though there may be significant (or tremendous!) job loss as companies continue to downsize, there's often evidence of significant job growth in other sectors of the very same industry—or in businesses that are closely linked to a familiar industry.

The Three Career Slopes

Advanced	Develop radically new approaches to what you do, where, and for whom you do it.
Intermediate	Branch out gradually into new areas or employment fields.
Beginner	Adapt little or no change, either on a personal skill level or in terms of exploring new employment fields.

Exploring a Middle-of-the-Road Strategy

Let's look at a few specific examples in detail that will illustrate how the "middle path" can help you manage change in your career in the best possible manner.

Looking Beyond Job Titles

As these words are being written, the field of telecommunications is on the verge of some dramatic growth. All these companies have been downsizing steadily, with telephone operators, in particular, losing their jobs to advanced technology that performs call-handling work people used to do.

Talk to informed analysts, though, and a fair number of them will tell you that the field as a whole appears to be poised for employment growth. Why? Well, the word "telecommunications" now embraces any number of industries. We're no longer talking solely about traditional phone service, but also voice communications technologies (such as that used to provide wireless communication with cellular phones), data transmission and processing (technology that makes it easier for users to access and use information), and image forwarding devices (ranging from facsimile machines to cable television). Added to these are all sorts of hybrid technologies that link telephones with computers, plus specialized products such as alphanumeric pagers. It's clear that, as the world shrinks, the role of telecommunications is growing—and will continue to grow. New fiber optic networks will revolutionize the way voice, video, and data are transmitted.

So, despite the job losses experienced recently by many in the field, the rising tide of demand for telecommunications "product" is impossible to ignore. Telephone bills have been rising at twice the rate of inflation, and much of the growth is in long-distance communication. *Title fixation* makes less sense for people in this field than it ever did. Displaced phone operators are better off highlighting their ability to manage data systems, work customers through problems, and (not infrequently) manage conflict over the phone.

The bad news: The industry doesn't need as many telephone operators as it once did. The good news: A new wave of teleservice representatives now take product orders, provide customer support for a wide variety of communications products, perform financial transactions, and so forth. The telecommunications traffic levels in the years to come are very likely to require "information professionals" aplenty—people who know how to manage new systems and are committed to expanding their skills in order to do so.

So take a hint from the telecommunications industry. Ask yourself: What new problems can I solve? How are those problems connected to my past experience? Dig down beneath your job title to the skills you've developed over the years.

Job Jargon
Title fixation is the attempt to cling to a single, narrowly defined job, typically one with a familiar label, despite important changes that have taken place in the industry in which you are looking for work.

Career Counsel
Simply keeping an eye out for companies that advertise about openings that mirror your last job title isn't enough. Ask yourself, "How can what you do be applied to other areas?"

Looking Beyond Industry Stereotypes

Much has been written about the changes within the U.S. steel industry. Most of the commentary has focused on job loss. One industry giant, for instance, cut back from a workforce of 120,000 to 20,000 in just 10 years. Many people have assumed that the industry simply collapsed under pressure from foreign competitors.

But not much attention has been paid to the rise of the mini-mills. These are small, highly automated operations that use advanced technology and recycled materials to

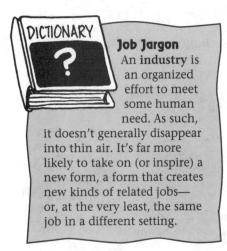

Job Jargon
An **industry** is an organized effort to meet some human need. As such, it doesn't generally disappear into thin air. It's far more likely to take on (or inspire) a new form, a form that creates new kinds of related jobs—or, at the very least, the same job in a different setting.

turn out customized products in smaller batches, and for a greater variety of clients, compared to the plants of the old behemoths did. The truth is that global competition and new technology have completely reconfigured the industry in the United States.

While the new steel industry may not provide the same level of employment as the old, it's important to note that the *industry* itself has not simply gone away. It will continue to evolve—and, almost certainly, continue to affect new industries in ways of interest to displaced employees. The same can be said for virtually every industry that undergoes restructuring and downsizing.

The moral: Keep an open mind as you evaluate industries and companies. Even "declining" industries may have a place for you.

Looking Beyond Industry "Downturns"

When the U.S. airline industry was deregulated in the 1970s, there was widespread fear that the industry would become dominated by several prime carriers, while other, smaller airlines were driven into obsolescence. And that's what happened—for a while. But as the dust has cleared over a couple of decades of deregulation, there's been an unexpected development.

Smaller, regional airlines have popped up all around the country. These niche market airlines have been employing pilots who lost their jobs with established airlines. In fact, some analysts believe that it was the availability of these "surplused" veteran pilots that gave rise to the niche market airlines in the first place.

As usual, the employment patterns in related industries are worth examining closely. In one instance, the failure of a second-tier airline in the aftermath of deregulation prompted a large travel agency to open a major office in the airline's home city. The company recruited the defunct airline's reservation staff as the core group for a service that makes travel arrangements for membership-oriented groups such as the Texaco Travel Club. Today, the travel company employs more than 500 workers, and the airline is flying again as a niche market carrier!

The moral: When an industry goes through a downturn, there's often a phoenix that rises from the ashes.

Nothing is static. Industries change and evolve. They encounter new market realities and new technological events, and they find new ways to operate. As they do so, they have profound effects on other industries. Companies (and economies) find ways to adapt to new market situations and new technologies. And nowadays, workers must adapt, too.

You should know how people and industries are now using the technology that has helped you develop your skill base. At first, breakthrough technology is typically used to do more of what people used to do before it was invented (say, work on budgets or balance a checkbook with a computer, or make a trip across town with a car). Eventually, though, successful inventions spawn new industries of their own (like Internet service providers or fast-food restaurants).

History is replete with tales of rising and falling technologies, revolutionary changes in the way people make a living. The difference today is that these revolutions are happening much faster than they ever did before.

Jobs versus Skills

In the midst of this changing economic scene, the one constant element is job-performance skills—if we know how to use them. Jobs solve problems. And, like industries, jobs don't stay in one place for long.

The first stage of any job is an employer's need. Someone wants help in meeting a special and identifiable need.

The next stage is finding *skills* to meet the need. Often, however, the skills that emerge to meet a need don't form new job roles. They're added to existing occupations.

The third stage of the process occurs when the skills take the form of an identifiable occupation, one with a dollar commitment in the company budget. That's not a development you can always count on. And given the rate of change in today's economy, you probably shouldn't count on an individual job staying in that budget forever, either!

Consider the task of word processing. When word processing technology emerged as a broad-based, everyday workplace reality in the '80s, it was assumed that many companies would employ full-time word processors. Instead, most people now use word processing in other jobs. This is a skill that has been added to existing occupations.

The days of being able to rely on a few unchanging skills for an entire lifetime in the workforce should be considered long past. We need to develop new skills continuously and select carefully the skills we hope to add to our repertoire. Whenever we

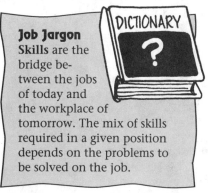

Job Jargon
Skills are the bridge between the jobs of today and the workplace of tomorrow. The mix of skills required in a given position depends on the problems to be solved on the job.

Career Counsel
Jobs have profiles that can be compared to human personalities. They're shaped by the mix of skills required to solve the problems being addressed. By focusing on skills you can translate to other work environments and industry settings, you will be in a much better position to manage change in your career.

consider entering a program of retraining, it's important to pay attention to the needs we see around us and the skills that are likely to help us address them, as well as the bridges we can build from our skills.

How to Build a Bridge

When I entered the field of journalism at 50, I found that the years I spent in career counseling sharpened my ability to draw out and evaluate information from others—a useful ability of great value in a brand new industry. Interviewing was a transferable skill that I used to bridge the gap between counseling and writing while I learned other skills, as well.

Most of the good jobs emerging in today's new economy call for combinations of skills, some of which you'll have and others you'll need to develop. So it's important to have a feel for the kinds of skills that come naturally to you—and to develop a strategy for learning other skills that may not come so easily. That's the only way to build on your strengths in a changing workplace.

Career Counsel
Employers large and small need people who can adapt well to new environments, and commit to update their own skills by continually enlarging on "core strengths," just as today's companies must do.

He Who Snoozes, Loses

Huge corporations have now realized the importance of *diversifying* their operations. What does diversifying mean? It means learning how to refine a basic set of experiences and abilities, so that shifting direction, when the time comes to do so, is less traumatic than it would otherwise be. This technique is emerging as a strategy for corporate survival, not merely corporate growth, in the new economy. It's about time individual employees, whose futures once depended on the predictable paths traced by big employers, adapted the strategy for themselves.

Adapt and You Shall Survive

To illustrate this idea, let's look briefly, once again, at the field of telecommunications. MCI is well known today as a long-distance carrier. They're the folks who battle with AT&T for the loyalty of customers who want to talk to Aunt Agnes after Thanksgiving dinner. Long-distance service is their prime source of revenue—their core business.

But that wasn't always the case. MCI started out 26 years ago as a microwave communications company serving truckers. ("MCI" stands for Microwave Communications, Inc.) After a 1984 court ruling broke up the phone monopoly, they branched into the long-distance business.

Today MCI appears to be broadening its horizons once again. The company now has 175 different product lines, many of which have more to do with the rapidly expanding information services industry than with telephone service. One of their products, InfoMCI, is a database-searching news retrieval service. That's a far cry from discount long distance.

These days, shifting industries is par for the course for agile (read: competitive) corporations. MCI's CEO, Bert Roberts, calls it "leveraging core skills into new markets." In the case of MCI, that means the ability to move data at high speeds over electronic networks. That's the nub of what they've learned to do.

If It's Good Enough for Big Companies, It's Good Enough for You

Most of you could benefit by applying the principles of corporate strategic planning to your own careers.

On the one hand, you should learn to keep an eye on your *core skills*. If the field in which you've been working levels off (such as the residential long-distance market has for MCI and others in the industry), perhaps you can transfer some of your skills. As I mentioned, I've done that with interviewing, a skill I learned in counseling and transferred to my career as a journalist.

The second lesson from the world of corporate planning is that if you try to take your core skill into new markets—a la MCI's venture into the information industry—you'd best not ignore your core business, the original application of your core abilities that's working for you right now.

The idea is to use your skill base to open new doors without shutting the old ones just as MCI did. As a soundly managed company must, you need to spend your critical resources (in this case, time and energy) wisely to expand your opportunities for the future.

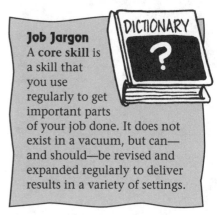

Job Jargon
A **core skill** is a skill that you use regularly to get important parts of your job done. It does not exist in a vacuum, but can—and should—be revised and expanded regularly to deliver results in a variety of settings.

A Balancing Act

As anyone who's shifted careers will testify, changing fields is a balancing act. It's generally important to keep one foot in a familiar field, and perhaps keep earning a living within that field, while you explore new directions with your core skills.

The rule of thumb: Don't ignore your core business. If you're changing fields, experiment and refine...but don't forget to keep your focus on what you know best. Don't give up your long-distance business in order to focus on those exciting new ventures.

The Least You Need to Know

➤ The best approach to career changing is probably the "middle path"—building on your existing skills.

➤ Fixating on job titles is a big mistake.

➤ Jobs are the solutions to problems, and problems, in today's economy, are constantly changing.

➤ Skills need constant revision. New skills should be added to the mix to meet the needs of a changing economy.

➤ Don't overlook the importance of maintaining your "core skills"—the skills you've used regularly to get important parts of your job done.

Thinking Like an Employer

Whatever the industry or organization you eventually decide to approach, you're going to want to emphasize one critical objective: adding clear value to the average day of the potential employer. In this chapter, you'll learn the best ways to focus on doing just that.

A Brief Refresher

Any attempt to clarify the type of value you can add to an organization, or the people it serves, should be rooted in the realities of today's workforce. Take a moment now to review three vitally important points from earlier in the book.

➤ The U.S. labor market has undergone a radical structural change in the past couple of decades that has caught many people by surprise in mid-career.

➤ For workers who are not happy with the way new realities of the employment world have unfolded in their own working lives, there are three helpful questions that will help you clarify how (and why) you want to change careers: Am I unemployed? Am I misemployed? Am I mismanaged?

➤ If, after reviewing your situation, you decide that you want to change careers, the best strategy to pursue is to take charge of your own career—to become your own CEO and think like a recruiter. Part of thinking like a CEO is addressing key questions about the direction of the economy in the area you're looking at by continually asking "Where's the market?", "Where am I?", and "How can I make a connection?"

Career Counsel
Your perceived attitude toward work and "fit" with the job will show prospective employers you're committed to embracing the culture and delivering positive results.

As you've seen, you'll be using your own core competencies and your natural networks as tools that will help you decide how best to conduct a "trial search" in an industry that can benefit from what you have to offer. For the ideas behind that "trial search" to work for you on a larger scale, however, you're going to need to be able to discuss, intelligently and with little or no prompting, the value you represent as a potential employee. You're going to have to demonstrate your ability to think about what most of today's employers want—results.

Bet You Didn't Know
In 1995, a group called the National Center on the Educational Quality of the Workforce asked a nationwide sample of employers how they picked entry-level workers. Of 11 possible factors, the top 6 all pertained to the applicant's personality and experience in the workforce, outranking academic concerns.

Results Are the Name of the Game

If you think about it, results are the foundation of every satisfying career. Nobody (or at any rate, hardly anybody) would feel like thanking the heavens for a career that consisted of work that made no positive impact whatsoever on anyone else's life. You and I must find a way to deliver something useful, to make something positive happen, in order to make a living. Specifically, we must add *value*, or deliver results, by rearranging and exploiting the resources and raw materials at our disposal.

Creating useful information from raw data that people otherwise would be unable to understand is a good example of adding value. So is taking care of a customer's needs and making that customer feel valued in the process; so is building loyalty to an organization by polling current customers about how well a new program is working out for them.

In the course of your career, you'll doubtless find yourself adding value in unique ways. In the process, you'll usually turn out some distinctive products.

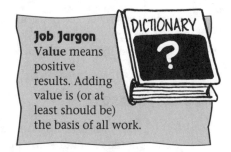

Job Jargon
Value means positive results. Adding value is (or at least should be) the basis of all work.

> **Bet You Didn't Know**
>
> "The return from your work must be the satisfaction which that work brings you and the world's need of that work. With this, life is heaven, or as near to heaven as you can get. Without this—with work which you despise, which bores you, and which the world does not need—this life is hell."
>
> —William E. B. (W.E.B) Du Bois

Of People and Products

When I talk about "products," I don't just mean tangible things like pieces of furniture or magazine articles. Sometimes the products of your work appear in the form of other people who've grown and developed, thanks to your influence.

Not long ago, I met with a young accountant and computer specialist who had just lost his job. Bob was a "typical" accountant—his social skills needed a little work, and he seemed genuinely terrified at the prospect of talking to other people about what he'd done for a living. In addition, having just been fired, he was in shock. To make a long story short, he was having a lot of trouble focusing on any accomplishments he could point to in the job he'd lost until the subject turned to people rather than abstract ideas.

When I asked him to think about his relations with coworkers, all kinds of examples of workplace value started rolling off of his tongue. "When Eileen came on board as a temp worker," he told me, "she was withdrawn and surly. But gradually, I got through to her and I taught her everything I know about accounting. Now she's working full-time and handling the finances of her department."

That insight was the jump-start Bob needed to focus on specific accomplishments for which he could rightfully claim responsibility. He had trained this young woman in the organization's computer system. He had helped her become acquainted with the schedules, requirements, and reporting procedures of many people who worked in the organization. And he had helped her improve her work attitude.

Once Bob started to focus on people, he began to get his bearings about the type of value he had provided in the past and was capable of adding now. He told me, "That's the kind of work I'd like to build on. I'd like to help other people develop, in the way I trained Eileen."

Try It Yourself!

Take a moment now and do exactly what Bob did. Think about the people whose lives you've made easier at some point in your career and precisely what it was that you did that made them walk away from the exchange thinking, "This is great! Now I can..." There's nothing *wrong* with focusing on products, services, or solutions first. But you, like Bob, may find it's easier to look at the question in terms of people you improved as the result of what you did on the job.

Stop reading now and focus on the value you've added in past work settings. If you've made it this far in the book, you probably already have an instinctive sense of the value you've added and can add. Now it's time to formalize things. Take a few moments to jot down, in a notebook or on a loose sheet of paper, the names of some people whose lives and careers you've improved or made better as a result of contributions on the job. How did they benefit from working with you? What did you do to improve their situation? Why did interacting with you make the situation better? Does that suggest the kinds of people with whom you'd like to work with in the future?

Job Jargon
An **informed interview** is an employment interview in which you participate effectively and completely, and ask questions yourself of the prospective employer.

Toward the Informed Interview

The next question, of course, is how the kinds of skills you've identified match up with the needs of an organization. Later in the book, you'll learn how to build on the basic familiarity with prospective employers you've developed during your "trial search" and turn it into what I call an *informed interview*—the kind of interview an independent contractor knows how to conduct.

Questions Employers Like to Hear

In the course of helping displaced workers find job opportunities, I've spent many hours talking with employers in growing industries. A couple of years ago, I met with Pete Savage, the CEO of a San Diego digital communications company called Applied Digital Access.

We began by talking about the needs in his organization. He described technical needs—skills in advanced circuit design, C++ object-oriented programming, and the like. I took notes furiously on all the technical stuff, hoping it would be of use to the unemployed aerospace workers whom I was trying to help.

As the meeting seemed to be drawing to a close, I picked up my notepad, thanked Savage, and headed for the door. I thought we were done. But we weren't. Pete Savage had a whole lot more to tell me about the value he likes to see potential employees demonstrate, and much of what followed had precious little to do with technical requirements. Savage (who's one of the best spokespeople I know of for the diamond-shaped business culture), demanded a certain outlook from those whom he considered hiring. I'll outline them in detail for you here, because each has a direct impact on the way Savage—and tens of thousands of employers like him—perceive value.

The following definitions of value will help you spot a diamond-shaped organization when you see one. They'll also help you make the most of your contacts with these new-mode employers, who represent some of the most exciting employment opportunities out there.

Value Means...Producing in Chaos

"We deliberately run the company one step to the left of chaos," Savage told me, "because if you don't do things differently every time, somebody's going to write a manual on how to do it."

That's true of many of today's high-growth employers, who aren't interested in hearing about how superbly you can perform under optimum conditions, but when things are falling down around your ears. Take a few minutes now to comb through your background. Take out your legal page and write down the details of an experience you've had where you came through like a hero despite the fact that you had to chart your own course as you went along. Then, be ready to use the anecdotes you develop in discussions with high-growth employers.

How I Saved the Day

_____

_____

_____

_____

_____

_____

Value Means...Carrying the Ball over the Goal Line Yourself

Work Alert!
Even if you were a manager in a past career incarnation, you should be prepared to look at a semi-managerial job if you're trying to find work in a diamond-shaped company in a high-growth industry. It's not that there are no more managers there, but there sure aren't many who are being paid to keep track of the work of other people on a full-time basis.

"We don't have many managers," Savage told me, echoing a common refrain among diamond-shaped company leaders. And for some people, that's a problem. When we've hired people from the telephone companies, we often found that they expected to have other people do the work while they just kept track of it. Around here, we don't compartmentalize jobs. If you're going to manage a project, you'd better be prepared to do your own cost accounting and write your own system specs plus your own correspondence. Besides, our secretaries all have college degrees and make $30,000 a year. They have other responsibilities. We all do our own typing."

Whatever job you're interested in a high-growth company, odds are good that the employer you speak to will be more eager to hear about what you can do on your own than about how accomplished you are at keeping the "support staff" busy. These days, it bears repeating, there usually is no support staff to speak of.

Take a moment now and think of a time when there was no administrative or clerical help available to you, but you somehow managed to complete an important project more or less on your own. Write the details out in your legal pad.

All by Myself

_____

_____

_____

_____

_____

_____

Value Means...Asking About What You're Up Against

Savage is an entrepreneur. That means he constantly asks questions about the market in which his company operates and the resources available to him to meet the needs of that market. But he doesn't want to be the only person in the company asking such questions and immediately passing along important answers.

He told one applicant, "You may be used to preparing for annual audits, but around here, we expect that as soon as you know something, you'll e-mail it to everyone in the company."

Develop a keen sense of curiosity—and don't be afraid to ask the right questions! "When people come here from other companies," Savage told me, "we watch to see whether they look around and recognize what an adjustment they're going to have to make. We hire the people who ask questions."

Take a moment now to find a situation in your work background that benefited from your taking the initiative to ask basic questions, while developing a workable strategy for coping with those facts. That instinct is one that entrepreneurs and "independent contractors" must share in today's workplace.

Write down the details of your results-through-questioning story in your legal pad. Be prepared to talk about it with new business contacts.

How My Questions Got Results

_____

_____

_____

_____

_____

_____

Two-Way Streets

Remember: The kind of value today's employers are looking for isn't the ability to do what you're told until something interesting happens. The kind of value I'm talking about delivering is generally more rooted in self-direction, accountability, and a certain awareness of both market realities and internal obstacles. By developing success stories along the lines suggested in this chapter, you'll be helping to assume responsibility for a positive outcome during your "informed interview" with the prospective employer...and, eventually, on the job.

Sometimes, of course, delivering value for an employer has a whole lot to do with getting the most out of a particular technical skill. But what if you don't yet have that skill?

In this chapter, you learned what today's new-mode employers are looking for. In the next chapter, you'll start finding out how to broaden your skill base when the specific technical skills you possess don't match up with the requirements of the employers you're most eager to learn about.

The Least You Need to Know

➤ Workers must add value, or deliver results, by rearranging and exploiting the resources and raw materials at their disposal.

➤ One good way to isolate value you've delivered on the job is to think of people who benefited from working with you.

➤ Today's employers are interested in the fact that you can perform under any conditions as well as start and finish assignments on your own.

➤ As an independent contractor in today's economy, the best results are obtained when you have all the information you need. Before you tackle the problem to be solved, ask questions first.

Chapter 13

Recycling Skills

In This Chapter

➤ Professional recycling

➤ Inside-out learning

➤ Outside-in learning

Can I tell you an old vaudeville joke? A fellow awakens from anesthesia after undergoing surgery on his shoulder. His arm is encased in a cast, hoisted straight up in the air, and tethered to a rack above his bed. Just then, his doctor walks in. "Doc, doc," the patient cries. "I got a question for you. When I get over this, will I be able to play the violin?"

The physician hovers over his bed. "Sir, I can assure you the operation was a complete success. Of course, you'll be able to play the violin."

The patient looks up in wonder. "Gee, ain't that somethin'? I never could before!"

I know that joke's a groaner but it illustrates something important. Wouldn't it be great if we could take some kind of medication—maybe even go through a surgical procedure—and come through with all the up-to-date knowledge we need in our careers? Maybe someday there'll be a breakthrough like that. Say, a Windows 95 serum, or a laser-based therapy that will automatically upgrade you from DoorJam 7.4 (which you just learned) to DoorJam 8.0 (which is suddenly all the rage).

Until then, however, Americans will continue to grapple with skills that go stale in mid-career. I call this "professional recycling." It's the process of revising and updating existing skills. When it comes to recycling skills, there are some principles that can help you keep your head above water when the workplace seems to be rushing downstream toward some new technological revolution. In this chapter, you'll look at effective strategies for organizing new learning.

Learning "Inside Out"

I've worked with adult learners for years, and have come to believe there are two basic ways to approach the business of *professional recycling* and picking up new skills. I think both strategies can be vitally important to the course of your career.

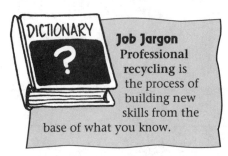

Job Jargon
Professional recycling is the process of building new skills from the base of what you know.

The Inside Out approach is a great strategy for the long-term. It's just a matter of following our deepest interests—our "passions," some would say—throughout the course of our careers. Remember the exercise on peak moments in learning? What I'm talking about here is simply building on those experiences and maximizing our mountaintop moments in learning.

Here's an example. In the early '90s, Mihaly Csikszentmihalyi (that's pronounced CHIK-sent-me-high), a psychology professor at the University of Chicago, wrote a fascinating book entitled, simply, *FLOW* (New York: Harper Collins, 1990). Mike (which is what everybody calls him, in lieu of trying to pronounce his Hungarian name) wrote his doctoral dissertation on a group of young artists he once met in Chicago. These young people were barely getting by, but they made a deep impression on him because of their motivation. It seemed their rewards were not money or even prospective fame, but the process of creativity itself. They were totally absorbed in their work.

Csikszentmihalyi went on to study other people who had that same sense of absorption in some area of their lives. He called the condition *flow*. It's "the state by which people are so involved in an activity that nothing else seems to matter; the experience itself is so enjoyable that people will do it even at great cost, for the sheer sake of doing it."

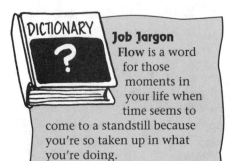

Job Jargon
Flow is a word for those moments in your life when time seems to come to a standstill because you're so taken up in what you're doing.

When you're experiencing flow, you may forget to eat at regular times. And if a paycheck is late, that doesn't stop what you're doing.

It's worth noting that Csikszentmihalyi found people had three times the incidence of flow experiences when they were at work, compared to after-hours. (The least absorbing experience was watching television.)

> **Bet You Didn't Know**
>
> Here's an example of a person in flow—someone whose vocation is so compelling that it permeates the rest of his life.
>
> Csikszentmihalyi writes, "During the ceremony celebrating the unveiling of Chicago's huge, outdoor Picasso sculpture in the plaza across from City Hall, I happened to be standing next to a personal-injury lawyer with whom I was acquainted. As the inaugural speech droned on, I noticed a look of intense concentration on his face, and that his lips were moving. Asked what he was thinking, he answered that he was trying to estimate the amount of money the city was going to have to pay to settle suits involving children who got hurt climbing the sculpture."

Turning On to Inside Out

Ron Gross, the adult learning expert, describes the same process in different terms. He quotes the British philosopher, Alfred North Whitehead, who thought of learning as a three-cycle process. It starts with a stage of "romance." Whitehead believed that true learning always begins with "a ferment already stirring in the mind." As we might say today, you need to be "turned on" by the subject before you can really learn it.

Whitehead called the second phase the stage of "precision." That's when you gain mastery over the subject matter. The third stage is "generalization"—when you apply your knowledge and put it to work in the world.

How It May Work

Gross described how his daughter Liz grew up with a deep interest in responding to various sorts of emergencies. In college, she'd run a telephone crisis help line. Later, she looked for opportunities to ride along in ambulances as an assistant to emergency medical technicians.

That was Liz Whitehead's phase one—the stage of romance. (As it happened, Liz met her future husband when they were riding an ambulance, and if that's not romance…) Phase two, for her, was nursing school—the stage of precision. Her love of helping people in emergencies got her through that program. Today, in phase three, generalization, she serves on a county health board and works in emergency services.

> **Career Counsel**
>
> Some experts are convinced that true learning starts from the heart. We have to care about the subject—have some feeling for it inside ourselves—before we can expect to master it. "Learning without romance is like sex without foreplay," writer Ron Gross observes wryly.

So that's one approach: Start from the heart. Go with the gut, when it comes to learning. But is that the final word in expanding or developing your skill base? I think not—sometimes learning is more mandatory than that.

Outside-In Learning

As the world turns, the workplace keeps changing. The job to which you and I apply our current skills today is sure to require a different set of skills tomorrow. And that's where the follow-your-bliss career philosophies come up short. Sooner or later, you're going to find it necessary to learn some skills that don't ignite your passions—at least, not at first. You will learn those skills not because you want to but because you have to, in order to get or keep a job. This is what I call the Outside-In school of learning.

A few years ago, I met a stimulating fellow named Tony Stubbs who'd launched a computer school based on the philosophy of "just-in-time training." Stubbs is an Englishman with a couple of degrees in computer science from the University of London. But he abandoned the British Isles and found his way to Colorado.

Attracted to the fast pace of American life, he set out to teach computer skills at the same aggressive clip. When I visited Compu-Skills, the school he founded, Stubbs was offering courses in 20 popular software programs. They were crash-and-burn courses. I took one of his courses in the spreadsheet program, Excel. The instructor packed two week's worth of information into an eight-hour day. By the time the class ended, my head was spinning with 16 different ways to format a spreadsheet and my wrist ached from mouse-clicking. I stumbled out of the classroom in a fog.

The Power of "Need to Know"

Later, I complained to Stubbs about his instructional format. He laughed. "Everything we do," he told me, "is based on the principle of 'need to know.' Most people don't benefit from long-term courses that cover everything they might conceivably need one day. People learn best when they're presented with the skills they needed yesterday. The other principle we follow is 'use it or lose it.' That's the heart of skills retention. It's important that our students return to work and put their skills into practice right away."

I saw that principle at work in my fellow students. Most of them were office workers who had arrived at work one day to find their computers loaded with a new spreadsheet program—Excel. After spending a few days fumbling around with the Help screen and the manual, they were prime candidates for one of Stubbs' crash courses.

Hands On!

There was one other interesting wrinkle in his program. Stubbs' instructors doubled as on-site consultants. For about $75 an hour, they'd come out to your office and provide one-on-one tutoring for special problems you encountered after the class.

Compare that scenario to a traditional academic course with its 16 weeks of classes—butt-in-chair, attendance charts, letter grades, and all the rest. For the person who needs some new skills yesterday, the crash course with an instructor who doubles as on-site consultant makes much more sense to me.

And the just-in-time format is terrific for the instructors, too. One of my former career clients, Marty, wanted to start a consulting practice, but had a difficult time marketing his services. Like most technically oriented individuals, selling was not his forte. So I introduced him to Stubbs, and soon Marty was teaching classes. Then he began meeting corporate clients who were sending employees to his classes. Soon he was doing on-site consulting for the corporations. It was the most painless path to marketing imaginable.

Inside Out or Outside In?

That's the question I hear from lots of people who are contemplating career changes: Which approach is best? The truth is that, today, most people need both strategies for upgrading skills as the workplace changes.

The emphasis you give to the two approaches will depend largely on your own circumstances and the requirements of the prospective employers whom you contact. You can increase the odds that both inside-out and outside-in learning will deliver results you can use by targeting your own learning style effectively.

Work Alert! Don't just enroll in any course that covers what you need to learn! Think about your options carefully, and find out how the course is being taught. Find a format that suits your strong-suits as a learner.

Assume, for the sake of argument, that you have some pretty good word processing skills. And let's say your goal is to expand your ability to use the computer to compose written documents into the ability to use a new graphic design program, one that simply doesn't come naturally to you.

To get a reading on your strengths, ask yourself some basic questions. Think about your best experiences in education for a moment. Then ask yourself:

Do you usually remember more from a class when you:

    A) Do not take notes, but listen very closely

    B) Sit near the front of the room and watch the speaker

    or

    C) Take notes, whether or not you ever look at them again

---

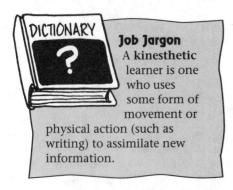

Job Jargon
A **kinesthetic** learner is one who uses some form of movement or physical action (such as writing) to assimilate new information.

If you answered A), you're likely an auditory learner. If you answered B), you may be a visual learner. If C), your learning style may be *kinesthetic*. It's a matter of whether you prefer to receive information through your ears or eyes or sense of touch.

On-the-Job Training (You Hope)

Gloria Frender, an educational consultant and author of *Learning To Learn*, cautions that people learn in different ways. She recommends this procedure when training employees on-site. 1) Tell them the procedure to follow. 2) Write out the instructions for them to read. 3) Have the employees write the instructions and repeat them to you. That way you'll touch bases with all three types of learners—auditory, visual, and kinesthetic. The same advice could apply to trainers in virtually any setting, I think, but it's certainly worth bearing in mind if you're on the receiving end of skill recycling that takes place on the job.

If you are the person to be trained, ask the trainer to give you the information you need in a way that best suits your style. Remember, individuals learn differently. And there's no reason not to take full advantage of your learning strengths!

Course Matters

From this chapter, you've learned that there are two approaches to building skills—inside-out and outside-in. The first is (usually) a long-term affair, an ongoing process of development and challenge guided by what truly inspires you. The second is more intense, more narrowly focused, and briefer. Both types of learning are worth considering in terms of both formal continuing education you initiate and training offered by an employer.

Is a continuing education program right for you? If so, what kind? In the next chapter, you'll learn how to make the best continuing choices for your situation.

The Least You Need to Know

➤ Professional recycling is the process of taking what you've learned and using it to learn something new.

➤ Being in flow—experiencing learning that's guided by a personal sense of passion— is best described as "inside-out" learning.

➤ Skills you learn because you have to in order to get or keep a job can be acquired through "outside-in" learning.

➤ Your personal learning style should play a strong role in determining the direction of your professional recycling efforts.

Chapter 14

A Matter of Degrees

In This Chapter

➤ The pros and cons of higher learning

➤ Finding out what needs strengthening

➤ Strategies to consider for expanding your skills

Maybe you're giving some serious thought to going back to college. It's a natural impulse for a career changer, especially if you find yourself unemployed, misemployed, or mismanaged around September or January—the times of year we've all been taught to register for courses. Early autumn is an especially apt time for the academic juices to start flowing.

But before you do anything rash and string a new series of initials after your name, let me pose a few questions and offer a bit of advice. The idea in this chapter is to help you make decisions that could expand your "degree" of leverage in the labor market, while avoiding some other kinds of decisions that might do little more than complicate your life.

Questions and More Questions

Here are some questions you should consider before you embark on the trail of higher learning. Don't worry, they start out easy. Do you still have that dog-eared legal pad you've been using throughout this book? Do you still remember how to draw a straight

Work Alert!
If you decide to pursue an educational program, you should do so because it adds measurable value to your skill base—not because it's "something to do next," or because of pressure from family or friends.

line down the middle of it? If so, give yourself an A. Find a blank page, and mark the two new headings "What" and "Where."

The Power of "What?"

Under "What" on the left side, make some notes on the kinds of skills you might lack in opening the next chapter in your career. If you've been out doing some information interviewing, chances are you've begun to pick up some insight on what skills you lack. This is the place to put your thoughts in order.

How Much Knowledge?

After you've made some notes under "What," you might find a few basic questions helpful. How much do you need in the way of new skills? Is it an increment of knowledge? Something like a formal course in, say, water law? Or is it just an overview—the kind of savvy you might pick up just by reading a book or two?

So that's one question. How much knowledge is required?

What Needs Strengthening?

Here's another question. What kind of ability do you need? Years ago, when I was directing an individualized University Without Walls program in Chicago, I met with a young woman who was considering a career in special education. The UWW program used a system of learning contracts to help students focus their objectives.

"Well, Erma," I asked her, "what is it you'd like to work on this term?" She thought a minute. Then she said, "These kids are just bugging me with all their needs. There's one thing I've begun to realize. If I'm going to go into this field, I sure need to develop more patience."

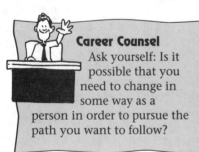

Career Counsel
Ask yourself: Is it possible that you need to change in some way as a person in order to pursue the path you want to follow?

So we made up a learning contract that included an internship with a good supervisor, in addition to her readings, to help her address that goal. The academic work alone, reading and writing papers, wouldn't have done it.

That's question two. Is it cognitive knowledge you need? Or do you need some new behavioral traits?

What Kind of Sheepskin?

Finally, and this is a question with a big Q: Do you need an academic credential? Do you really need that alphabet soup of initials after your name?

Some people do either because the work that interests them requires it (say, it's not enough to have completed three courses in water law; you have to be a J.D. with three courses in water law). For others, it might be a matter of personal need for recognition and status.

When I was 30 years old, I had a powerful need to have a doctorate of some kind. My father-in-law was a "Doctor." So was my brother-in-law. By jingo, I had to have a way of hearing people call me that, too. Today, at 60, I find those motives laughable. But they were very real to me at the time.

The Power of "How?"

Now for the big question: How will you acquire the skills you've identified?

The point is, you'll need to make some decisions about the approach you'll take to your new learning. Here are three options to consider: 1) go it alone, 2) go with a professional association or product vendor, or 3) go the full academic route.

On Your Own

For adults, I believe the first option to consider is always self-managed learning. That's because the vast majority of adult learning is independent. Some years ago, a Canadian educator, Alan Tough, did a broad-ranging study of adult *learning projects* in Chicago. Almost any kind of content could qualify. But he required that the projects consume at least eight hours of time in the course of a year, in increments of at least one hour. In other words, a day's labor in segments as long as a typical television program.

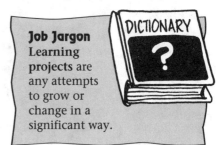

Job Jargon
Learning projects are any attempts to grow or change in a significant way.

By that definition, Tough found an amazing amount of learning transpiring, at every echelon of life in Chicago. Most of it was work-related—lawyers researching cases, teachers preparing for classes.

➤ Two-thirds of the adults' learning projects were carried on independently.

➤ Only 1 percent were motivated by a desire to earn academic credit.

Sometimes, if you're stumped for cocktail-party conversation, try asking people the questions Tough did. Ask them what they've been learning, why, and how. You'll find that almost everyone is busy learning something and that very few adults are interested in academic credit for their labors. Most people are learning what they need to on their own.

Help Me Get My Feet Back on the Ground...

If it seems that you need some support in your learning process, that studying independently won't meet your needs, look for an alliance of people who are interested in the issues you want to learn. For career-related learning, that often means finding a good trade association.

During the past 15 or 20 years, there's been a major shift in continuing education away from colleges and toward professional associations. Today it's common to find professional groups publishing training courses, proctoring exams, and awarding certificates in fields that range from hotel operations to processing health insurance claims.

The reasons for this movement are probably twofold. In the first place, as I've already commented, job-related skills are changing so rapidly that most universities are having a hard time keeping faculty members' skills in step with the times.

(One of the strategies they've used to update yesterday's skills is to employ practicing professionals in various fields as part-time instructors. That's why it's common to find community colleges where one-half to three-quarters of the faculty are on part-time status.) The other reason trade groups are taking over training for themselves is that they very often don't need academic institutions as they once did. Colleges, after all, are late entrants to the training scene. Prior to the industrial revolution and, for the most part, until this century, on-the-job training was handled by associations of workers such as craft guilds. The guilds ran rigid programs of apprenticeship, but people who had not paid their dues as apprentices could sometimes circumvent the system and find someone to teach them on the job. You could say we're simply returning to a very old (and very effective) employment pattern, one that's a heck of a lot less expensive than getting an advanced degree.

Bet You Didn't Know

William Lovett, a 17th century English craftsman, was apprenticed as a rope-maker but couldn't find any work in his field. So Lovett signed on as a carpenter or cabinet-maker. He got the training he needed in his new crafts by plying his coworkers with kegs of ale.

Today we seem to be re-creating systems of work that prevailed before the rise of mass-production factories. Today's William Lovetts are likely to appeal to professional associations, whether or not they offer an ale for an education.

The best way to find out whether a certificate issued by an association will serve as well as a college credential in your new career is simply to ask the people you meet in the course of network interviewing.

Training offered by product vendors is a bit more tricky to evaluate. Generally, this kind of training is readily available and essentially free to employees of firms using a given product. I've taken a number of courses of this kind while researching newspaper columns and most of my fellow students have been using the technology we've studied on their jobs. That's one of the benefits of working at the high end of the labor market.

Work Alert! There is a downside to vendor-sponsored training. If the product sold by the vendor loses market share, so do the skills to use it!

In some cases, vendors become so successful that they can charge tuition for individuals to be trained on their product. Many federally-funded job training centers have paid for this kind of training, partly because it's short-term and favored under government guidelines.

Pomp and Circumstance

How about higher education? First, take a look at the plus side of the equation. Say what you will, a credential can come in handy in this life, especially in employment and career matters. If you have both A) a degree, and B) the good sense to know when and where not to display it, there's a good chance your formal education will occasionally benefit you.

The advantage of accredited college courses is that they go on for weeks at a time, which is good if the subject matter that interests you merits it. Organic chemistry or biblical Hebrew probably are not topics to be covered in a weekend workshop. To build up "reserve skills" in a field—the kind of knowledge you know you're going to need to go back to again and again—you may want to take full advantage of a four-year college curriculum.

Bet You Didn't Know

The Index of Majors and Graduate Degrees (The College Board) gives a fine overview of what's offered where in America's 3,200 colleges and universities. It's available for $16 in local bookstores, or call (212) 713-8000.

Then again, you may not need that kind of information in your new career. If you don't, committing to a four-year program could be a serious waste of time and money.

Since the stakes are so high when it comes to selecting the right course of action in this area, you're going to want to look in depth at all the pros and cons.

The Sad Truth About Higher Learning

In many parts of the world today, academic credentials are often not worth much in the marketplace. One survey found that recommendations by teachers ranked dead last among 11 factors cited by employers making a hire.

The problem is paradoxical because, given the direction our economy is heading, information and the ability to solve complex problems are as important as ever. As Peter Cappelli puts it in *Change at Work*, "the labor market is reducing the rewards to brawn and increasing the rewards to brains."

Degree-Mania

> ### Bet You Didn't Know
>
> The U.S. Department of Labor projects that the number of jobs requiring a college degree will rise by 39 percent between the years 1990 and 2005. That compares to a projected 20 percent increase in the overall numbers of jobs. (Bureau of Labor Statistics)

The increased need for college degrees has a way of rising and falling according to the current available supply of college grads. When graduates are plentiful, as they were when hordes of baby boomers were entering the labor market, employers raised the bar of academic requirements. A job that once required a high school diploma now called for a college degree instead.

Today, in many parts of the country, there's a glut of college graduates on the market. Some analysts estimate that only 70 percent of today's college grads will find a job that requires four years of postsecondary skills.

Two Years and Out

Those figures have given rise to a different scenario for life after high school. People who run two-year community colleges have begun to trumpet the notion that all most workers need is two years' training after high school, since that's enough to learn the skills most jobs require.

Well, there's something to be said for that view and many Americans are voting with their feet to support it. Of the record number of new students who are entering two-year community colleges, some 20 percent already hold four-year undergraduate degrees. Why are they lining up at the two-year schools? To get short-term, targeted training in the (mostly technical) skills they need to update on their jobs.

That's an approach to continuing education that I find makes sense. Go down to the community college for a term or two of desktop publishing, if you want to learn to publish a newsletter. But don't stick around for a two-year Associate of Arts degree. What's the point? Just get your training and get on with it. Indeed, last time I checked, the percentage of community college students who were completing those two-year degrees was going down. I suspect that a number of those non-grads from the community colleges already had four-year degrees.

But it's important to note that the kinds of technical skills community colleges specialize in are changing all the time. Every year, about one-third of the technical skills we use turn obsolescent. So, in order to stay current in this society, what most people need is not a single, two-year, Associate of Arts—but the equivalent of a new A.A. degree every decade.

Beyond Narrow Skills

I believe that, despite the fact that a degree is no longer an instant entrée to high-end employment, something resembling a four-year college education is a good investment for most people. There are several reasons for this.

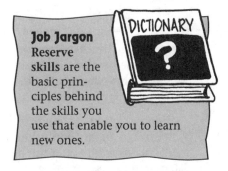

Job Jargon
Reserve skills are the basic principles behind the skills you use that enable you to learn new ones.

First, while employers today need workers with current, job-specific skills (not laggards like me who do their word processing in WordStar), they don't need an armada of workers with narrow skills. They need *reserve skills*—the kinds of core competencies one learns in a good college program.

Another argument is that studies have shown that people who get themselves into a high-end work environment are most likely to get retrained. Whether this is fair is a point to argue, but the trend is undeniable. One recent survey of large employing organizations found that professional and technical workers were almost twice as likely to receive formal training away from their work stations as were production workers.

Career Counsel
Although the market value of many college courses is debatable, there's one exception. According to Peter Cappelli in *Change at Work*, an individual level of achievement in math is "a powerful indicator of later earning capacity."

Today, as the line between blue collar and white collar jobs fades and as whole layers of supervisory positions are eliminated from organizations, there's a growing trend to try to get more education further down the line. If it takes a degree—carefully chosen and supported by the people you talk to during your trial job search—for you to take advantage of that process later on, the time and expense may be worth it.

One final point in favor of a (carefully selected) four-year degree is that there are some marks of character that employers may strongly associate with college grads. I've heard

Work Alert!
One of the criticisms of higher educa- tion is that it often leaves its students ill-prepared for certain aspects of the real world. For instance, journalism students typically don't study personnel management. As a result, organizations habitually promote good writers into positions as editors where they become bad managers.

human resource managers comment that people who graduate from college demonstrate two traits: 1) they have the ability to complete what they started, and 2) they are flexible enough to satisfy the requirements of a variety of professors. Both of those qualities are likely to contribute to success in the workplace, they say.

Don't Buy the Okey-Doke!

So those are some of the arguments, pro and con. The best advice is to make your own thoughtful decision when it comes to an advanced degree and not to be bamboozled by the sales pitch of a specific educational institution.

Finding a college that will allow you to build a degree plan from a combination of courses that makes sense to you is a terrific idea if you know which courses will help you meet your career goals. Again, the best way to make those decisions is to ask good questions in the process of network interviewing. I'd be cautious in following the recommendations of faculty members or placement officers who may or not know conditions in the labor market.

Another option for adult students with specialized learning interests is a growing group of alternative higher education institutions that have sprung up in the last 30 years. These schools generally offer the opportunity to study one-on-one with mentors in the field, integrating academic theory with practical experience. They also award academic credit for skills and knowledge acquired outside the classroom. The best clearinghouse of information on programs of this kind is the Chicago-based Council for Adult and Experi- ential Education. You can contact them by calling (312) 922-5909.

Bet You Didn't Know

A recent study of occupations in America compared the top 30 occupa- tions (measured by numbers of workers) in the years 1900, 1960, and 1995. Here are some interesting outcomes:

Of the top 30 occupations in 1995, most are comparatively recent entrants. Only 12 of the 1995 top 30 were on the leaders' list in 1960, and only eight in 1900.

In 1900, 75 percent of the American workforce was employed in one of the top 30 jobs. But in 1995, the proportion had shrunk to less than one-half. What that means is that most of us need to be prepared for a workplace in which job titles come and go.

And Don't Forget...

There are countless education alternatives in our society. Today, education is everywhere, spilling out beyond the walls of traditional colleges. From CD-ROMs that teach reading readiness to pre-schoolers to alternative short-course schools such as what CompuSkills offers, Americans have unprecedented new and expanded learning resources.

Logging On

The fastest-growing form of education is electronic—courses beamed across the Internet. Not long ago, only a few colleges were sticking a toe into cyberspace. What a change!

Recently, I interviewed an English instructor about one of his composition students. She was singing lead in a country and western band appearing in Holiday Inns all across the Midwest. Equipped with her laptop computer, she could receive and send out writing assignments. The singer had made a grade of A in her first course and was signing up for another.

According to Robert Tucker, a higher education researcher based in Phoenix, more than 50 percent of the nation's four-year colleges now offer courses on the Internet to more than a million students. According to a recent article in *Forbes Magazine*, that number of cyberlearners will triple by the end of the century.

> **Career Counsel**
>
> "Non-traditional education helps someone be more flexible. There's nothing wrong with a traditional education (but) too many people 'go by the book.' It doesn't matter if one is in a corporation, a university, or a film crew, the person who can think outside the system while using the system is the one to watch."
>
> —Rita Mae Brown (Author, *Rubyfruit Jungle*, and graduate of the nontraditional Union Institute based in Cincinnati)

Want to Learn? Watch TV!

For those who find interacting with a keyboard and computer monitor an unsatisfying alternative to flesh and blood instructors and students, yet who can't see their way clear to enroll in traditional classes, telecourses may offer a middle-range option. Some even allow you to arrange for formal college credit!

Most of the television courses available today are a far cry from the old "sunrise semester" classes where students had to stagger out of bed to watch boring lectures by professors who appeared as talking heads. I've previewed some spectacular TV courses, such as Destinos, a Spanish class structured like a 52-week soap opera and photographed on-site in Spain.

Educators who work with telecourses suggest that students train themselves to view the lessons actively, drawing out ideas from the lessons rather than simply sponging up the videos from the couch. They also suggest taking notes, and taping broadcasts so that you can rewind the tape when necessary for review.

Get Involved!

Finally, here's another good way to pick up new skills and one that you may not have thought of. Take on a volunteer assignment. It's an opportunity to network in social service organizations, if that's your bent. But you can also learn to use certain office equipment, or accounting systems, or learn to turn out a newsletter, or sharpen up a foreign language.

Bet You Didn't Know

United Way, the social service umbrella organization, has produced a computer program to match volunteers with agencies and assignments where one can learn specific skills—say, database management on Excel. The computer program is called Matchpoint and is available at various local United Way organizations. For information, call (800) 593-5654.

The downside of volunteering if one is job-hunting is that most agencies now require a three-to-six month commitment in order to recoup their investment in training. That doesn't leave much time for pounding the pavement. However, it's often possible to arrange one's schedule to free up daytime hours.

One United Way volunteer coordinator reports, "We recommend that people treat a volunteer assignment like a full-time job. When you call on an agency, dress as you would for a job interview. After all, that agency is becoming part of your professional network."

It Never Ends!

The watchword of the new economy is lifelong learning, and the bottom line message is that it's never too late to start. Nor is it ever too early! A few years ago, I went to see former Secretary of Labor Robert Reich at his home in Cambridge, Massachusetts. I was trying to line up a lecture appearance for Reich in Denver and needed to go over some details of the arrangements.

Reich asked me to come over at something like 7:00 a.m., but he forgot he'd made the appointment. When I arrived, he and his wife and two small sons were having breakfast in the kitchen. They invited me to join them and we were having an enjoyable discussion over cornflakes and coffee when suddenly his three-year-old started wailing.

I wheeled around to see if he'd taken a header out of his high chair. Nope. The little tyke was seated in front of a full-sized computer, and the program he was working on had crashed. He stopped sobbing as his mother re-booted it.

Some days, I wish someone could do the same for me.

The Least You Need to Know

➤ For adults, the first option to consider is always self-managed learning.

➤ Community colleges may be a valuable resource for expanding your skills whether or not you go for a degree.

➤ Alternative higher education institutions generally offer the opportunity to study one-on-one with mentors in the field, integrating academic theory with practical experience.

➤ You should consider taking on a volunteer assignment that expands your skills.

➤ The best advice is to make your own thoughtful decision when it comes to an advanced degree and not be taken in by the rhetoric of a specific educational institution.

Chapter 15

Big Employers, Small Employers

In This Chapter

➤ Your professional profile

➤ What big companies look for

➤ What small companies look for

➤ How to send the right signals

Which prospective employer appeals more to you: Amalgamated Worldwide Widgets, the industry behemoth, or Solo Widget Technologies, the hot new startup that offers all the triumph—and all the long hours, uncertainty, and heartaches—of a dynamic small firm? In this chapter, you learn about how a company's size and guiding culture should influence your career choices.

The Lunch Date

Juan had looked forward to the meeting for a month. A college friend had set up lunch with a couple of guys he'd said were real comers. They worked for a large corporation in one of the hot new industries of the '90s—satellite digital TV.

Juan had done his homework on satellite TV. He knew some of the technical terminology and had a sense of how the satellite operators stacked up against cable companies in the fight for cyberspace. Now he had some questions to address to see if there was a place for his accounting skills in the industry.

But, 10 minutes into the first course, he began to feel queasy about his new acquaintances. And by the time the waiter brought out the dessert tray, he was dead-sure he didn't want to work at that company.

"The only thing they talked about was office politics," Juan reflected. "It seemed all these guys cared about was pumping their image. Their company was having a reception that night. 'Man, I hope when the CEO walks up to me, he remembers my name,' one of 'em said. 'That would score some points with my boss.'

"Hey, that was enough for me," Juan sighed. "I couldn't wait to get away from those guys."

Mismatched Mindsets

Juan's experience is not unusual. He found himself in a work environment that didn't suit his own outlook on life. The same thing just as easily could have happened to a career changer who encountered a fast-moving, bare-bones *entrepreneurial* style for the first time.

Job Jargon
An entrepreneur is a person who creates and manages an enterprise or business.

For all one might say about the transformation of American business culture—the shift from pyramids to diamonds—there are plenty of signs that the timeworn, traditional corporate culture is alive and kicking. There are lots of workplaces where people appear to build careers on schmooze-ability rather than tangible skills. For lots of people (including me), that kind of workplace doesn't hold much excitement.

So, this is a good time to ask which kind of environment you belong in. Although Juan's story paints the corporate culture of some larger organizations in an unflattering light, that doesn't mean you can't find a home in some large organization. Some people find happiness in what outsiders refer to as "the corporate life." Others opt for smaller firms, where the allegiance is more to industries than to organizations.

Whenever you find yourself in a new organization—working there or exploring it—there are five basic questions that can quickly orient you to the shape and culture of that organization.

1. *What* are these people doing here? What product or service are they trying to provide?

2. *How* are they doing the work? What technology and management procedures are they using?

3. *Who* is doing the work? Are these people all about the same age, from the same ethnic group, of the same gender, with the same educational background, etc.?

4. *Where* is the work centered? Is this the corporate headquarters or a branch office? Are other companies in the same industry located here? Is this community an industry center?

5. *Why* is the work being done here, by these people, and in this way? Are there particular advantages to this location, or is the work likely to shift elsewhere?

Take good notes on what you find out. Then put your feet up and take time to reflect on who you are.

Questions Revisited

This is a good time to review some of those bedrock questions we began the book with.

➤ What does work mean to you? Is it a job and just a small piece of your life? Or a career that you treat as a series of stops along a track that follow a logical sequence? Or a vocation, which is something you feel called to do?

➤ "What needs doing?" Is that the way you view your work? Or, "Where's the market?" That's if you're more pragmatic. Whichever track you take, the next question is, "What can you do? Where are you?" And then, "What are your links with the market—to a place where someone needs what you can do? How can you make a connection?"

➤ I've asked you a number of questions about your skills, for that's the main bridge to new fields. As you've looked back over the peak moments in your prior work, I've prompted you to ask this question about your accomplishments to get at your core competencies: "What were you doing when you did that?" It's a way to find your core competencies.

➤ Above all, I've concentrated on the message that you need to be as self-reliant as possible in today's new economy. You need to be a business enterprise of your own, capable of managing your own affairs. That's the way I've charted the patterns of skills you need today: projecting, producing, and promoting. If you're strong and skilled in one part of that complex, you still need to pay attention to the sides where you may be weaker.

➤ And, finally, I've stressed the need for new learning. That's not just learning hard skills, such as object-oriented programming in C++ if you're in software development, but being open to learning entirely new ways of working as the employment environment changes.

So, look at every one of those factors as you consider where in the world of work it seems that you belong. The more focused you are on your future direction, the more clearly you'll be able to present your background in meaningful terms—highlighting the skills you want to transfer, and leaving out the parts that don't fit.

Brand Management for Yourself

To put it another way, the more focused you are, the more you'll present a strong and persuasive brand image—what I call a *professional profile*.

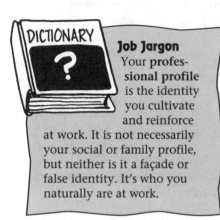

Job Jargon
Your **professional profile** is the identity you cultivate and reinforce at work. It is not necessarily your social or family profile, but neither is it a façade or false identity. It's who you naturally are at work.

Corporations constantly consider their public profiles, and today's mobile employees should, too. Think of Apple Computers, when they were trying to wrestle some market share from IBM—that stodgy bunch that used to go around in white shirts and dark suits. Apple Computers chose a multi-colored apple with a bite missing to convey the idea of creativity.

Corporations also pay attention to elements of their profile that they leave out. When the Walt Disney Corporation decided to turn out R-rated pictures, such as *Down and Out in Beverly Hills*, they created a special subsidiary, Touchstone Films. It was a way to keep Mickey Mouse and his clean-cut cohorts clear of half-clothed characters in the adult films.

Bet You Didn't Know

Just as you must in your career search, professional athletes must pay attention to the profiles they project. There's a legendary story in the NBA of a player who ruined his chances for high-end product endorsements when he appeared in a hot dog commercial.

Pay attention to your profile, and make it a strong one. If there's an off-camera side of you—such as my secret life as a part-time sportswriter—keep it out of view on those occasions when it could muddy the profile people need to have of you.

Expect a larger, hierarchical employer to look for people who...

➤ Play it safe and avoid risk.

➤ Embrace fixed, clearly defined work structures.

➤ Expect to be able to control events.

➤ Look for security.

➤ Work well with support staff.

➤ Have a passion for anonymity.

Expect a smaller, more market-driven employer to look for people who...

➤ Love risk and realize they'll be penalized for not taking it.

➤ Embrace fluid, loosely defined work structures.

➤ Expect very little control over events.

➤ Value compensation and the respect of their technical peers over security.

➤ Need no support staff.

➤ Have a passion for new technology.

(Source: Dave Lovely, Human Resources Manager, Maxtor Corporation)

When you have your product profile clear, find a way to present yourself in the market that feels comfortable to you. If it's easier to express yourself in writing rather than over the phone, write a note to the person you're calling, indicating the purpose of your call before dialing her up. The idea is to play to your strengths and stay clear of those weaknesses we all have.

In his biography of Henry Ford, Robert Lacey reports that the eminent inventor was a dreadful public speaker. "Fluent and persuasive in the presence of two or three respectful listeners, Ford could become tongue-tied and awkward in front of a crowd. He fidgeted and stammered, and his self-confidence evaporated."

To make matters worse, Ford was no better communicating in print. He read with difficulty and couldn't spell a lick. But, according to Lacey, Ford found another way to reach the public. "Henry was wondrously at ease with the press. Set a reporter in front of Henry Ford with a notepad and the carmaker became a fountain of quips and quotes..."

Paul Edwards, the author of eight books on self-employment, puts it this way. "The point is to find your own style: something that is natural and effective for you... Your marketing style should feel like a dessert should taste."

Career Counsel
The professional profile that comes most naturally and easily to you—attentive to details or freewheeling and risk-oriented, hierarchical or independent—will have a great deal to do with the success of your career-change campaign.

The Vanishing Manager?

If you do opt for the corporate life, be aware that there's a lot of experimentation going on among the diminishing ranks of corporate managers. According to one study, the number of organizational layers between CEO and shop floor (or the equivalent) in American corporations shrank by one-third in the 1980s. Companies that had employed nine tiers of managers in 1981 had only four to six levels in 1991.

> ## Bet You Didn't Know
>
> Management gurus such as Stephen Covey of Provo, Utah draw huge crowds these days with seminars on transforming the American corporation. Covey touts some time-worn but leading-edge values. What's the best way to cope with a changing business environment? He recommends committing yourself to principles that don't change, such as trust. "To the degree you can build trust in an organization, you don't have to supervise people," he advises employers, and the message is worth remembering for employees and career changers, too. But the best advice is this: If you do head into a big corporation, don't try to do so as a full-time manager. Go in with a specialty—some area in which you can offer leadership—and build other skills around it.

Big Company, Small Company

The best maxim to follow in organizations of any size is Henry Kaiser's timeless "Find a need and fill it." If you devote most of your attention to identifying unmet needs in industries and organizations and concentrate on what needs doing, you'll be much more likely to find your way to a place where someone needs what you can do than if you confine yourself to job postings.

I'm always struck by some of the inventive ways people I've met come up with employment opportunities—often by creating their own jobs, or even their own companies! Here are a few recent examples.

Issues, Anyone?

Garth Johnston got a master's degree in the field of intellectual history some years ago from the University of Minnesota. Now, if there's one unmarketable academic major I can think of, it's intellectual history. That's the kind of field you find on the resumes of minimum-wage clerks in bookstores.

But Garth loved that field, and he wanted to do something with his training when he burned out on a career in government work some time in his 40s. He'd become involved with a local chapter of the World Future Society, and one evening at a meeting a light bulb went on. "Wow—I could do this for a living!" he thought. He suddenly saw that people who were "futurists" were doing nothing but practicing the discipline of history in reverse. So he started his own organization and called it the Colorado Issues Network. He began holding seminars on emerging trends that could affect businesses and signing up organizations as members.

For some years, now, he's made his living that way. The meetings are held in the facilities of member groups. He sponsors seminars by outside speakers and sometimes hooks up with national figures through teleconferencing technology. Ask any of his members and they'll tell you: The Issues Network is one of the most stimulating outfits around. (Just don't tell them it's an exercise in intellectual history.)

Work Alert! Don't let your degree or choice of major stop you from pursuing what you really want to do.

Pink Slip? Who Cares?

Consider the case of Ron Harmon. He spoke at a seminar I attended on defense conversion. Harmon was a young engineer who had lost his job with Ball Aerospace. One morning, he was out jogging when he had an interesting idea. He'd been at his daughter's school at a PTA meeting the night before and had heard teachers complaining that they couldn't keep up with all the new technology that was being thrust upon them.

"Hmm," he thought, as he trotted along. "That's one thing I could help them with. As an engineer, I understand how software's put together. Engineers know how to learn software." As fate would have it, later that day he received his pink slip.

The last time I talked with him, Harmon was investigating a career change into education—not as a classroom teacher, per se, but as an on-site instructional media specialist who would use one of his core competencies in engineering to help public school teachers. He could help them keep up with the demands of learning new technology.

The Power of the "Dead-End Job"

Then there's Bonita, who graduated a few years ago from one of America's leading liberal arts colleges. The school was one that offered students the opportunity to design their own interdisciplinary majors, and that's what Bonita did. She put together a degree program in outdoor education and had a good time completing her studies.

Once out of school, however, the fun times came to a skidding stop. Bonita and her academic advisors had given no thought to whatever it was she might do for a living with her degree. In desperation, she took a minimum-wage job with a cut-rate outdoor sporting gear retail outlet.

The store environment was Spartan and the job was boring. Most of the time, Bonita worked the cash register. But after a few months, she began having conversations with some of the customers who wanted to find excursions into the wilderness outside town. So she worked up a proposal and took it to the store, suggesting she start up a new department where rafting, horseback riding, and climbing trips could be made available to customers.

The managers gave her proposal some thought and decided that they liked the idea. They were outdoor-types themselves and were feeling burned out on running a bargain-basement, "category-killer" store. So they approved the proposal and helped her come up with marketing materials. Within a couple of months, she was using her skills. Her program was up and running.

Could You Do That?

What are some other fields in which a person with ingenuity can match cultures with groups that have specific problems—and then go on to create a job that connects with unmet needs? Here are two broad possibilities—your own research could lead you to dozens more.

Words, Words, Words

Anyone with a foreign-language skill might pay attention to the phenomenal growth in the number of recent immigrants in America's service industries. A few years ago, I found myself stuck for 10 minutes in a hotel parking lot. It seemed to be taking everyone a long time to pay the cashier.

As I drove up to the exit, the attendant greeted me with a smile. "Zodt your zighedt?" he asked me.

I said, "Huh?" Then, "Oh, yeah. I've got my ticket right here."

That was in California. The next week, I was in a restaurant in Florida. I watched a young waiter carrying around a dessert tray. Finally he came over to me. As he set the tray down, he confided that he was trying to learn English on the job. "Now, take this dessert." He pointed to the menu—Oreo Pie. "It's really good, but I can't pronounce it."

Career Counsel

In the U.S., there's an urgent need for bilingual personnel who focus on core skills necessary for a particular industry (such as hotel management) and can also train others to work effectively in an English-language environment.

In the United States, an estimated 1,972 legal immigrants arrive every day. The number of illegal immigrants is unknown. Whether their status is legal or illegal, many of these people are well educated (some 20 percent have college degrees). But most are struggling to learn the English language—often in service-sector jobs that demand basic language skills. In another day, they'd be working in factories where jobs were segmented and language skills weren't always all that vital. Nowadays, those routine factory jobs are history, and qualified teachers of English as a second language may be able to benefit as a result.

Information, Please

New patterns are emerging in the rapidly changing field of information technology. The other night, I heard a talk by Troy Bettinger of the Colorado Technical Recruiters Network. Bettinger believes that many of the highly sought-after infotech people of the near future will be specialists in various industries who happen to have a bent for computers and are willing to learn the tools that apply to their fields.

Want an example of how this would work? Not long ago, I had a couple of clients: One was a hotel manager who got tired of working that field's customary 60-hour weeks, and the other held a comparably demanding position in the restaurant field. Both were convinced it was time to find something else to do for a living. "I've never met a successful person in my profession who wasn't divorced," the hotel worker lamented. "You can't work these hours and have a real life." Both went on to become marketing reps to information technology companies with clients in their (former) field.

Bettinger put it well. "It's a lot easier to teach computer technology to people who know the business where it's to be used, than it is to teach someone with computer skills the basics of the business," he said.

In Reinventing the Corporation, John Naisbitt quotes futurist Barbara Marx Hubbard: "For the job you want, no one is hiring and the pay is nil. That's why we all must learn to be entrepreneurial." Fortunately, there are some good role models out there.

Drum Roll, Please...

So far in this book, you've learned a great deal about your own core competencies, the problems they're likely to solve for other people, and the best ways to find out how what you have to offer matches up with the outside world. You've even learned about the missions and culture of prospective employers in particular industries, thanks to your "trial search." In the next chapter of this book, you'll take everything you've learned so far and use it to formalize your career goal.

The Least You Need to Know

➤ Your professional profile probably lends itself either to a large, hierarchical organization or a smaller, more flexible one. You need to know which environment works for you.

➤ Managing your profile—and sending the right (honest) messages about the work you do—is an important part of career success.

➤ Some people find happiness in what outsiders refer to as "the corporate life." Others opt for smaller firms, where the allegiance is more to industries than to organizations.

➤ If you do head into a big corporation, don't try to do so as a full-time manager. Blend your managerial skills with some other specialty.

➤ The best maxim to follow in organizations of any size is probably Henry Kaiser's timeless "Find a need and fill it."

Chapter 16

Goals 101

In This Chapter

➤ What you should be asking yourself

➤ What to do if your goal isn't clear

➤ What your goal might sound like

Do you remember how, a little earlier in the book, you developed a strategy for a "trial search" within a field that seemed to make sense for you? Now it's time to take a look at the results of that preliminary search and find out whether or not the industry you selected as the target of your "trial search" should be the focus of your career goal.

Taking the Initiative

Twenty years ago, the key to finding good work was to develop a great deal of experience within a particular, narrowly defined industry, and to demonstrate a willingness to sell oneself to an employer who happened to be passing out jobs in that field. Today, as I've noted repeatedly in this book, most good work takes the form of projects, rather than jobs—at least initially. That's the kind of work that needs doing in most organizations: "How can we network these computers?" "What's the market for our product in Malaysia?"

Work Alert!
Having a career goal you can commit to is *not* the same as having a specific job title you're eager to call your own.

Lots of career-changers get hung up on the terminology associated with a particular job. That's a great way to shut out opportunities.

"On the average, how many senior citizens are using the Internet to arrange travel plans during the course of a day?" Taking the initiative and finding a way to provide useful answers to questions such as these is often the best way to enter a new career field.

But to find that kind of work, you have to understand the needs of an industry or organization and you also have to be able to propose a realistic solution to those needs.

In this chapter, you'll work through questionnaires about the needs you highlighted during your "trial search" with prospective employers, and the potential solutions you might provide. They'll help you to confirm the "fit" of the industry you've already selected on a provisional basis.

But I Don't Know Enough About the Industry!

If you still feel that you don't have an adequate grasp of the problems facing the industry you selected for your "trial search," you will probably want to conduct some further research before proceeding with the questionnaires and worksheets that follow. At this point, a trip to the library is your best bet.

We'll be looking in detail at library research techniques in Chapter 18. (That's where you'll be learning about using the library to get the information you need on particular employers.) For now, though, you should devote at least a day to researching the biggest library in your area (they're usually the best) and do the following:

Work Alert!
The Internet can be a great way to track down facts about a particular organization or industry, but it can also be a remarkable time-waster. If you decide to supplement library research with online data searches, schedule particular blocks of time and then carefully evaluate what you've actually learned during that hour before committing more time.

➤ Make friends with a reference librarian and tell him or her you're interested in finding out about the challenges facing top decision-makers in your industry of choice. See what information resources he or she suggests.

➤ Ask for a look at relevant trade publications. Think in terms of your industry, the industry it buys from, and the industry it sells to. (For instance, if you're trying to win a job in the publishing industry, take a look at trade magazines directed at both publishers and commercial printers.)

➤ Check the *Reader's Guide to Periodical Literature* or the library's online article database for recent articles of interest to people in your target industry.

➤ Finally, ask the librarian for information on average salaries in the industry or work area you're focusing on.

You'll be looking in greater depth at some more focused library research techniques a little later on in the book. For now, your goal is to solidify, or expand, the information you've gathered during your "trial search" campaign with potential employers.

Once you've done that, you're ready to move on to…

Questions About Your Career Goals

Take a look at the questions that appear in the following boxes. Use the research, insights, and "gut feel" you've developed during discussions with employers and library research to provide the most complete answers you can.

Much of what follows will be familiar to you. That's good! Take advantage of this opportunity to formalize, and commit to your legal pad the answers to key questions you've considered earlier in the book.

If you find that you're consistently coming up short on the answers to these questions, the odds are good that you need to find out more about the industry you're focusing on.

Career Counsel
Reference librarians are a resource too often overlooked by careershifters. These folks are usually highly qualified to help you track down information on trends and key players in the industry you're trying to learn more about. Ask for their help!

Work Alert!
Some people pick careers based solely on economic trends, and by mid-life most of them are miserable, even if they've succeeded in their chosen fields. The problem is, they haven't really chosen those fields. They've only settled for them.

Part One: Where's the Market?

1. What are the names of five major employers in the field you've been exploring? (They don't have to be employers you could see yourself working for, although the more who fall into that category, the better. If you've uncovered information on more than five employers, select the five most promising.)

   Employer #1 _____

   Employer #2 _____

   Employer #3 _____

   Employer #4 _____

   Employer #5 _____

   continues

continued

2. What needs doing at these organizations? What pressing problems did your discussions or library research uncover? For instance, is every organization you spoke to trying to figure out how to keep its computers from going haywire on January 1, 2000? (Go into as much detail here as you can. Are consumer patterns changing? Is there a new technology that's changing the way end users think about what these organizations do or produce? Is a new product release in the works? Is a new group of consumers being developed?)

What needs doing at Employer #1: _____

_____

_____

_____

What needs doing at Employer #2: _____

_____

_____

_____

What needs doing at Employer #3: _____

_____

_____

_____

What needs doing at Employer #4: _____

_____

_____

_____

What needs doing at Employer #5: _____

_____

_____

_____

3. How does the general salary information you've been able to uncover for this industry/work area compare with your financial requirements? And what about opportunities for professional growth? What's the learning/earning equation? (If you can't make a living in this industry or grow within it, it doesn't make much sense to try to pursue a career here!)

_____

_____

_____

_____

4. Of the problems, needs, and objectives you listed in #2, which make the most difference to you? Which give you the greatest feeling of energy when you think about trying to solve them? (Go into as much detail as you like about as many different topics as you like.)

_____

_____

_____

_____

Part Two: Where Are You?

5. What skills would you have to possess in order to help solve the problems that interest you (the ones you outlined in #4)? Leave aside for the moment your own experience on the job. Focus on the aptitudes that would be required for someone else to attack the problems you've just outlined, and don't leave anything out. (Be ruthlessly honest here, and try to use as much of the specific feedback from personal interviews conducted during your "trial search" as you possibly can.)

_____

_____

_____

_____

6. What can you do? What skills have you already developed a high proficiency in? What are the core competencies—skills you strongly associate with "peak moments" in your life—that relate to work you've already performed? What, in other words, are the skills behind your job title? (Try thinking about people you've worked with who benefited as a result. What happened to those people? How did you help them to achieve important goals?)

_____

_____

_____

_____

continues

151

continued

7. Now identify the areas of overlap between #5 and #6 above. What skills do you have that are already highly relevant to the job of solving the problems identified in #3? (Again, be as brutally honest with yourself as you can, and don't list skills that prospective employers have told you don't appear strong enough yet.)

_____

_____

_____

_____

8. Where is your current skill set lacking—at least in terms of your ability to attack the problems that inspire you within the industry you've selected? WARNING: Engaging in wishful thinking here, as opposed to hard analysis, can make your career-change process take much longer than it should! (If, during a face-to-face meeting, a prospective employer isolated an area where you need to grow professionally, be sure to list it here, along with any other skill gaps you've identified.)

_____

_____

_____

_____

_____

And finally...

Part Three: How Can You Connect?

9. What have you been learning? (More often than not, our careers are renewed through the warm-blooded stuff we're still learning rather than the skills we have down cold. Whatever their age, most people have some sort of growing edge to their interests, whether it's a new computer program or an after-hours hobby. As you look at the skills you've developed thus far in your career, where do you see your interests growing?)

_____

_____

_____

_____

10. How much of what you just outlined in the question above is likely to bring you closer to the goal of erasing the "skill gaps" you identified in #8? (In other words, what are you already doing, because you choose to, that will bring you closer to the goal of possessing a skill set that matches up precisely with the problems you'd like to solve in the target industry?)

    _____

    _____

    _____

    _____

11. Having reviewed the options for expanding your educational and skill horizons that appear in Chapter 14, which appear to you to be the most realistic, given your aim of solving the problems you outlined in #3? (Make the best decision for your situation, and think long and hard before committing yourself to an expensive, time-consuming course of formal academic study in order to enter this industry.)

    _____

    _____

    _____

    _____

12. If you were to describe to a prospective employer the top three reasons you're the right person to solve the problems that interest you, how would you do so?

    _____

    _____

    _____

    _____

Two Alternatives

If you've taken an appropriate amount of time to develop truthful, accurate responses to all of the questions you just read, odds are good that you now find yourself in one of two situations.

Situation One: You Don't Fit in

Career Counsel
If, after completing the questionnaires you are still uncertain about your career goal, ask yourself: "Who are three to four people whom I admire? What kind of work is each person doing?" Select people five to ten years older than you are. How did these people get where they were going? Do you want to go there? Can any of them provide advice or guidance?

Career Counsel
If you haven't yet found a match with an industry that makes sense for you, that's not a black mark against you. It just means you're careful about what you invest your time, effort, and energy in pursuing. See Appendix B for ideas on career fields you may want to consider exploring.

There's a mismatch somewhere. Perhaps your research and face-to-face interviews weren't able to identify any pressing problems that needed solving. (This is either a sign of an industry that's in very steep decline or, what's more likely, a tell-tale sign that you need to do some more exploring about the field in question.)

Or perhaps the problems you've identified simply don't resonate for you—they don't carry a great deal of meaning, and there's not much about the industry that gets you excited. It could be, too, that your research leads you to conclude that the field you've selected simply isn't lucrative enough for you to pursue it further, or doesn't offer you enough opportunities for new learning.

Perhaps you've decided that the gap between your current skill base and the skills required to solve the problems you've identified is just too large. If you have a passion for aeronautical engineering, but you have no technical experience in the field, there's no shame in admitting that you're not willing (at the moment) to invest the time and money necessary to gain the skills you'd need to make a contribution in this area.

In all of the preceding cases—indeed, in any situation in which your honest assessment leads you to believe that you aren't yet ready to commit to a career goal—the remedy is straightforward: Do more digging! Meet with some more people, make another trip to the library. Find another set of problems that represents a more impressive match for your situation.

You shouldn't try to move on with the advice that appears in the following chapters of this book until you can take the questionnaire again, and move out of "mismatch mode."

Situation Two: You Know Where You Belong

You've identified an industry that makes sense for you. You also have a good fix on the problems you're personally motivated to solve, and you have a workable, realistic strategy for overcoming any skill gaps that may exist.

Basically, you're in good shape as far as your objective goes. You're ready to commit to your career goal—and talk about it intelligently with prospective employers. That means you're ready to make the most out of the chapters that follow in this book.

Your career goal may sound something like this:

➤ "My goal is to have a career in sports medicine, working for a professional team or individual clients. Because the top jobs in that field seem to require a degree in physical therapy, I plan to take the necessary courses to get into a top-rated physical therapy program rather than a short-term exercise physiology program. Then I'll look for an internship with a local pro team."

➤ "My goal is to work hard and make a lot of money in the computer field during the next few years so that I can retire and raise llamas in New Mexico. To accomplish that, I plan to brush up on my COBOL skills so I can hire out as a programmer to redo computer systems that are slated to crash on the first day of the year 2000. I realize that my COBOL skills will lose value once the crisis is past, but hey, come 2001, I'll be off with my llamas."

➤ "As a single parent, I need to bring in some income and provide good housing for little Jeff and Nellie. Someday I'd like to get my real estate broker's license, but I can't afford a rollercoaster income right now. I've found there's a need for apart-ment managers in my area. The pay isn't outstanding, but you can get free housing on the premises, and you can train for the field within 12 months. There's a com-munity college down the street that offers a program in apartment management; I'm going to look into it next week."

If those kinds of statements now come easily to you, congratulations! You know where you're going. In the next chapter, you'll find out how to focus like a laser beam on particular employers.

What Now?

As you've seen, you'll be using your own core competencies and your natural networks as tools that will help you decide how best to conduct a "trial search" in an industry that can benefit from what you have to offer. For the ideas behind that "trial search" to work for you on a larger scale, however, you're going to need to be able to discuss, intelligently and with little or no prompting, the value you represent as a potential employee. You're going to have to demonstrate, in other words, your ability to think about what most of today's employers want—results.

The Least You Need to Know

➤ Focus on the essentials and don't get hung up on the title assigned by one company to the person who typically does what you want to do.

➤ Ask yourself key questions that focus on "Where are you?"

➤ Ask yourself key questions that focus on "Where's the market?"

➤ Ask yourself key questions that focus on "How can you connect?"

➤ Formulate a realistic, workable career goal before you proceed with later chapters of this book.

Part 3
Connections

Lights, camera, action! Learn the best ways to reach out to employers within your target industries—and what to do if that offer you're after doesn't materialize right away. This part of the book will show you the best means of entry to today's companies.

Chapter 17

How Not to Conduct a Job Search in Today's Economy

In This Chapter

➤ Reaching out

➤ Avoiding the common pitfalls of the job search

➤ What good initial phone contact sounds like

You've narrowed the field. You know what type of industry you want to enter, and you have a good fix on the types of problems you feel qualified to solve. If there are skill gaps for you to fill, you now have a sense of the most realistic ways for you to fill them. The question now becomes: How do you make direct contact with potential employers within your chosen field?

In this chapter, we'll look at some of the best strategies for expanding your "trial search" into the real thing. We'll also take a look at the techniques you should stay away from—unless you have unlimited amounts of time, effort, and energy to spend on the job search!

Emphasize Solutions, Not Positions!

I've said it several times in this book, but the message bears repeating: Focusing on short-term projects rather than full-time positions is the most effective way to find a niche in a new field. There's a very good likelihood that, by taking an active approach to expanding your natural network of contacts (that is, the work-related connections you already have), you can focus in on the problems of prospective employers by means of phone or face-to-face interviews. Once you've gotten "on the radar screen," you'll be in an excellent position to find out about short-term opportunities. These "find-a-need-and-fill-it" assignments serve as two-way auditions: You're auditioning for the company, and, just as important, the company is auditioning for you.

Career Counsel

Remember: There may or may not be a formal job opening at a particular company within your target industry, but there is sure to be a pressing problem attached to a decision-maker who's looking for a quick, relatively inexpensive, hassle-free solution.

This book isn't a job search guide, but I do want to give you some information on what does and doesn't work when you're contacting potential employers. The first message is: Don't be afraid of juggling short-term assignments, or of presenting yourself as someone who is happy to do so! This is part of the entrepreneurial approach: delivering solutions to a wide range of contacts in your target industry, rather than immediately trying to find a way to "fit in" in a single organization.

What Doesn't Work

Sometimes, when it comes to a career search, a cautionary note or two on what *not to do* is just as important as any advice you may receive on what *to do*.

Here's a list of "tactics" some career changers have used to get seriously sidetracked. If you're smart, you'll avoid them like the plague.

Burying Yourself in the Want Ads

I've already talked about the danger of fixating on want ads earlier in this book. The instinct to spend precious time poring through countless dense columns of small print is so strong that I feel it's worth reinforcing the point.

The temptation to spend an entire morning reviewing various want ads is particularly strong among career changers who make a habit of reading the morning paper! The want ads have their place—but that place *isn't* the center of your job search. If necessary, save the paper for the end of the day, and read it when it's time to unwind.

Falling Prey to Tunnel Vision

"He said he was interested!"

"She said she wanted to look at my resume!"

"He said he'd call me next week!"

When these kinds of results come up in your networking campaign, they're very good news…usually. What comes as a surprise to many job seekers is that positive words from prospective employers can also be very *bad* news for your job search campaign if they bring about enough euphoria, tension, or distraction to keep you from doing whatever is necessary to turn up the next job lead.

Lots of job seekers I've met have superb time-management skills right up until they get the first nibble—at which point their ability to get the very most out of an hour suddenly plummets. They find themselves unable to make more calls, send out more letters, or visit more trade events, because they've got one thing, and only one thing, on their mind: that nibble!

> ### Bet You Didn't Know
>
> A sales trainer I know has a saying: "The sale that you think can't fall through usually does." His point is that the process of prospecting for sales leads needs to be continuous, to make up for all those "sure-thing" contacts that don't turn into revenue. The same point holds true for your job search.

The contact that definitely represents your dream assignment with that dream organization may result in tangible progress. But don't spend an hour of your day daydreaming about what the contact you talked to yesterday had to say. Get back on the horse and keep riding. You need lots of leads like that.

Getting too Casual

One of the most common mistakes career seekers make is to forget that the business of finding a job is a business.

You've read, at various points in this book, about the importance of taking an entrepreneurial approach to career management. That means taking on the role of the independent contractor and accepting full responsibility for both the results one delivers and the job of developing a proactive "marketing campaign." That's your strategy for reaching out to prospective employers. An entrepreneurial approach also means paying close attention to the messages prospective employers receive when they make contact with you.

Keep-It-Professional Checklists

During in-person meetings with professional contacts and prospective employers, do you:

➤ Dress the part? (Your attire should be one notch above that of the typical daily attire of a successful person who currently occupies the position you want.)

➤ Groom yourself immaculately? (No, you don't have to plunk down $85 for the perfect hairstyle before every meeting. Yes, your hair should be neat, clean, and attractive, and your hands—especially your fingernails—should look clean and well cared for.)

➤ Pay close attention to personal hygiene? (If breath or body odor is a problem, virtually nothing else you say or do will reverse the negative first impression you'll make with your contact.)

➤ Speak slowly, clearly, and appropriately? (Sure, you're excited, but don't run off at the mouth—and don't use inappropriate terminology or technical jargon that may put off your contact.)

At home, do you:

➤ Make sure your answering machine or service is on at all times? (These days, if people can't leave a message, it's a definite negative.)

➤ Make sure your answering machine message is positive and professional-sounding? (No jokes. No rock and roll or other inappropriate music. No non sequiturs. No children. You need to make a powerful, competent first impression with professional contacts. If it wouldn't show up on company voice-mail, it shouldn't show up on your message.)

➤ Set aside a (more or less) soundproof environment in which you can take calls related to your work? (Dogs barking, horns blaring, or children crying in the background send the wrong message.)

➤ Limit or eliminate speakerphone use? (Answering the phone "on speaker" gives the caller the impression that he or she has dialed a wrong number and reached Venus. Putting someone else "on speaker" without permission is rude.)

Getting too Weird for the Market

There's a fine line between conducting a creative networking and self-marketing campaign and ticking people off. Make sure you stay on the right side of that line.

Is there anything wrong with confidently phrased, creatively formatted letters for contacts who don't yet know how wonderful you are? Of course not.

I've heard lots of stories about job seekers who sent gifts or tongue-in-cheek props to prospective contacts and "got in the door" as a result. Intelligently applied to an industry you know well through person-to-person and library research, this may make sense. But get a good sense of the culture you're trying to enter into before you get too creative, and remember that the boundaries for what is and isn't acceptable will vary.

> **Career Counsel**
> If you're in doubt about the appropriateness of a "creative" contact campaign, talk to someone you know in the industry and ask how it would go over at their employer.

Terrifying or Infuriating the Decision-Maker

At all costs, avoid threatening or steadily more annoying "creative" campaigns. I heard of one aspiring broadcaster who developed a mail campaign based on sending steadily larger balls to presidents of major outfits in his target industry. On the first day, the president would receive a Ping-Pong ball. On the second day, he'd receive a tennis ball. On the third day, he'd receive a basketball. It continued for a week or so, until by the fifth day the poor CEO's secretary had to contend with one of those oversized activity balls toddlers push around living rooms!

I'll have to paraphrase this mail campaign's theme. It went something like: You'd have to have a lot of...let's say "courage"...to miss out on the opportunity of hiring me. This is the kind of "creative" campaign you probably want to avoid—unless you're applying for a job as a "shock-jock" on the morning radio.

Sounding Like You're Desperate

Did you ever hear that country-and-western song that advises struggling musicians to "sing like you don't need the money"? There's something to be said for taking a similar approach to the process of contacting people during your job search. Yes, there will be some times when you have to state outright that you're exploring career opportunities within your industry of choice—there's no percentage in misleading people, and everything to lose by doing so. At the same time, the way you state what you're looking for can make all the difference in the world.

Let's assume, for the sake of argument, that you're facing the dreaded task of calling someone you don't know about professional opportunities. (I recommend that you exploit your natural network to the fullest in this situation, so that there's at least a 50/50 chance you can use a personal referral when approaching your contact.) Consider the difference between the following dialogues:

> **Career Counsel**
> Setting up a "sideline" business—even a modest one—allows you to say honestly that you're self-employed and looking for new clients. Consulting is a great umbrella for short-term assignments that could turn into full-time jobs.

DIALOGUE A:

You: John Smith, please.

Contact: This is he.

You: Oh, good. I finally got through! This is Anna Palika calling. I'm an experienced technical editor, and I've got a record 13 years of achievement in a number of high-pressure materials-publication environments. I've been talking to some close friends of mine about professional opportunities in your industry, and one of them, Nadia Muhammed, said she knows your cousin Ralph. I've been making calls to lots of employers, Mr. Smith, but you're the first supervisor I've been able to reach. This is great. I've heard wonderful things about your company.

Contact: So you're looking for a job?

You: Yes. I was wondering if I could stop by for an hour or so to discuss any openings you might have now at ABC Company?

DIALOGUE B:

You: John Smith, please.

Contact: This is he.

You: Mr. Smith, thanks for taking my call. Nadia Muhammed, a mutual friend of ours, suggested I get in touch with you. This is Anna Palika. Nadia told me that one of the big projects that you're working on at ABC Company is the new release of Shutterbug version 6.2, which Nadia tells me is due out this fall. The reason for my call is to find out what plans you have for developing the manual and support materials that will accompany that project.

Contact: Well, we haven't really made any firm plans as of yet. The project's still in development. Are you looking for a job?

You: Well, I probably wouldn't turn one down if I were lucky enough to get an offer from your company, but I'll tell you why I ask about the new Shutterbug release—I operate a freelance writing business. I was senior technical editor at Tenalco for four years.

Contact: Yeah, I heard about the downsizing campaign there.

You: My position was eliminated. That's how I got started working on my own. Actually, that was a very positive step for me. Anyway, the point of this call is to see if there was anything I could suggest in the way of a bid for freelance writing and composition services on that upcoming release. To tell you the truth, your company has always been of interest to me. I use your ByteWrite word procesing software. I'd love to drop by and take a look at the place and see how the project's progressing and talk about your plans for materials development.

Dos and Don'ts

Now, let's get one thing straight—no script can guarantee you a positive response from a networking contact. But by the same token, some scripts are a heck of a lot more likely to result in negative responses than others, and for my money, I'd take Dialogue B over Dialogue A any day of the week—regardless of which side of the telephone I had to be on! So you see the difference?

Here's a list of classic "don't let this happen to you" mistakes that the first dialogue engages in—and the second scenario neatly avoids.

DIALOGUE A	DIALOGUE B
Uses the words "I" and "me" repeatedly in opening statement.	Focuses opening statement on employer, and openly expresses concern for the value of the employer's time.
Neglects to mention name of referral until call is well underway.	Mentions referral's name before mentioning own name.
Replies with honest "yes" answer when asked, "Are you looking for a job?"	Puts "yes" answer to the question, "Are you looking for a job?" in the proper context.
Asks for interview that almost certainly carries no benefit for the contact.	Asks for interview that carries clear benefit for the contact.
Shows little or no evidence of research.	Shows evidence of solid research.

Words to the Wise

Finally, here are two vitally important points:

1. The job search is a little like being a salesperson, and that means you need to have a lot of "prospects" at any given moment to result in a single "sale" at some point down the line. Your goal is to generate leads—lots of leads—so that one of them can turn into the opportunity that's right for you. But you ought to be "pre-qualified"—there should be a rationale for the contact, as in Dialogue B. There's a point of connection behind the call.

Career Counsel
A single "no" does not a career catastrophe make. Think of the job search as a marketing campaign akin to selling a house. You don't need everyone to agree to purchase your home—you just need one person with the right offer.

2. You have the right to contact anyone within the target organization (not just the personnel office) to discuss proposals likely to benefit that organization. Don't apologize for reaching out as an entrepreneur and suggesting something that could be helpful for the company in question. Don't take rejection as a personal affront; it's only a rejection of your proposal. And, when one opportunity doesn't work out, don't forget the most powerful four-letter word in the language: NEXT!

The Least You Need to Know

➤ Don't rely on help wanted ads as your primary source of action. They make you dependent on someone else's actions, and you may end up wasting valuable time.

➤ Don't fall prey to tunnel vision.

➤ Keep it professional.

➤ Don't get too wacky.

➤ Don't intimidate decision-makers.

➤ Develop an effective phone presentation.

Chapter 18

Getting the Information You Need

In This Chapter

➤ Getting the most from your library

➤ Advice on electronic research and job searching

➤ Resources you can use

In the last chapter, you got an idea of what does and doesn't work in the targeted career search—a strategic venture into new directions. Now you need to find out more about a particular employer. How do you track down the information that will give you the lowdown on problems you can solve—and make networking, if not exactly a snap, at least a more comfortable series of discussions?

You hit the right branch of the right library for everything it's worth, for starters. There you'll be able to gather information about a specific hiring organization and you'll also be able to find supporting facts about a new job role you've learned about, the industry you've selected, and late-breaking market trends that showed up in this morning's paper.

In this chapter, you're going to learn what you should be looking for at the library— where to get just the information you need to support your industry-specific contact campaign.

What About the Internet?

You read right. The best place to begin your in-depth search for information—the search that will be supporting your quest for employment in your target industry—is a good library. I make that statement with some confidence, and in spite of everything we all hear these days about the impact of the Internet on career networking.

These days, almost all libraries are hooked onto the Internet, and they're often staffed with people who know how to help you make sense of it. That's a big plus, since anyone who's ever spent significant amounts of time online can tell you that cyberspace is one of the world's great time-vacuums. Career changers in general, and career changers who are between jobs in particular, tend to be short on time. So appealing to the experienced staffers at a good library first, before you commit time (and money) to making an Internet service provider a major information resource, is a pretty sound idea.

Let's leave the question of cyberspace aside for a moment, though. (Don't worry, you'll be coming back to this issue: You'll find a review of Internet job-searching strategies at the end of this chapter, and a listing of some of the most important online employment resources at the end of the book.) The point to bear in mind now, is that those time-tested institutions—libraries, with their stacks of books and journals—are anything but outmoded. In fact, they should be your first line of attack.

> ## Bet You Didn't Know
>
> It's doubtful that libraries will ever be put out of business by other information sources such as CD-ROMs and online services. In the future, I expect they'll co-exist, along with other devices we can't yet see. Information resources will be multi-modal, like our transportation systems—planes, trains, and automobiles. We'll use one to get to another, depending on the task.

Your Primary Resource Is (Gasp!) Human

So, head off for a visit to your local library. As I've already suggested, one of the best resources in that institution—and a prime reason the institution will not go away during our lifetimes—is the troop of trained professionals who are on duty there to assist you. Librarians are a stellar, if often overlooked, resource for career changers.

Recently, I spent some time with Esther Gil, Business Reference Librarian at the University of Denver. It has a big business school and a good array of directories. All the tools cited in this chapter are available at her institution—and, I'll warrant, at a major library worth traveling to in your area.

If you can't find out at least *some* key information about important employers within your target industry by using the following resources, the facts you're trying to track down are probably classified!

Business Directories

Many of these are available in both printed and CD-ROM formats.

Standard Industrial Classification Manual. Defines and outlines SIC system used to gather information by industry, product, and establishment.

Career Counsel
If you live in a small community or a rural area, you may have an exceptional local library nearby. Then again, you may not. If you're left with slim pickings, find your way to a library that has access to the kinds of resources that are listed in this chapter.

➤ *Million Dollar Directory.* Includes 160,000 private and public companies arranged alphabetically, geographically, and by SIC code.

➤ Business directory for your state. Where available, these are commonly compiled from the *Yellow Pages*, listing businesses by city, ZIP code, and SIC code.

➤ *Contacts Influential.* A directory, available for certain states, that lists key personnel (such as chief financial officers) in addition to business directory information.

➤ Directory of manufacturers for your state. Where available, lists all manufacturing firms in a given state. Arranged alphabetically, by location, and by SIC code.

➤ *Thomas Registry of American Manufacturers.* A 29-volume set with 150,000 private and public companies listed under product and service headings. Provides company profile and a catalogue file.

➤ *Dun's Directory of Service Companies.* Includes companies whose primary source of income is from a service, rather than a manufactured product. Companies are listed alphabetically, geographically, and by SIC.

➤ *Standard & Poor's Register of Corporations, Directors, and Executives.* Includes 55,000 private and public companies and 450,000 officers, directors, and other principals.

➤ *Directory of Corporate Affiliations.* Contains over 118,000 companies. Lists parent companies and U.S. and international subsidiaries. Indexes include company names, geographic location, SIC, and personnel. Has separate international volume.

➤ *Standard Directory of Advertisers.* Classified and Geographical editions of 17,000 advertising companies that do national or regional advertising. The Classified edition arranges companies by 51 product classifications. The Geographical edition arranges them by state and city.

➤ *International Directory of Company Histories.* Thirteen volumes. Contains histories of over 2,000 companies.

Company Information

Again, some of this material is available in both printed format and via CD-ROM.

➤ *Moody's Manuals*. Company financial information compiled from 10Ks and annual reports. Includes history, description, lists of officers, and basic financial data.

➤ *S&P Stock Reports*. Two page overview of financial information and outlook for *publicly* held companies exchanged on the New York Stock Exchange, American Stock Exchange, and NASDAQ.

Job Jargon
A public company is one that sells stock and is publicly traded.

➤ *S&P Corporation Records*. Company information compiled from 10Ks and other filings with the Securities and Exchange Commission SEC filings. Includes most current information on financial data, management changes, etc. Updated semimonthly.

➤ *Value Line Investment Survey and Expanded Edition*. Analyzes company performance. Arranged by industry group, with overview of industry's performance. Covers NYSE, ASE, and some NASDAQ companies.

Printed Indexes

Resources in this category include:

➤ *Accounting and Tax Index,* 1992–present; *Accountant's Index,* 1986–1991. Indexes books, pamphlets, government documents, and journal articles in accounting and related fields. Includes information on accounting standards and tax regulations.

➤ *Statistical Reference Index (SRI),* 1986–present. Comprehensive, descriptive index for statistics gathered by trade associations, business organizations, research centers, commercial publishers, and state governments.

Career Counsel
Enlisting the aid of a qualified reference librarian will help you make sense of the mountain of data available on a target company within your chosen industry.

➤ *American Statistics Index (ASI),* 1980–present. ASI indexes statistics gathered by the federal government, some of which may be relevant to your target industry.

➤ Index *to International Statistics,* 1983–present. Indexes statistical publications of international intergovernmental agencies. Issued in two volumes, titled Index and Abstract.

➤ *Work Related Abstracts*, 1973–present. Divided into two parts—Abstracts and Subject Index—this service extracts significant material from over 250 management, labor, government, professional, and academic periodicals. Consult the subject heading list (separate volume) for appropriate indexing terms and then go to the index at the back of the main volume for the appropriate abstract and citation.

Business Information Handbooks

Resources in this category include:

➤ *Handbook of Business Information: A Guide for Librarians, Students, and Researchers,* by Diane Wheeler Strauss. Clear and concise discussion of business sources, including online services.

➤ *Business Information: How to Find It, How To Use It,* by Michael R. Lavin. Discussion of sources, with practical advice.

➤ *Using Government Information Sources: Print and Electronic, Second Edition,* by Jean L. Sears. Searching by subjects and agencies, finding statistics, using special techniques.

Directories for Market Analysis/Demographics

➤ *Statistical Abstract of the United States.* U.S. Bureau of the Census annual publication. Answers many statistical questions on industrial, social, political, and economic topics. Gives sources of further information and overview for each section.

➤ *American Statistics Index* (ASI) and *Statistical Reference Index (SRI).* Comprehensive, descriptive indexes that are similar in format but differ in the source of their data. ASI indexes statistics gathered by the federal government, while SRI data comes from trade associations, business organizations, research centers, commercial publishers, and state governments.

➤ *Demographics USA.* Published as part of Sales and Marketing Management. Contains statistics on population, effective buying power, retail sales by product, and five-year sales projections.

➤ *Simmons Study of Media and Markets.* Surveys 23,555 adults to measure "ownership, purchase of, and use of hundreds of specific products and services, media exposure (TV program viewing, radio listening, magazine and newspaper reading) and the demographic characteristics of individuals and households." Multi-volume set.

➤ *Editor and Publisher Market Guide* (annual). Marketing information for every city where a daily newspaper is published. Describes population and commerce.

➤ *Direct Marketing Market Place.* Networking source of direct marketing industry. Includes over 9,700 different organizations.

➤ *Leo Burnett Worldwide Advertising and Media Fact Book.* Contains basic media information, country-by-country, throughout the world.

➤ *Sourcebook of ZIP Code Demographics.* Profiles each ZIP code area for age, demographics, housing, and income.

➤ *U.S. Industrial Outlook.* Annual publication by the U.S. Department of Commerce. In-depth review and projections for more than 350 industries, with narratives and statistical tables.

➤ *Standard & Poor's Industry Surveys.* Prime source of information on major industries. Includes composite company information.

➤ *Service Industries USA.* Industry analyses, statistics, and leading organizations. A comprehensive guide to economic activity in 150 service industries, both profit and nonprofit. Includes 4,000 leading organizations and covers data for 620 major metropolitan areas.

➤ *County Business Patterns.* Statistics on employment and wages for each of the SIC categories compiled by the federal government, by state and county. More useful at the state level, as data is obscured at the county level in many cases to protect the privacy of major employers, due to government regulations.

➤ *Encyclopedia of Associations.* Most comprehensive source of information available on trade associations and similar groups. Published by Gale Research, Inc.

Career Development and Job Search Directories

Resources in this category include:

➤ *Professional Careers Sourcebook: An Information Guide for Career Planning.* Profiles of more than 110 professions including job descriptions, requirements, and so on.

➤ *Encyclopedia of Careers and Vocational Guidance.* Four-volume set on industries and professional and technical careers.

➤ *Occupational Outlook Handbook.* Annual publication of U.S. Department of Labor, Bureau of Labor Statistics. Basic career information primarily addressed to guidance counselors and high school students. More useful when consulted as a review of job requirements and worthwhile courses of study than as a summary of the employment outlook in any particular field.

➤ *Specialty Occupational Outlook: Professions.* Published by Gale Research, Inc.; provides in-depth information on 150 additional careers, beyond *Occupational Outlook Handbook* data.

➤ *Index of Majors and Graduate Degrees*. Annual publication by The College Board, outlining 580 majors at 2,900 colleges with degree programs at all levels: certificate, associate, bachelor's, master's, doctoral, professional.

Print Guides to Electronic Databases

These are helpful resources for those planning to track down business information online.

➤ *The Internet Business*, by Sandra Eddy, et. al. SYBEX, 1996.

➤ *Internet Business 500*, by Ryan Bernard. Ventana, 1995.

➤ *Prentice Hall Directory of Online Business Information*, by Christopher Engholm and Scott Grimes. 1997.

Online Electronic Databases

These are databases you access through a computer that links to another computer.

➤ FirstSearch. This is a series of 14 online databases available through various libraries. The databases include: ABI/INFORM (citations to over 1,000 business periodicals, with full-text to some entries; 150-word abstracts can be searched by subject, classification codes, geographical area); GPO Monthly Catalog (an index to U.S. government publications from July 1976 to present); Business Dateline (citations on regional business articles); Business Industry (facts, figures, and key events).

➤ Information Access Companies (IAC). Another broad compendium of online databases. Includes Business and Company Profiles (indexes business publications and provides directory information for approximately 150,000 private companies; full-text/full-image provided for some entries); Business Index (indexes business publications, including articles from the *Wall Street Journal* and *New York Times*; offers the option of fee-based document delivery by fax or printer).

➤ Colorado Alliance of Research Libraries (CARL). Nationwide online system that includes catalogs of member libraries, online indexes to periodicals, and access to remote systems.

➤ NEXIS, the business component of LEXIS/NEXIS, offers full-text documents from newspapers, journals, trade publications, wire services, newsletters, and so on. (LEXIS is for legal research.)

CD-ROM Databases

These are databases you access through a computer that uses a CD-ROM player. Most are updated on a regular basis.

➤ Predicasts F & S Index—U.S. and International. Covers U.S. and international business trade journals. Some citations include full text of articles.

➤ National Trade Data Bank. A CD-ROM database issued monthly by the U.S. Department of Commerce. Contains over 100,000 documents including export/import statistics, market research reports, country analysis, CIA World Factbook, trade barrier data, foreign exchange rates, and so on.

➤ ABI/INFORM. Provides indexing and abstracting to 800 business journals, featuring 150 word abstracts. Can be searched by subject, classification codes, and geographic area.

Data Overload? Naaah...

After you've spent a day or two in the library with resources like the ones listed above, you'll be in a much better position to talk intelligently with professional contacts about the current trends and problems faced by particular employers in your target industry. And bear in mind—by doing *any* research about a target company, you're setting yourself apart from the vast majority of job-seekers, who don't bother to learn much more than the name of the CEO and the logo.

Your aim, of course, is not to snow your contacts with random facts and figures, but to be able to lead into conversations with remarks like this:

"I've noticed that your company is trying to crack the Eastern European market. I've got some experience in export work, myself, but I'm curious: What's the biggest hurdle your organization faces in taking on something like that?"

or:

"I understand that more restaurants are started up than any other type of business. But half of them fail or change ownership within the first five years. My research tells me that you're doing some innovative work on site selection here at Bagel Baby."

You say you're hungry for even more information about opportunities in your target industry—information you can track down yourself by surfing the Net? You're not alone! Assuming that you've put in your time in the stacks, and perhaps gotten a few pointers from an expert on how to connect to cyberspace without inheriting phone and access bills that leave you feeling faint, you may now want to explore that leading-edge resource: the Internet.

> ## Bet You Didn't Know
>
> In September, 1993, Margaret Riley was a circulation librarian at Worcester Polytechnic Institute in the outer reaches of Massachusetts. She spent her days monitoring the photocopiers and answering routine queries from patrons. But one day the head librarian made an announcement that would change Margaret's life. She asked if anyone on the staff would be willing to spend some time with a growing network of hyperlinked computers—the Internet.
>
> Riley volunteered and the rest is history. By the following year, she had broken into print, producing a publication for students who were looking for jobs: *Employment Opportunities and Job Resources on the Internet.* Today, Riley works full-time operating one of the best-known job search Web sites on the Internet: **http://www.dbm.com/jobguide**.
>
> That's how fast careers can change in the age of technology.

Does Anyone Get Hired via the Internet?

I don't know if anyone has a fix on how much hiring is going on via the Internet these days. But it's clear that a lot of companies are at least screening job seekers that way. And there are a host of opportunists out there, offering to hook candidates up with the right kinds of employers. I found 43 career-related Web sites in a recent library listing; everything from Employment in Australia to Careers in Management Consulting. (See Appendix A for a listing of some of the most important Internet employment resources.)

Who Are You, Anyway?

With all the site-probing and resume-posting out there in cyberspace these days, some important questions remain. What kinds of career-changers can benefit from a process as anonymous as the Internet—a system that makes initial connections between employers and employees pretty much sight unseen?

Recently, I received an e-mail from the media relations office of Real Madrid, a world-class soccer team I hope to see this fall when my wife and I are in Spain. The e-mail included an update on the schedule. I've also been able to track down some fascinating information about Saskatchewan, where I'll be traveling soon. All of a sudden, I'm globally connected! That's pretty intoxicating.

Work Alert!
The Internet may represent a serious productivity vacuum for you. As anyone who recently has gone cybersurfing knows, there's a seductive quality about the Internet. It's an exciting resource for all kinds of information—maybe too much information.

Handle with Care!

Isn't it fun to surf the Net? And isn't it easy to waste a lot of time that way? If you're seriously interested in finding new employment, the Internet is a resource to consider using—with great care, for certain predetermined periods of time.

Why do I add all of these disclaimers? Well for one thing, the Net is a lot like the help wanted ads. It puts you in a passive mode. That's why it should be used like the want ads—as a secondary strategy, a backup to something else that puts you in an active role. Checking in with the want ads every now and then is one thing. Investing all your hopes in them is quite another. Another problem, of course, is the "hypnotic factor." You click to one cool site, which links to another cool site, which links to another...then you look up from your screen and realize that four and a half hours have passed!

Pluses and Minuses

The upside of job-seeking via the Internet is that it's so precise. Today's search engines are a phenomenal weapon in the battle with information overload. Learn a few principles of database searching, and you can scan scads of material in milliseconds.

The downside of the Internet is that its supreme isolation. It's an easy escape from the harrowing challenge of picking up the phone and actually calling somebody. Or writing a letter that promises a follow-up call at a certain date and time. Or (gasp!) scheduling an interview with a stranger. The Internet is a seductive substitute for interactions and relationships with real people.

It's ersatz interaction.

So Is the Internet Bad?

No, the Internet isn't evil. It's only a huge potential waste of time if you get addicted to it, which is surprisingly easy to do.

So, how *should* you use the Internet in looking for employment? Here are some pointers from Perry Ford, a colleague of mine, who has run seminars on job searches over the Internet for some time.

Here are a few of his Ford's Dos and Don'ts on this topic.

DO Start Big

Begin with a megasite like Monster or Career Mosaic (your search engine will point you toward these sites) and learn to use their keyword search operations. Use the program to refine your terminology regarding your skills and the kinds of jobs you're looking for.

If you've been calling yourself a "programmer," perhaps the term employers in your target industry use is "systems analyst." If one of your skills is "training," they may say "performance improvement" instead. Learn the lingo. The more you know about the keywords a potential employer is using to pull (and exclude) posted online resumes, the more effective your own targeted resume will be.

DO Focus on Highly Relevant Newsgroups

"Once you can talk the talk, the place you want to be is the newsgroups," notes Ford. "They're essentially bulletin boards, and you can access them through a site such as Career Mosaic."

Ford compares the highly focused newsgroups to Internet chat rooms in that they're interactive. (They don't, however, take place in real time.) "But these newsgroups are all business," he notes. "They're the places where smaller employers are likely to post jobs, and if you don't have your terminology down to the point where it sounds like you know their industry, you'll be out in the cold. Those newsgroups can be unforgiving."

DO Use the Internet for Specific Company Research

"When you contact an employer," says Ford, "if you've seen their Web site and got good information from it, say so. People view their sites with a lot of pride." He's seen a number of people prepare effectively for interviews by tapping into Internet sites. One of his clients applied for a job as a senior accountant with Toys R Us. "By the time she went in for the interview, she knew more about the company than their interviewer," Ford recalls. "She understood their corporate mission statement, their organizational structure, and the way they'd structured their jobs. Needless to say, she was hired."

DON'T Waste Time with Virtual Job Fairs

"Those programs," Ford advises, "give the impression you can interact with somebody representing an employer in real time, but you can't. An online job fair is no different from filing an application online."

DON'T Think the Internet Is the Only Place for a Job Search

I may be pounding this point into the ground, but it deserves to be well and truly pounded: *Getting a job or a new career requires more than sitting in front of a computer screen.* Don't be misled on this point by today's cyber-entrepreneurs.

The other day, I came across this heading for jobs in higher education on one of the megasites: "The Ivy League wants you. Get a job in academe this week." The implication appears to be that anyone with an Internet account can move from pumping gas at the local service station to teaching Shakespeare 101 in front of the freshman class at Brown. If you believe that, I've got a bridge in Brooklyn you may be interested in acquiring.

There's one exception to all of this advice, and it's a big one: If you are a purebred professional in a technical field, and if you can identify the companies that are hungering for your brand of technology, then you may want to make the Internet your primary medium. Many high-tech companies like to meet prospective employees first over the Internet.

However, personal networking still can be vital in targeting a prospective high-tech employer. Try to intervew someone in the organization to find out how the company frames its hiring needs.

Online or in person, the same rule applies: If you want to make effective contact with an employer, first do your homework.

The Least You Need to Know

➤ The biggest branch of a major metropolitan library system is an excellent place to track down information about your target companies.

➤ A qualified reference librarian can point you toward a wealth of resources that will supply key information about the companies you will be contacting.

➤ Not all libraries are equal, and neither are all librarians.

➤ Use the Internet intelligently—and remember that getting a job requires doing more than sitting in front of a computer screen.

Chapter 19

Letting the World Know on Paper

In This Chapter

➤ How to assemble your resume

➤ What it should look like

➤ When to send it (and when not to)

In Chapter 17, you got an idea of what you should and shouldn't do in your person-to-person networking campaign. In this chapter, you learn how to craft your "on-paper" representation of yourself—your resume—so that it sends the right message to people in your target industry.

Culture Connections

An e-mail message came up on my monitor recently. A large delegation of Japanese business professionals was coming to town for a big economic conference. Would anyone volunteer to take some of the visitors to a Colorado Rockies game? Free box seats provided.

Gee, a Rockies game? At no cost? When I could be cleaning out my sock drawer? The sacrifices we make for the cause of world peace and brotherhood! It took me all of 10 seconds to zap back my message and sign up.

Career Counsel
Resumes are a well-established convention. Nothing more and nothing less. While it's certainly important to know how to construct a good resume, there are many occasions when the resume is best kept under wraps. Flashing a resume may convey a message that you don't want to send ("Hire me! I'm desperate!), and may actually interfere with effective communication.

Later, the person who was coordinating the event sent a follow-up message: "Be sure to bring plenty of business cards." But that wasn't all. She went on to outline the protocol of exchanging business cards with the Japanese.

"Hold the card in both hands and take time to read it. Act impressed. Sometimes a Japanese contact will speak the person's title out loud. If you're have a meeting with the individual, or are even just having lunch with him, place the card on the table in front of you. Keep it in view. Above all, don't stick it in your pocket, the way we Americans do."

An experience like that is a good reminder of how business cultures differ around the globe. We can recognize how a hand gesture that represents a greeting in one society may be seen as obscene in the next. Or how a business card can convey a much clearer sense of status in one country than another.

Use It, Don't Abuse It

There's an art to using a resume as part of an effective career-change campaign, an art that's similar to finding out the protocol a foreign visitor is used to. You'll behave differently with a visiting Saudi Arabian business person than you will with a visiting Japanese business person; you should behave differently when interacting with the representatives of High-Tech Solutions than you would when interacting with the representatives of Staid Old Banking Corporation. Each should receive a resume from you only when the time is right; the resume should highlight particular skills, interests, and aptitudes of interest to that employer.

Work Alert!
Handing a resume to a brand new contact is likely to stereotype you as a desperate job-seeker and make his or her eyes glaze over.

Like any art, this one requires practice and continual refinement. How do you do it?

Surprise: You're the Expert!

Here's an overview of how to use a resume in a career campaign, followed by a few samples. Remember that writing a resume is more of an art than a science, and that any advice you receive from me or any other resume-doctor may be countered by the next "expert" down the street. Your own knowledge of the company, its culture, and its requirements should probably play as large a role in the development of your resume as any set of rules you find in a book like this.

I know of one woman who got a job with an advertising firm by scrawling her "resume" on a clean hamburger wrapper—and warning that if she didn't get the offer, she might become the burger-flipping queen of the upper Midwest! That was a good ploy for an advertising agency, but probably not the best way to sidle up to a law firm.

All the same, you should take a moment now to review a few generally reliable resume guidelines. Some of what follows is inspired by the sage advice of the recruiters at Robert Half. When it comes to writing resumes and cover letters, I always take the counsel of headhunters very seriously—those are the folks who are constantly evaluating them. At the same time, I never assume that the advice they give stays fresh for very long.

Career Counsel
If you can, get feedback on your resume from a recruiter or human resources professional within your target industry.

Work Alert!
Resume etiquette can change radically from company to company. Get a sense of the corporate culture before you develop a resume for a particular opportunity.

Length

A standard resume runs one page. But if you need an extra page to describe important aspects of your career, use it. Because stapling pages looks a little tacky, it's a good idea to run a two-page resume back to back. Type *(over)* on the bottom of the first page.

Layout

Keep the layout of your resume simple and uncluttered. Because resumes are typically read very quickly—30 seconds or less is the norm—it's a good idea to leave lots of white space between paragraphs and to set your word processor with wide margins.

Opening Paragraph

A resume is a lot like a news story. Nothing is more important than the lead. It tells the reader why the rest of the resume should be read. But how to begin is the puzzling question. For the experienced person in mid-career, it's generally a good idea to lead with a Summary statement rather than an Objective. That makes you sound a bit more in control of your professional destiny. Use an Objective if you're new to the marketplace or your targeted field.

Whichever opening you opt for, be sure to define yourself in the market. Give yourself an identity. Create a strong brand image. Don't leave others guessing what it is you hope to do with your college degree in Latin American studies and three years experience in the Peace Corps coaching an African soccer team.

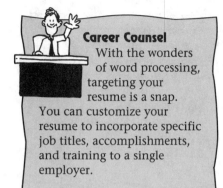

Career Counsel
With the wonders of word processing, targeting your resume is a snap. You can customize your resume to incorporate specific job titles, accomplishments, and training to a single employer.

For example: "Summary: International sports marketing specialist" or maybe "Summary: Multilingual soccer coach." The important thing is to specify the way you want folks to see you. If you're new to the field of your dreams, you may decide to say "Objective: College soccer coaching position."

Remember that it's perfectly acceptable—indeed, strongly advised by many career authorities—to develop a targeted resume for each opportunity that comes your way. Some aggressive career counselors even suggest that you make whatever excuses necessary to delay submitting a resume until you've had the chance to tailor your resume around a formal written job description. That's certainly a better strategy than passing out a "plain vanilla" resume to every one of your contacts as the starting point of the relationship!

Professional Experience

Work Alert!
A recruiter friend told me recently that her major client throws out any resume that has a time gap of longer than two years between jobs, education, or other work-related activity.

"Professional Experience" is a better heading than "Work History"...unless it sounds too high-falutin' and inflated for the kind of work you've done. Begin with your most recent job, and describe each position briefly—three or four lines, max. Place dates along the right margin, by years, not months. Listing months weighs down the chronology, and makes employers think things like "Where the hell were you in September?"

Which brings us to a key question: What about gaps in your career? Try to account for every time period of a year or so— whether you were taking courses or "consulting," which can be a pretty good euphemism for a spate of unemployment.

Education

Here, I'd also include certifications and licensure that support your goals. This is a good place to enumerate core competencies. If you have an unusual degree, list your areas of concentration—so many courses in accounting, for instance.

Here's another effective technique following my earlier discussion of careers and core competencies. "My degree in _____ enables me to _____." (I once worked with an educational psychologist who had a terrific knack for classifying clients according to their learning styles. She'd draw up wonderfully clear charts in all sorts of vivid colors. And where'd she learn to do that? Her undergraduate degree was in geology. She'd developed her skills in classifying and arranging ideas from sorting out strata of rocks! This is another example of a transferable skill. A resume is a good place to point them out.)

Accomplishments

Be sure to include at some point—either in your job history or as a separate section—some indication of how you've done throughout the course of your career. Focus on the positives. Did you recruit 70 people, 68 of whom were subsequently fired? Better find something else to spotlight.

Here's an example of an eye-catching accomplishment: "Saved company $1.2 million by resolving bad debts from accounts payable department."

Bet You Didn't Know

The accomplishments on your resume needn't take the form of hard currency. One of my best jobs was directing a University Without Walls program on the south side of Chicago. I worked hard to help keep the academic quality of the program strong: 94 percent of the UWW students who came through that program were admitted to their graduate school of first choice. I'm proud of that accomplishment, and, if I were developing a resume for an adult education program, I might choose to share it on paper.

There's nothing wrong with trotting out your good deeds as long as they're objectively quantifiable. It's only when you start listing traits that sound like a Boy Scout litany—"cheerful, thrifty, brave, clean, and reverent"—that you can get into trouble. Leave the testimonials to your references.

Closing Paragraph

People remember the first and last items in a series much more than anything that comes in between. (Think of how you respond to the first or last preview of coming attractions at the movies.) So close with some sort of "grabber." Maybe Personal Interests, or New Learning. Include some sort of information that can't be said about hordes of other people. One of the worst ways to close is: "References Available on Request." Everybody can say that—we can all persuade an uncle to vouch for us.

Career Counsel

If you close with Personal Interests, include only those interests that demonstrate skills and traits that could affect job performance.

And Whatever You Do...

Above all, never include in a resume any information that is untrue. Every now and then, you'll read in the newspaper about some public official who claimed to hold a degree that he or she didn't actually complete. Careers are ruined that way.

I can think of a noted scholar who was nominated for an academic award in the late stages of his career. The man had written a book that was one of best-known works in his field. But when someone from the public relations office of his college called another school to clarify the date when the scholar had received his graduate degree, the place had no record of him as a student. Ultimately, in fact, it came to light that he had no academic credentials at all.

Did that fact reduce the quality of the writing and teaching he'd done for years? Of course not. But having been untruthful put a cracked and crumbling capstone on his career. So, be careful about what you put in your resume. And, whatever you do, be honest.

So How Do You Use It?

What's the use of a resume? Well, as we've seen, in a society that may require one for entrance to kindergarten before too long, it's a good idea to be able to formulate a resume that gets the reader nodding his or her head with interest. Here are some examples that do just that, following different formats:

Mel Smith
123 Main Street
Newtown, MA 01949
508/555-1212

SUMMARY OF QUALIFICATIONS:	Project Manager with extensive experience in high-performance applications, networks, and operating systems development.
CAPABILITIES:	**Technical Skills:** Have taken classes in C Programming, Object-Oriented C++, and UNIX; straight A grades. Quickly learn new operating systems, networks, applications, tools, languages, and hardware.
	Leadership Skills: Experienced in full range of software development leadership functions including defining project contractor, developing specifications, designing, constructing, testing, and integration. Have a history of high productivity, high-quality, on-time projects. Effective at building strong bonds with team members, project management, users, and customers. Skilled at handling difficult people situations. Good at fostering stimulating learning environment. Proactive in detecting and resolving problems.

EMPLOYMENT:	Senior Engineer/Data Manager Howard Aerospace Eureka, California 1978–1995
	Programmer/Analyst U.S. Air Force Eureka, California 1967–1977
	Industrial Engineer/Aircraft Enhancement Specialist The Airtech Company Omaha, Nebraska 1966
EDUCATION:	B.A. Mathematics, Economics and Business Dearborn University Dearborn, Illinois 1965

Mel Smith uses a format that I often recommend, with two paragraphs of skills following a summary of qualifications. As a project manager, he's separated his technical from his managerial skills. The account of his employment is brief and to the point. In addition to the previous resume, he provided a summary of kudos from past employers as the "second page" of the resume. I recommended that he use the plaudits sparingly—probably only in the context of an interview with a prospective employer.

This kind of resume is often called a functional/chronological format, because the chronology of work history follows the description of functions the individual wants to perform. Highlighting the hybrid skills of leadership and technical competence is very important in Mel's case, because that's the special kind of project management niche he hopes to find.

Lou Thomas
4000 Lake Trail
Minnetonka, 55343
612/555-1212

Professional Summary

Broadly based career in program management, product development, electronics manufacturing, and corporate restructuring. Management of product development in printers, copiers, and optical recording. Executive management in high technology manufacturing, including introduction of SNF into volume manufacturing at Bigtech.

continues

continued

Selected Work History and Accomplishments

Techstore Corporation

Director of Manufacturing for Direct Access Storage Devices (DASD), 1993–1996

➤ Responsible for group of 85 employees and $20 million budget to both produce the Berrison project in Arizona and to transfer all production to Jamaica by year's end.

➤ Met 1996 Berrison delivery, cost, and asset management goals in Arizona, producing about $230 million in revenue.

➤ Transferred Berrison production to Jamaica, consolidated two organizations into one that totaled 170 people, and downsized by 30 percent without disrupting critical revenue stream.

➤ Reduced test cycle time by 16 percent.

American Business Technology

Mechanical Engineer, 1989–1993

➤ Developed a paper handling system for a drum-type ink jet printer that was capable of simultaneous loading and unloading of paper.

➤ Spearheaded the resolution of mirror-lens reproduction problems, allowing introduction of Magna Doc copier.

➤ Developed a cleaning system for new reproduction process capable of performing without maintenance for 175,000 copies.

➤ Resolved wear and stress problems on high-speed mechanisms through a variety of analytical and experimental techniques.

Education

Master of Science in Mechanical Engineering, Minnesota Institute of Technology

Bachelor of Science in Mechanical Engineering, Minnesota Institute of Technology

Lou Thomas's resume takes a more straightforward, chronological approach. This is a man who has had a successful career in high-tech manufacturing, rising to a senior level. This kind of resume works well—if there is a logical next rung waiting on the ladder.

If there isn't—or if, perhaps because of age, you've topped out in your career—then the chronological resume may stand in your way. You may need to rethink a way to use your background in some other role. When you do, you'll probably need to put together a resume of the Mel Smith variety, showing how you'd like to perform.

Maria Diaz
123 Bonita Way
Silver City, NM 88061
505/555-7676

OBJECTIVE:	Professional position emphasizing mathematics, leading to statistical analysis.
EDUCATION:	B.A. Magna Cum Laude Mathematics/Computer Science, University of New Mexico, Albuquerque, New Mexico, June, 1995. Minor: Women's Studies. Overall gradepoint average: 3.8 (4.0 scale).
RELATIONAL SKILLS:	Extensive experience in leadership roles involving organizational skills, conflict resolution, interpersonal relations, and problem-solving. High comfort level speaking to groups and composing written documentation. Strong analytical and critical-thinking skills.
WORK EXPERIENCE:	BankEast Federal Savings Bank, January, 1987–May, 1994; Teller/Customer Service Representative.
	First Episcopal Church of Santa Fe, April 1983–October 1986; full bookkeeper.
	Navajo Construction and Supply, Inc., July 1980–April 1983; full bookkeeper.
OTHER EXPERIENCE:	Committee for the Reevaluation of Text Materials, Albuquerque Board of Education,1990–present.
	Financial Secretary, First Episcopal Church of Santa Fe (part-time volunteer position), two years.
HONORS:	Blue Board Honor Society, University of New Mexico.
	Who's Who Among Students in American Colleges, 1994.

"All knowledge is of itself some value. There is nothing so minute or inconsiderable that I would not rather know it than not."

—Samuel Johnson

The third resume, by Maria Diaz, starts with an objective, unlike the other two. That makes sense in Maria's case, since she's trying to establish herself in a field where she has little relevant work experience. Notice, too, that she places her education and a paragraph on "people skills" above her work history, and trots out all her academic honors near the bottom. Her work history is somewhat buried in the middle of the resume, which is just as well. She doesn't disguise the series of run-of-the-mill jobs she held as a working mother while her kids were in school. But now that she's completed her own college degree and is starting a career of her own, it's time to lead with her strongest suit—which is her academic training.

Notice that Maria closes with an interesting quote. That's a good example of ending the resume with something that's a conversation starter, rather than a yawner like "References Available on Request." The technique also suggests that one has enough chutzpah to display some convictions and stand out from the crowd.

And the $64,000 Question Is...

What's the bottom line in all of this? Do resumes land jobs? My answer is twofold. You probably can't land the job you want without a good resume. At the same time, you can't expect the resume to do the whole job for you.

Here are some dos and don'ts to bear in mind in the resume game.

DO Develop a "Basic Resume" That Only You See

This way, you force yourself to describe yourself within the confines of one page. In addition to serving as a template for later, customized resumes, this document helps you focus on a 30-second to 2-minute verbal summary, and avoid the considerable hazards of autobiographical overkill.

DO Use Your Resume as a Visual Aid

Don't think of it as an application. Think of it as a prop to appeal to during your interview. You'll find more on interviewing techniques in the next chapter, but for now think of deploying a resume as a graphic artist might unwrap a portfolio of logos she'd designed. It's a visual aid in the interview process.

DO Forward Targeted Resumes to Networking Allies

Drop off a resume in the course of a conversation with anyone in your network who is likely to be motivated to point you toward a job or contractual assignment. Target the resume, to the best of your ability, to the industry and organization that will be reviewing it. Bear in mind, though, that a resume connotes "job-seeker."

DON'T Distribute Resumes Randomly

Don't pass resumes out at a professional meeting, for example, or mail them indiscriminately to your relatives and friends. There are few things in this world that strike such terror in the hearts of close associates as the knowledge that someone they know is out of a job. (More on this point in the next chapter.)

DON'T Mail Resumes

At least, not if you can possibly help it. "Send me a resume"—that's tantamount to dismissal. Try every stratagem you can to set up—even a brief interview in the person's office instead. Then leave the resume as a calling card.

If none of this works, you might consider sending a very brief letter that dramatically summarizes your credentials—perhaps a skills summary that looks something like this:

[Date]

[Address]

Dear Mr. Smith:

Thanks for taking the time to talk with me on Thursday afternoon about opportunities at WidgetMaster.

As you requested, I'm sending along a summary of my qualifications for the position of Widget Inspector.

Your Needs	**What I Offer**
Three years of experience on WidgetPro software	Four years of experience on WidgetPro software
Four years of experience in engineering environment	Five years of experience in engineering environment

continues

---

continued

| Certification in Widget Analysis | Recently completed course in Widget Analysis at Middleton State College |

This opportunity is a very exciting one and I look forward to discussing it with you in detail.

Sincerely,

Jane Smith

617/555-1212

P.S.: I'll plan to call you at 8:00 a.m. on July 13 to discuss this opening, and the possibility of performing contract work at WidgetCo further.

DON'T Send Electronic Gobbledygook

In other words, don't get too fancy if you're filing a resume on the Internet. Use a straight ASCII format, and a copy/paste editing process rather than an attachment (which may require special software to be read).

DON'T Mistake a Resume for a Career Search

> **Career Counsel**
> If you send a resume to a large-scale, technical employer that does a ton of recruiting and screening over the Internet, be sure to do enough homework to identify the keywords they're likely to program into their optical screening devices.

Don't ever base a career-change campaign solely on your resume, unless you know, and have solid proof, that you're in serious demand within your target industry. In other words, if the mere mention of your skills can't carry the day in your career, don't expect that your resume will. For the vast majority of job-seekers, a good deal of preliminary and follow-up work will be necessary.

The occasional exception to this rule is advertising, marketing, and public relations. I've seen professionals in those fields hired on the basis of a compelling resume as a demonstration of their marketing skills. For the rest of us, a resume is basically a shrewdly designed visual aid to be used during the course of an interview, and a calling card to leave behind us.

The Least You Need to Know

➤ Remember that you may turn off some contacts by giving them a resume early on in your relationship.

➤ Get feedback from people whose experience you respect, but remember that your own research and instincts must guide the development of your resume.

➤ Pick the right resume format for your situation.

➤ Don't send resumes to just anyone. Make targeted, quality mailings.

➤ Don't rely on your resume alone. It's your personal ad: You are the product.

Chapter 20

Letting the World Know in Person

In This Chapter

➤ Strategizing the interview

➤ Targeting your research (even more)

➤ Building bridges

In the last chapter, you found out how to develop a resume that makes sense for your job search campaign, and how you should (and shouldn't) use that document on the networking front. In this chapter, you find out how to conduct, not just any interview, but an informed interview, with decision-makers in your target industry.

This Is for Real!

It's not that you were completely nonchalant about the contacts you developed during your "trial search," but the fact is, you hadn't made a commitment to your target industry at that point. Now that you have a definite career changing goal, and an interview in which you "crash and burn" in front of a key decision-maker will set you back a step or two.

Accordingly, you will want to make the very best impression you can during your contacts with professionals in your chosen field.

How do you pull it off? By keeping your mindset positive and enthusiastic—and by ruthlessly targeting your efforts. By targeting, I mean making a commitment never to walk in the door to an interview without having developed an exhaustive portfolio of information about the target firm!

Two Models

Remember that there are, broadly speaking, two kinds of organizations at which you may be interviewing. There's the classic pyramid corporation with the elaborate, many-tiered hierarchy. For this employer, the basic idea will be to look up the mission statement, see where you resonate with it, and let your contacts know that you've done your research.

There's also the diamond organization, where everything's in motion, and the job you're "applying" for may still be an idea in someone's mind. In this kind of company, your best bet is to ask lots of questions, propose projects, and basically act like a partner, rather than a supplicant.

You'll want to be supportive and creative when dealing with contacts at pyramid-shaped organizations, as well, but your discussions with people at diamond-shaped organizations are likely to sound like colleague-to-colleague talks a lot sooner than the other interviews will.

During the interview, you must follow through on an unshakable commitment to be relentlessly positive.

Interviewing is not an adversarial process. Think of it as a collaborative effort—still sales-oriented and persuasive, but not a contest. Be prepared to fill, tactfully, any knowledge or procedural gaps that may arise during your discussions.

Answer honestly but intelligently. Emphasize the positive. Show your understanding and respect for the goals and strategies of people you've worked with in the past, and tie all that together with what you can do for this company now.

The Stakes Are High!

When a professional salesperson tries to win over a big account, an account that could mean tens of thousands of dollars in commission revenue, he or she will usually conduct an all-out research campaign on the company in question, doing whatever it takes to find out that company's mission, current position in the marketplace, patterns of decision-making, and current strategic approach. I know one salesperson who did so much research on a target company that his contact asked him, at the end of the first sales call, "Are you sure you haven't worked here before?"

Part of being an independent professional is committing to doing the kind of research that shakes people out of their rut and makes them ask you, "Have you ever worked here before?" That's an informed interview—the kind that wins contacts and alliances. By taking advantage of the library resources and Internet job-searching techniques listed in Chapter 18, you should also strongly consider the following steps:

For Pyramid-Shaped Organizations:

➤ Contact the prospective employer directly to obtain a copy of any relevant employment materials (such as job description, project outlines, or contract worker guidelines). The people at the reception desk will usually be able to point you toward someone who can supply this kind of information.

➤ Contact the employer's corporate information office (or equivalent) for corporate summaries, mission statements, or press releases.

➤ Contact the employer's marketing department (or equivalent) for brochures, catalogs, newsletters, or other printed materials that will let you know who this company is trying to reach out to.

For Diamond-Shaped Organizations:

➤ Conduct appropriate information interviewing with people who know the target company or industry well enough to give you some insights on where it's headed. (You may need to do a fair amount of this to compensate for the lack of formal, printed material at diamond-shaped organizations.)

That's a Lot of Work!

Yep. Preparing for a targeted, informed interview takes some preparation. But it carries one serious advantage over *not* developing such a collection of data: It works.

There's little or nothing you can do that will impress a prospective employer more than being able to speak intelligently about the overall goals of the organization, and about the obstacles that key players face as they try to attain those goals.

Remember, your aim is to fulfill the role of an independent professional—and that means taking on the sales (promotion) function with full commitment. Any good salesperson will tell you that up-front research pays off handsomely on key accounts. And if this prospective employer isn't a key account, nobody is! After all, this organization represents not tens of thousands of dollars in potential income, but *hundreds* of thousands of dollars in salary over the years!

So What Do I Do?

One good principle to remember before we talk about specific interview strategies: When in doubt, focus on your plan! Talk about what you'd do to make the widgets ship faster or keep the customers happier or reduce costs in the accounting department.

➤ When you're not sure whether or not the prospective employer is considering you for a full-time job or short-term contract work, *focus on your plan.* Make statements and ask questions that demonstrate your orientation toward tangible solutions for that particular employer.

➤ When you're asked a question that really throws you, give it your best shot, then *relate the topic to your plan.*

➤ When you're asked about your past experience, detail what you've done and then *connect your past accomplishments to your current plan for this employer.*

Here's an example: "Yes, as you see, I was a high school guidance counselor. And I'll tell you how I think that experience can help me as a sales manager. I've read a lot and spoken with a number of people in this field. What they all tell me is that you want a supportive, nurturing person in this role. As I understand it, you don't necessarily want another competitive sales type. I know how to help people reach their goals, and I'm results-oriented. You'll notice that a high percentage of students at my school went on to college. I believe the principal will tell you I had a lot to do with that."

Do the Research!

I heard a story about a top executive who was being interviewed for the job of president of a Fortune 1000 firm. As part of his interview, he prepared a detailed business plan outlining goals and battle plans for a number of years into the future. Later, when he was told that the job offer had gone to someone else, he made a point of mailing his business plan to the person who'd interviewed him—and expressing his hope that the work he'd done could benefit the person who took on the president's job. Not long afterward, the "failed" applicant received a call from his contact informing him that the person they'd offered the job to had declined. Based on the work our hero had put into his formal written plan, they'd now decided to offer him the job!

You could do worse than to follow that example. Do the research. Find out about the challenges the target organization is facing. Develop a thorough, written plan that will help address the problem. Submit it as one professional to another during the interview.

How to Shine When the Spotlight Is on You

There are a couple of basic techniques that are almost always helpful in professional interviewing settings. Let's take a look at them now.

First, it's important to prepare a brief summary of your background—two minutes long is a good rule of thumb. Summarize your background in the light of the work you're there to discuss. Yes, this means you'll need to provide different "bios" for different employers.

Remember the Deion Sanders principle? (He's the athlete who won fame and glory in both major league baseball and the NFL.) If you're interviewing for a position as a center fielder, don't arrive wearing your football helmet. And if you want to be a defensive back and punt returner, leave your baseball bat at home. Always be selective in presenting your background. Concentrate on the skills you have that are needed in the environment at hand.

I spoke earlier in the book about the importance of developing concise self-descriptive statements, and of how much practice it takes to deliver these statements comfortably and confidently. You should take a few moments now to review and revise your self-descriptive statement, and to point it directly toward the company and industry you're now targeting.

Don't forget to practice saying your mini-biography aloud. Most of us are simply not accustomed to summarizing the highlights of our lives and speaking persuasively about them within a small "time window."

Career Counsel
The interview request "Tell me about yourself" isn't a query from someone who's eager to prepare the outline of your soon-to-be-published biography—it's a test to see how you handle the task of prioritizing many years of personal and professional experience into a few concise sentences!

Don't Let This Happen to You

I remember a fellow who had a job interview where the personnel manager began with that daunting directive, "Tell me about yourself." Harry took a deep breath and began to recount his life story, almost from the moment of conception.

"I was just hitting my stride, about the eighth grade," he told me, "when I heard a beeper go off. The H.R. director took out her pager and spun around in her chair to pick up the phone. When she got up, her face was ashen. 'There's a crisis at the plant,' she told me, as she headed out the door. 'I'm afraid our interview's over. Leave your resume on my desk.'

"And that was my moment in the sun," Harry recalled. "My life story ended at the eighth grade."

The Right Life Story

The moral of the story might be summed up in a few basic rules of journalism. When telling an important story, such as that of your life:

➤ Put the important stuff up front.

➤ Use active verbs.

➤ Employ one idea per sentence.

Don't overestimate the attention span of your audience. When it comes to verbal autobiographies, less is always more. Practice your life summary until you know it by heart, can present it while snowboarding, can maintain good eye contact with your interviewer as you say it, and can modify it to meet the interests of your audience du jour.

Any Questions?

There are lots of interview books out there that will walk you through responses for specific tricky interview questions. Although their advice is often on-target, there's always the danger that a "canned" response will do your cause far more harm than good on the interview front. I say think before you answer, admit what you don't know, and try like the devil to find a way to point your answer to your plan for the organization. That's pretty much my whole strategy on handling "tough interview questions."

Career Counsel
By doing research ahead of time, and asking intelligent questions during the interview, you'll be demonstrating that you fit in at the target organization. By acting as though you already are a member of the team, chances are you'll increase your likelihood of becoming a member of the team.

Turning the Tables

The questions *you* ask can have just as great an impact as the questions you are asked—and perhaps even more.

I recommend that you go into an interview with a list of questions pertaining to the people you're there to see. Doing preliminary research will help you grasp their needs in a general way—and you'll certainly make a stronger positive impression if your questions make it clear that you've done your homework.

Continue your research in the interview process. Make it your goal to spend three-quarters of the time asking questions and—this is vitally important!—taking notes.

So What Do You Ask?

The focus of your questions should be on the skill mix the organization needs. Look for signs of problems, if that kind of information is forthcoming. Concentrate on ways to add value.

"You indicated in your ad that you want to explore some new markets for your adult education program. Can you give me some idea of how enrollment has been holding up?"

"Are all your courses at fixed times, in formal classes? Have you ever explored the flex-course approach, where people can study at their own pace? I had some experience with that format and it worked pretty well at Siwash State."

Interviewers Who Need a Clue

Finally, and this is a tricky but important point—don't ever assume that the person who is interviewing you has all the answers. That's especially true in the case of personnel workers who do nothing but interview job candidates all day. They may know much more about interviewing than about the industry they're in.

Ironically, the people who bear the most responsibility for hiring decisions may have the weakest skills in the organization when it comes to interviewing. That's because they're paid to run the department where a job is located, and that's the way they spend their time. They don't spend much time interviewing.

It's also possible that the head honcho in an organization may not be an expert in his or her industry. That's certainly worth knowing if you're presenting a business plan to the head of the outfit.

The other day I read a newspaper article about a fellow named Arnold Pohs who's president-elect of the National Cellular Phone Association. He's also head of one of the industry's largest companies. But Pohs told how he first learned of his industry. Someone called and told him of a new idea that had to do with something called "cellular."

"I said I was not interested in biotech," Pohs recalls. That was less than 15 years ago—an indication of how fast industries and technologies are changing these days. And that's why it's important to remember that every interview is basically an *exchange* of information, whether between an employer and an employee, or a consultant and a client. Even if you're talking to the president of the company, your aim isn't (and can't be) simply to pass the test by providing perfect answers to an uninterrupted series of questions.

Show some poise and confidence during the meeting. Carry your end of the load. Try to help the interviewer feel comfortable in a process he may not have mastered. Help him or her enjoy the interview process.

What You're Trying to Get Across

Earlier, you identified some of your most important skills by thinking of ways you'd helped people on the job. Before you step in the door for the interview, you must ask yourself: How do the skills you've identified in this way match the needs of an organization? Where does what you can do result in the solution to someone's problem? That's the point of interviewing—the kind of information that an interview is intended to find out.

To participate effectively in an interview, you need to work with your contact to help find an answer to that kind of question. And that means that you need to assume an active and direct role in the process by tactfully and sensitively "interviewing the interviewer."

Career Counsel
A job interview is a two-way transaction. It's not a final exam, but a consultation that has the potential to benefit both parties. It's like any other conversation in which we share responsibility for the process and the outcome.

Bet You Didn't Know

It turns out that the standards an interviewer uses for hiring may be different for entry-level and experienced employees.

Dennis Benson, a researcher who heads Appropriate Solutions in Columbus, Ohio conducted follow-up interviews of two kinds of participants in federal employment programs. One batch consisted of inexperienced workers. The others were people in mid-career who had lost their jobs.

Here are the top five factors that the employers cited for not hiring the inexperienced job candidates. 1) Poor Personal Appearance, 2) Bad Attitude, 3) Poor Work History, 4) Inadequate Communication Skills, 5) Lack of Technical Skills.

No surprises there. But, when Benson asked employers why they failed to hire experienced workers, the order came out this way: 1) and 2) Lack of Technical Skills and Inadequate Communication Skills (tie), 3) Poor Work History, 4) Lack of Experience, 5) Poor Personal Appearance and Poor Work Ethic (tie).

Intriguing Variations

To close this chapter, let me share with you a few of the more innovative ideas I've heard about from real-life job seekers who found a way to make contact with potential employers during interviews. Not all of what follows may suit your style or the industry you've selected, but it's always worth knowing what's made a positive difference on the job search front for other applicants.

Some Interesting Ways People Have Built Alliances During Job Interviews:

➤ If an employer—especially an employer in a diamond-shaped organization—seems reluctant to hire you on a permanent basis, offer an employment plan. Propose a project that you could complete on an interim basis—one that has the potential to lead into full-time employment. Offer all the specifics and see what happens.

➤ Bring a portfolio of past projects that directly relate to the problems your contact faces.

➤ Develop a prototype of the idea or product you'd use to solve the contact's problem, and bring it with you during the interview.

➤ Hand in a detailed report highlighting a potential new profit center for the company.

In the end, your objective is to come across as an innovative, independent professional, someone who's a valuable prospect for the team. Speak as one colleague to another and never leave yourself in a "one-down" position—and you'll be fine.

The Least You Need to Know

➤ Adjust your strategy for pyramid- and diamond-shaped organizations.

➤ Practice (again) telling your life story concisely.

➤ Be prepared to ask intelligent questions about possible solutions to the dilemmas faced by decision-makers.

➤ Envision the interview as a collaborative process between equals. (It's sort of like a first date.)

➤ When in doubt, focus on your plan.

HI, I WAS JUST CALLING TO CHECK IN ON...

Chapter 21

Following Up

In This Chapter

➤ What to do when they don't call back

➤ What not to do when they don't call back

➤ Evaluating the offer

You've had the interview, and it was a triumph. You're positive you knocked 'em cold with your answers to the most intimidating questions. Or, perhaps the meeting was more like a casual conversation—a meeting of peers. You met with an old colleague. You sat down and carved out a position for yourself over lunch. Things seemed to be going swimmingly.

In either case, however, the problem you're confronting now is threatening to disrupt that carefully cultivated optimism. Since the last hearty handshake, you haven't heard a word. The people at your target company haven't called and haven't written. What should you do now? In this chapter, we'll take a look at some possible strategies.

Immediately After the Interview

What do you do at the end of an interview? Some folks have been known to head home and then stew, staring at the mailbox waiting for a letter to appear, or glaring at the phone that hasn't yet rung. Here's a better idea.

Take a few moments to jot down the essentials of the meeting you just conducted. You're going to want to be able to appeal to the specifics of this meeting at a later date. So grab that familiar legal pad and jot down as many details as you can remember about:

➤ The high point of the meeting. (Focus on this first. Give yourself credit where credit is due.)

➤ The general sequence of events. (Take a moment or two to remind yourself of exactly what happened during the interview, when it happened, and how you felt as the meeting progressed. You may *think* it will be easy to recall all this material tomorrow morning or tomorrow afternoon, but it won't.)

➤ The low point of the meeting. (Is there anything you did that you'd like to make a point of *not* repeating in future interviews?)

➤ The questions you were asked. (Were there any that surprised you?)

➤ The answers you gave. (Which appeared to go over best? Did any appear to leave your conversational partner feeling uneasy or less than satisfied?)

Work Alert!
Don't beat yourself up about some aspect of your interview performance that left you feeling dissatisfied. Learn from your mistakes and then let them be. Replaying a subpar response to an interview question is a great way to lower your self-esteem and lose energy for approaching the next opportunity.

➤ The names of everyone with whom you met. (If you have to use phonetic spellings for now, do so. You can confirm the correct spellings afterward.)

➤ The specifics you and your contact agreed on about what would happen next. (Did your contact agree to talk with his or her superior? That means you didn't meet with the decision-maker.)

➤ Any other points that seem worth recording for later reference. (What new projects or initiatives did your contact discuss? What new obstacles to the organization's goals did you uncover? How has the organization traditionally handled contract or full-time work with people in your area?)

Now What?

Establishing a workable strategy for following up after an interview is always a tough call. You want to hear what the people you spoke with decided. Maybe even slather a bit of frosting on the cake. But, on the other hand, you don't want to pester your would-be employer.

What should you do next? Here's some sage advice.

By all means, follow up an interview with a note within a week. But don't simply send a thank-you note. Don't just thank them for their time or rhapsodize about how good the Caesar salad was.

Instead, go back into your research mode and dig up some data that will take your interview a step further. Are they looking at a new spreadsheet accounting software package? Find some relevant articles in your accounting trade journal and send them a copy to build on your discussion.

If you still haven't heard anything the following week, do some more digging and send them something more. Unlike sending a thank-you note, this is a technique you can exercise more than once. The idea is a familiar one: Begin to behave as though you were already a member of the team. Demonstrate some ways you can help them solve problems.

Finally, don't sit still while you're waiting for a response. Try your best to turn your energies (and, perhaps, your frustration) in a positive direction. Focus on the next prospective employer, and the next interview in your career campaign.

What's in the Letter?

So you're going to send the employer a note. Again, this is not a thank-you note exactly (although you should express your gratitude for the person's willingness to sit down with you). It's a friendly colleague-to-colleague letter that touches on some highlights of your discussion and attempts to move the relationship forward.

"Here are some of the ways in which it seems to me I can benefit your organization," you might say. Include a few bullet points to summarize the interview. Then add a few additional points for further discussion. Follow the letter with a phone call to ask if the employer would like to schedule another meeting.

Here's one example of what the letter might look like:

Dear Ms. Importanto:

It was a pleasure to speak with you recently about your export plans at ABC Corporation. Thanks for taking the time to meet with me.

I found your company's plans to expand into Central America particularly exciting. I think my export experience in this part of the world at my previous employer, Hillside National, puts me in an excellent position to help you develop this market for ABC.

After our interview, I found an interesting article on public/private partnerships in Central America in a recent issue of *Forbes* magazine (enclosed).

continues

---

continued

I hope we can talk soon about how I can use my export knowledge, on a contract basis, to help ABC:

➤ Develop a workable strategy for market entry

➤ Identify the most important potential barriers to revenue growth

➤ Set up a network of industry and government contacts that will maximize efficiency for ABC

Sincerely,

Brent Allen

(508) 555-1234

Job Jargon
Taking a **proactive** approach on the job search front means taking the initiative to make suggestions and follow through on your own.

The real point of this strategy is not simply to share interesting articles or other information relevant to your discussion. The real aim, as you've seen, is to show that you're ready, willing, and eager to act like a member of the team—and to follow up for as long as it takes until there's tangible progress toward a goal that makes sense for both you and the organization.

In other words, you want to use your follow-up campaign as a model for the way you'd collaborate to take on this and other challenges and help solve problems once you're employed within the organization. You're using employment networking as an object lesson in how you get things done.

You're taking a *proactive* approach. You're moving forward—asserting yourself in the hiring process. Instead of squirming on your folding chair at the edge of the dance floor, you're taking the initiative and asking for a dance.

Mixed Signals

Time goes by. You sent a few letters. You still can't seem to move off of ground zero with this employer.

If you're still befuddled by the interview that led nowhere after going so well, turn to your network. Go back to the person who referred you to the company in question and ask whether he or she knows what's going on. Chances are, the delay you're experiencing is due to other items claiming the employer's attention. Nine times out of ten, it has nothing to do with you.

It bears repeating: Don't get sidetracked worrying about a single opportunity. Keep your focus on developing multiple leads at multiple organizations within your target industry.

What If They Say "No"?

Even the world's best follow-up campaign won't eliminate the possibility that the contact with whom you met may issue a brusque "thanks but no thanks" response to your inquiries about employment opportunities. But don't fret! Getting rejected after an interview is not the end of the world—not by a long shot.

That may sound like one of the most shameless rationalizations anyone has ever had the temerity to put forward about the world of employment, but it really is true. I'm not talking about getting rejected after a phone or mail contact, but after a face-to-face meeting. Once someone has taken the time to meet with you personally, you're on board. You're a possibility. Even a "no" answer with absolutely no daylight in this setting can't change the fact that the person with whom you spoke took time out of a busy day to meet with you. That means you're on the radar screen.

Don't give up! Develop a formal plan such as the one discussed in the previous chapter. This is a short-term project proposal, complete with benchmarks for quality assessment and start and end dates. Submit it to the appropriate person at the organization that rejected you. Think like an entrepreneur and make a proposal!

Career Counsel

An organization that tells you "no" may nevertheless contain one or more people with whom you connected strongly—perhaps someone who would have liked to have hired you, but couldn't do so. Try to incorporate such people within your "natural network" of employment contacts.

Work Alert!

Don't leave "thanks-but-no-thanks" organizations unattended! Once an employer devotes time and attention to an in-person interview, you should stay in contact. The truth is, your "reject file" is one of your very best sources of opportunity for professional employment.

To: Jean Importanto, ABC Industries

From: Brent Allen

Hi, Jean:

Thanks for bringing me up to date on the status of our talk last week.

Attached please find my formal proposal for a contract assignment in which ABC would retain my services to help it enter the Central American widget market.

continues

---

continued

DURATION: The assignment would begin September 1, 19XX, and conclude October 1, 19XX.

OBJECTIVE: ABC would retain me (Allen) to develop a detailed (100-page, with a three-page key summary section) report on:

➤ The countries that represent the best market for ABC's products

➤ The best strategy for market entry into those countries

➤ The most important potential barriers to ABC's revenue growth within the targeted countries

➤ A directory of industry and government contacts likely to be sympathetic to ABC's efforts. (Many of these contacts will arise from my own experience in the region.)

BENCHMARKS: I propose that the report be submitted directly to you for final review, and that any additional research or summaries you may require for final submission to the board of directors be completed on an hourly basis. (See COMPENSATION.)

HANDOFF POINTS: I propose that I submit my report to Melanie Greystone, who would evaluate it and either suggest areas for further research on my part, or pass it along to you.

COMPENSATION: I estimate that the initial draft of the report will require approximately 60 hours of my time to complete. I propose an hourly rate of $30 per hour.

What do you think?

Yeah! They Made an Offer!

Your efforts seem to have paid off. One of your target companies took you up on your suggestion concerning contract or full-time employment. Before you accept, remember that there's more than simply money at stake.

You need to focus not only on what you'll be earning but on what you'll be learning as a result of the opportunity before you. Will this job help you to expand your skills within the target industry? Will it bring you closer to solving the types of problems that you identified when you established your career goal?

Career Counsel
"No man ever listened himself out of a job."

—Calvin Coolidge

You may recall the importance of acting as your own executive recruiter. I've had quite a bit of contact with recruiters over the years and have learned how headhunters operate. When they're retained by a client firm, they launch into an intense process. As you may recall, this process has four phases—phases you owe it to yourself to try to replicate on your own in your career-change campaign.

Here's a brief refresher:

1. *Sourcing.* This means taking the employer's perspective and understanding the unmet needs of the organization—the skills and other traits required. You need to have some idea of the places where people pick up the skills and the arenas where employers find them.

2. *Recruiting.* This means finding methods of reaching out to establish contact between the job candidate (you) and the employer. This may include activities such as perusing Web sites and attending job fairs, but it also includes informal contacts within one's own natural network and in new arenas such as trade and professional associations.

3. *Hiring.* This corresponds to the job of negotiating any areas of disagreement that may arise, and that will have to be resolved, during the latter stages of the matching process.

4. *Retention.* This means establishing opportunities for advancement, recognition, and performance-based compensation once you're on the job.

Think about each of these four phases from your own perspective. Be your own recruiter. What is it you're looking for? What are the avenues of training and networking that could lead you to your ultimate objective?

Check It Out

The following checklist, inspired by a discussion with Kimberly Lucas of Robert Half International, Inc., is worth reviewing closely when your career-change campaign is successful and it's time to evaluate an offer.

Checklist One: Would you like this job?

❑ Will accepting this job improve the overall quality of your life?

❑ Will accepting this job likely lead to healthy relationships with colleagues and superiors?

❑ Will accepting this job mean exposing yourself to a pleasant set of working conditions?

❑ Will accepting this job mean accepting responsibilities that are realistic?

❑ Will accepting this job mean embracing a level of professional challenge you will enjoy?

❑ Will accepting this job mean embracing a day-to-day routine you will enjoy?

Checklist Two: Would you like what this job means for your career?

❏ Will accepting this job advance your broad career objectives?

❏ Will accepting this job mean exposure to more tasks and projects that truly interest you?

❏ Will accepting this job mean a likelihood of enhanced career prospects in the future?

Checklist Three: How many of the following are you being offered?

❏ Competitive salary (ask a good reference librarian to help you determine how this offer stacks up to that for comparable positions in the industry)

❏ Sign-up bonus

❏ Expense account

❏ Specialized employee assistance program

❏ Child care assistance

❏ Training programs

❏ Educational assistance (such as tuition reimbursements)

❏ Company auto or gasoline allowance

❏ Disability insurance

❏ Life insurance

❏ Stock options

❏ 401K plans

❏ Bonuses based on predetermined performance goals

❏ Pension plan

❏ Medical benefits

❏ Vision benefits

❏ Dental benefits

The bottom line is this: Balance the earning potential with the learning potential when it comes to evaluating a new position.

The Least You Need to Know

➤ You should use your follow-up efforts to show that you're ready, willing, and eager to act like a member of the team.

➤ You should strongly consider making an offer specifying the details of a contract-based assignment you'd take on for the target company.

➤ Even a post-interview rejection can lead to opportunity—so follow up on those "no" answers and stay on the prospective employer's radar screen.

➤ Think like an executive recruiter when the time comes to evaluate an offer.

➤ Always consider how much you will learn as well as earn before accepting a job offer.

Part 4
Challenges

Are you facing a special situation? This part of the book is for you. Here's where you'll find advice about what to do when people say you're too young, too old, or too new to the industry. You'll even learn what to do if you've been out of the workforce entirely for a long stretch of time.

Chapter 22

Advice for Older Workers

In This Chapter

➤ What you're up against

➤ Five workplace generations

➤ How to overcome stereotypes

In this chapter, you learn about the obstacles that face you as an older worker and the best ways to take advantage of some of the forms and values that affect the workplace today.

Why Work?

Why show up for work at this age? A temporary service firm in Denver, Senior Skills, lists these reasons motivating their older clientele:

Financial reward

Skill enhancement

Personal identity

Job Jargon
Ageism is discrimination based on a person's chronological age.

A sense of achievement

Social interaction

All of these are good reasons taken together. They represent a good summary of the reasons that may be guiding your own search for career satisfaction. But it might be there's a barrier between you and your objectives. It's called *ageism*, and your age may work against you.

What You're Up Against

Sometimes ageism gets very explicit. Tom Ryther, a former Minneapolis TV sportscaster, was fired by his station, KARE-TV, in 1991. Ryther was 53 at the time and had been with the station for over 12 years. He sued, claiming the termination was age-related. In 1997, the U.S. Supreme Court denied an appeal on the part of his former employer and issued a judgment: Even in industries such as television, where image is important, people can't be discriminated against because of their age, or even the perception that viewers prefer another type of person.

I'm not suggesting that you sue everyone you can think of in your target industry—that can be counterproductive, to say the least, but direct, blatant discrimination is a fact of life for many older workers.

It Doesn't Have to Be Obvious

Here's an example of age discrimination that's more covert or unconscious. When the University of Colorado in Boulder was seeking a successor to coach Bill McCartney in December 1994, the university hired a new coach named Rick Neuheisel over another candidate, named Bob Simmons, who happened to be black. (Simmons went on to become head football coach at Oklahoma State University.) At that point, civil rights activist Jesse Jackson attacked the University of Colorado charging race discrimination. There was indeed reason to consider the possibility of discrimination, but in my view it had less to do with race than age. Neuheisel, the man who got the job, was 33 at the time; Simmons was 46. Could this have been a factor? I don't know, but I do know how the new man was received by the local media.

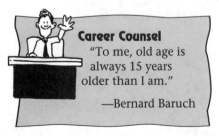

Career Counsel
"To me, old age is always 15 years older than I am."

—Bernard Baruch

The copy editor at the *Rocky Mountain News* who wrote the headline announcing the hiring decision broke the news this way: "CU Goes for a Young Gun: Assistant Coach Neuheisel, 33, to take over for McCartney." The story went on to state that Neuheiser was "the picture of what CU intends him to be: an energetic and dynamic recruiter." A university official was quoted as saying, "The youth of this country needs to look to leaders like this; he has a spark and a yen for life." (Unlike, say, the majority of 46-year-olds, who may need 24-hour geriatric care and frequent naps during games.)

That headline, that story, and that quote represent the kind of implicit, pre-emptive, covert valuing based on age that often takes place in this society. It's subtle. It's pervasive. And, for older workers, it's bad news.

Block That Stereotype!

If you're going to change careers in mid-stream, you may find that being 45 or higher is often seen, quite inaccurately, as lacking a "spark and a yen for life." The best way to dispel this myth is probably to demonstrate, in no uncertain terms, where your spark lies.

This brings us back to the fundamental question: What do you want to achieve? What are you passionate about? What gets you excited about work?

Some people continue to work simply because they don't have much of an idea about what else to do. It's certainly true that many younger workers lack clear goals—but they usually aren't relegated to the category of "used-up" in quite the same way that older workers who are uncertain about their objectives are.

So if you're an older worker, it behooves you to get goal-oriented, to be able to state with unusual specificity and conviction precisely what kinds of problems you're hoping to be able to solve in your next position.

Bet You Didn't Know

Habit can be a very dangerous thing. Just because you've *been* doing one type of work for the last, say, 15 years, doesn't mean you *should* be doing that work for the next 15 years.

"For a while, it looked like I was going to be stuck in Westerns. I figured out that I could make six a year, for sixty years, and then retire. I decided I didn't want it. So I started blinking my eyes every time a gun went off in the scenes. That got me out of Westerns."

—Robert Mitchum

The Road You'll Be Traveling

There comes a point in everyone's career where you have to ask: What have I done thus far? How do I feel about it? How much of what I've done do I want to keep doing? Of all the things I've done so far, is there anything that I'd just as soon let go of? If you're an older worker, and your initial answer to that last question is "not much," there's a good likelihood that you still have some goal evaluation to do. You may want to consider reviewing the strategies and exercises outlined in Chapter 16.

Creative Employment in Later Years

Fortunately, there is no shortage of examples of creative employment when it comes to older workers.

Presidents, Anyone?

The Registry for Interim College and University Presidents was founded by Tom Langevin. Tom was the former president of Capital University in Columbus, Ohio.

He retired and was eager to find something interesting to do after leaving the University. Earlier in his career, he had served as the Dean of a Lutheran-affiliated college in Nebraska. When the president of this school left, the trustees asked Langevin to serve as interim president, which he did for several years. (He couldn't be appointed on a permanent basis because he was not an ordained Lutheran minister.)

Career Counsel
The point for older workers is not to start from scratch, to reject all that's gone before, to begin learning from the ground up in a completely new field. Instead, the idea is to translate your experience and your core competencies into new forms.

Later, he reflected that there was no position that he had ever held where he'd been able to accomplish so much. The reason? People saw him as an interim leader—they knew he had no long-term ambitions, and did not represent a significant threat to any person or constituency within the institution. Langevin applied that lesson to his late-life work. That's how he came to set up the Registry—a temporary employment service for former college presidents!

The people his organization places are qualified to step in on an interim basis to head a college or university. (When I interviewed Langevin a few years ago, he had six or eight of these people placed, and was receiving a healthy chunk of the salary paid out by their educational institutions!)

ACE It!

Here's another example of creative employment in later years: Access Coordinators for the Elderly (ACE). This is a strategy to hire the so-called "young old" in key areas. Typically, these are people who are retired from social service positions (teachers, social service jobs, and the like) who are hired to serve as brokers of services for older Americans who live in certain apartments built with federal loans. In these buildings, it's a requirement that residents be self-sufficient. Those who work for ACE are people who are on call to find cleaning services, shopping, medical services, and just good old-fashioned companionship for residents.

That's been quite a successful program. In addition to offering seniors the help they need in selected areas, ACE has served as an employment opportunity for those who have retired from another service role. It's a good example of solving more than one problem at a time.

Bet You Didn't Know

You can contact Access Coordinators for the Elderly through the Colorado Finance and Housing Authority at 303/297-2432.

Computer Power

Yet another example is the Silver Fox Computer Club in Louisville, Kentucky. This organization offers computer instruction to people 55 and over—all those who serve as teachers must occupy the same age bracket. Like ACE, Silver Fox suggests that some of the most exciting career opportunities for older workers may lie in extending "what they're good at" to other older people.

What's the Right Kind of Job for Older Workers?

How do you know when a job or career opportunity makes sense for you as an older worker? I'd say that there are four characteristics for which you should be on the lookout.

The right position for you is likely to be *co-created*, *customized*, *composite*, and *caring*.

Co-Created

The right jobs for older workers usually aren't prefabricated. They're put together by employer and employee, collaboratively.

The older worker always needs to be in a position to help create a suitable work situation. The alternative—a low-skill job slapped together by an organization that is probably running out of younger workers—is unlikely to be rewarding, or to make use of your unique background and experiences.

Customized

Jobs that turn out well for older workers tend to have a very "tight fit." There's an extremely close match between the skills you offer and their precise application in the workplace. An example would be the hardware stores that now hire retired craft workers—plumbers, carpenters, and electricians—to handle questions from beginners about stock and materials. That's a big help, having someone like that on board.

A large bookstore in my area, the Tattered Cover, employs many former teachers—people who are

Job Jargon
Co-creation is the process of working with an employer to define the parameters of a job. One good category for older workers to explore on this score: temporary employment services. Some of these operations now specialize in placing older workers.

thoroughly familiar with particular subject areas. The closer you are to being an expert in a certain area, to being someone with deep practical experience and insights of interest to a motivated group of customers, the happier you, and the employer, are likely to be.

Composite

What does this mean? Simply that you should be prepared to have a number of balls up in the air at any given time.

I've had a composite career for quite a while now. I do research part of the time, I do writing part of the time, I lead workshops, I teach college courses, I do seminar work, and I occasionally do some one-on-one career counseling. Shifting gears and changing industries several times a year can be a very stimulating and enjoyable lifestyle.

The older worker may put together not one job, but a composite of several different jobs. Finding the right balance isn't always easy and neither is developing compensation arrangements that allow you to maintain the stability you need. (Questions about benefits tend to get tricky for those who pursue composite jobs.) But the rewards, I believe, are usually worth it. For most older workers, a composite arrangement easily beats the alternative of pursuing a single, numbing routine day after day.

Caring

Successful employment for the older worker comes down to doing something that you really care about. If you've been in four or five different career fields, it's important to separate the wheat from the chaff. You should make a commitment to do whatever it takes to allow yourself to continue only with those skills that are motivated skills—the skills that you really care about using.

Where Do You Fit In?

To make sense of where your own age group fits in the world of work and how other workers may relate to you, it helps to have a sense of how it relates to the other major age groups. The recent American workforce can be broken down into five major categories: Note the relative size of the various groups.

Organization Group—Born 1901–1924. Originally 63 million strong.

Silent Generation—Born 1925–1945. Originally 57 million strong.

Baby Boomers—Born 1946–1964. Originally 76 million strong.

Generation X—Born 1965–1977. Originally 34 million strong—a much smaller group, even considering the shorter time span.

The Echo Generation—Born 1978 and years following—projected to reach 74 million.

Strauss, William and Neil Howe, *Generations* (New York: Morrow, 1991).

Bradford, Lawrence (co-author), *Twenty-Something* (New York: Master Media, 1992).

Let's look at each of these groups in depth.

> **(!) Bet You Didn't Know**
>
> In 1940, of adults aged 25 and older, 13 percent had less than five years of total education. Only 4.6 percent had four years of college or more. In 1994, only 1.9 percent of adults 25 and over had less than five years of total education, and 22.2 percent had four or more years of college.

➤ *The Organization Group*—This is the "Organization Man," or "GI Bill" group, people born between 1909 and 1929. These are people for who the Great Depression and World War II were formative experiences. Strong work values include: Leadership, loyalty, self-sacrifice, and conformity to organizations—and, last but not least, strong gender-related work roles. Eric Hoffer called their success in World War II "the triumph of the squares." Many, but not all, of these workers are now retired.

➤ *The Silent Generation*—This is the group that followed the "GI Bill" workers, people born between 1925 and 1945. They're about two-thirds the size of the "GI Bill" workers, and half the size of the group that follows, the Baby Boomers. (They've always been outnumbered and, to a certain degree, overshadowed by those two groups.) Their work focus has typically been on mediation, sensitivity, and, to a certain degree, an instinct for reform and improvement. This group has produced more psychotherapists, and more service-oriented professionals, than has any other group in American history. It also had to come to terms with gender rules that began to change dramatically on both the personal and professional fronts in the 1960s and 1970s.

> **Work Alert!**
> Competing with Baby Boomers for key jobs is often a daunting proposition—primarily because the generation born between 1946 and 1964 is both well educated and highly career-focused.

➤ *Baby Boomers*—A huge, exceptionally well educated, and immensely powerful generation, these are the people born between 1946 and 1964. There's been a lot written about this group.

Basically, the value that comes to the fore here is self-expression (both in terms of idealism and personal ambition). One writer has written that the boomers "sometimes seem to see themselves as walking works of art." In addition to the elaboration of self, this group has focused intently on the value of the immediate. (The savings rates among boomers are quite low.) At work, self-sufficiency and independence are key values—values that may cause members of other groups to use terms like "self-absorption" or "careerism" when describing the boomers. Women take a much more active work role in this group than in the earlier two.

> ### Bet You Didn't Know
>
> The "Baby Boom" generation is not as wealthy as media stereotypes would have us believe—only a small fraction earns above $50,000 annually. The cultural, political, and social influence of the Boomers, however, is as advertised, massive.

➤ *Generation X*—These are individuals born between 1965 and 1977. This group is worthy of note primarily because its dominant work values are so striking: skepticism (sometimes bordering on cynicism), a search for family-like work communities (to replace actual family structures that may have left something to be desired), and an ongoing search for sensory stimulation (perhaps guided by an attention span profoundly influenced by commercial television). A character in the popular film *Hackers*, may have summed up the Gen-X outlook most accurately: "There's no right and wrong anymore—there's only fun and boring." Detachment and alienation figure prominently in Generation-X music and culture.

➤ *The Echo Generation*—These "post-X" people are, for the most part, workers whose influence and outlook is yet to be fully felt. One thing is certain: We can expect this group to significantly outnumber the Gen-Xers, leaving that group with imposingly large demographic groups both in front of it and behind it. That trademark cynicism may get even deeper as the years go by.

Surprise!

The "Organization" and "Silent Generation" groups of workers—that is, anyone beyond, say, his or her early 50s—shares a significant problem with the Generation X group. That problem is, being dwarfed by the immense size, ambition, and influence of the "Baby Boomer" generation. Boomers account for better than half of the workforce and about a third of the population. Competition for jobs is intense, both among themselves and with the outnumbered Silent Generation.

A Strategy You May Not Have Expected

My advice to older workers interacting with a Boomer-entrenched establishment is actually pretty simple: Stay out of their way. Follow the model of the interim college president—make it clear that you're not competing for the same positions, that you have no axe to grind, and that you aren't out to compete for leadership roles. Look for the "trusted elder" slot, rather than the "final authority" slot.

Leave those highly competitive (and, let's face it, highly draining) roles for the Boomers. Instead, try to function as a mentor, someone whose experience, background, and insight can help smooth the way for some other warrior.

Understand the skills you want to use. Find out where they're needed. Then point them toward someone (probably a Boomer) who stands to benefit—in a tangible, career-oriented way—from what you have to offer. Make it clear, overt, and unmistakable that you're not out to take over the world. You're out to help someone else take it over, and you've got a lot of experience to bring to bear in that regard.

Become an ally, and perhaps even a trusted advisor, but don't try to take over the show. And, when there's something new to learn, remember that it doesn't hurt to be a good novice! Take it from someone who knows. Most of my own mentors in the field of journalism are close to the age of my kids.

The Least You Need to Know

➤ Ageism is rampant in the workplace.

➤ One of the best ways to fight it is through clear and loudly broadcasted, goal orientation.

➤ Look for opportunities that are co-created, customized, composite, and based on caring.

➤ The five 20th-century work generations are the Organization Group, the Silent Generation, the Baby Boomers, Generation X, and the Echo Generation.

➤ You should strongly consider adopting a role that does not threaten entrenched (and intensely careerist) Baby Boomers—and consider instead taking on the role of the trusted ally or older advisor.

Chapter 23

Advice for Younger Workers

In This Chapter

➤ Overcoming stereotypes

➤ The employment landscape you face

➤ Degrees and internships

In the last chapter, you learned about some of the obstacles that face older career changers—and got a sense of the workplace traits and attitudes shared by members of the five most recent generational groups. In this chapter, you find out about some of the stereotypes hiring officials may have about younger workers, and you learn how to overcome them.

Ain't Gonna Work on Maggie's Farm No More

The short message for younger workers trying to establish a satisfying career is a familiar one: Don't depend on the organization!

In that regard, if you're under 27, you're likely well ahead of the game. The odds are that you've already developed a healthy skepticism about how much long-term commitment you should expect from employers. You're probably already aware of some of the ways in which your own career interests are likely to diverge from the long-term interests of employers in your target industry.

Lots of older workers need months or years of adjustment time to come to terms with the realities of the current marketplace. You, however, are likely to have a much more realistic attitude about today's world of work. That means you're better positioned to take the initiative yourself to track down and develop opportunities that make sense for who you are now within your field of choice.

Changes? Cool!

Work Alert!
If there was ever a group for which fixating on full-time white-collar jobs was a strategic error, it's today's younger workers. There are simply not enough jobs of that kind to match the graduates of America's 3,500 colleges are producing.

Many of today's younger workers are perfectly positioned to exploit their own adaptability. They're still experimenting with their careers. They're not bound to a single skill or routine. You may well fall into this category. If so, try to develop your experience, education, and skills in ways that will broadcast to potential employers the messages they want to hear:

"I can work flexibly within your organization!" "I don't have my heart set on being a manager! I can move easily from project to project!"

"I have a set of unique strengths that are directly applicable to problems you want to solve!"

"I'm really into this industry!"

Bet You Didn't Know

Perhaps you've wondered why there's a career bottleneck—why rewarding full-time openings can seem so hard to track down. Part of it has to do with the increasing life span of the population as a whole. The longer people live, the more of them may decide to stay on the job, often of necessity. Consider that the Baby Boomers have had the lowest savings rate of any generation in American history.

Consider that white males (the only group for which historical information is available) had an estimated life expectancy of 35 years in 1789; 40 years in 1861; 60 years in 1933; and 73 years as of this writing!

Your Reputation Precedes You

If you were born between 1965 and 1977, you should know that some older workers—particularly Baby Boomers—are likely to have a set of preconceived notions about the work attitudes of people in your age group. For better or for worse, you'll need to combat a number of stereotypes, and perhaps develop anecdotes that lay those stereotypes to rest.

The "Slacker" Thing

Boomers and Silent Generation workers are quick to summon up horror stories about younger workers who lack the necessary interest, attention, or commitment to meet basic professional standards. (These mature workers often don't stop to think about how career bottlenecks, massive downsizing campaigns, and the sad spectacle of watching the careers of many older colleagues come to a complete halt may have influenced the way their younger counterparts look at work.)

In talking to prospective employers, it's in your interest to focus on at least two or three instances from your own past that dramatically demonstrate your commitment to solving problems in an area of interest to you. When did you get up early, or stay up late, to solve a work-related problem? When did you go above and beyond the call of duty for a customer or client? Be ready to share the details of such stories with the people you talk to about career questions. They may need to be convinced of your dedication.

The "Changing Jobs" Thing

As a statistical matter, today's younger workers are far more likely to move from one job to another than, say, a Baby Boomer was at a comparable stage of his or her career. Younger workers are often faulted for this; in fact, they are only reflecting larger trends in the economy.

Throughout this book, I've reminded you that long-term employment security is pretty much a vestige of the past. In fact, it's a relic of the very recent past—what's really taking place in today's economy is a return to the contract-based employment model that prevailed in the early decades of this century. At the time of World War I, about half of all American workers had something less than lifetime employment. They, too, moved from job to job.

All the same, it's certainly true that many younger workers may be criticized that they won't "commit for the long haul." This stereotype can cost you when a full-time position that is pretty much perfect for you is on the line. If you come across an opening that looks like a stable professional opportunity in an area that matches your career goals, you should know that the employer is going to be looking for proof that you're just as committed to "sticking with it" as a competing older candidate would be. If you can do so honestly, you should offer that evidence, and perhaps make explicit estimates about the amount of time you'd feel comfortable working in the position in question. (A safe but persuasive response: "Obviously, I'd want to stay with the job for as long as I felt like I was growing. From what you've told me about the company, it sounds like that would be at least two to three years.")

Bet You Didn't Know

Younger workers may be easier to hire once they've proven themselves.

As most of us know from lamentations in the media, temporary employment has been growing at a record clip. According to recent data from the National Association of Temporary Services, the temp industry grew 27 percent during a recent one-year period. Many temp assignments serve as auditions for longer-term work or even full-time offers. Proven younger workers, whose salary requirements are generally lower than more experienced candidates, are often the most attractive candidates for these new "trade-up" positions when they materialize.

Accepting a temporary assignment with a company in your target field may just allow you to take advantage of, or even help design, a position that's right for you.

The "On the Clock" Thing

Older employers may get distracted about the issue of "ownership" of your time at work. He or she will be asking: Are you likely to commit all of your energy and attention to business matters, or are you likely to be "gossiping" with someone else on the staff? You should know that a good many employers have interpreted younger workers' needs for meaningful connection and reinforcement with colleagues as a desire to do as little as possible during the course of the average work day. As unfair as this is, it's something you're probably going to have to deal with in the employment world.

Baby Boomers and Generation X workers have been known to wage some titanic battles over the nature of work. Is the idea to get as much done during the course of a given day as possible—or to complete predetermined tasks, and then just hang out with coworkers in anticipation of the next "rush period"? Rather than open up this can of worms with a fresh contact, you'll probably want to send honest signals about your ability to manage your time wisely.

It's likely that your older contact has had conflicts with younger employees about the relationship between business time and business productivity. Ease his or her mind. Pass along an anecdote or two that illustrates your punctuality, time management skills, and willingness to focus with full attention on a task that's been passed your way.

Are You the Signpost for a Generation?

Rest assured that marketers are trying hard to reach customers in your age group. Can you help them in that task?

If so, you might target employers who are trying to focus on consumers of your own age. The same advice can be given to older workers—remember the Silver Fox Training Service? (Are you crazy for snowboards? If so, could you help launch a new brand?)

Take a good, long, look at your target industry. Do you represent the average customer or client within it? If so, are there aspects of your experience or personality that you should be highlighting in your meetings with contacts? Consider shining a spotlight on your:

➤ Awareness of current trends

➤ Sensitivity to what distinguishes major customer concerns from minor annoyances among your age group

➤ Direct experience as a customer with the product or service in question

Giving Yourself the Third Degree

Another piece of advice for younger workers: Don't try to advance your career prematurely simply by accumulating a lot of degrees.

That's because your professional opportunities may well be worse if you have an advanced degree (such as an MBA) and no real-world experience than if you had some ground-level work background, combined with a lesser degree. Many employers are extremely skeptical of resumes that feature little or nothing in the way of practical experience, but more degrees than a thermometer. Hiring officials may conclude that you're steeped in an organizational culture that doesn't emphasize experimentation and flexibility—namely, that of academia. So you should find some way to expand your roster of activities that demonstrates that you're capable of functioning productively in some other environment.

In short, try to keep your education and your experience in synch. Don't make the (common!) mistake of assuming that the best response to a job bottleneck in your field is simply to pile on lots of letters after your name.

Make the Most of Internships

I've stressed throughout this book that career changers need to focus on projects, not on jobs. That's just as true for younger workers as it is for people who are in mid-career. It will be easier for you to learn the business in your chosen field incrementally if you arrange an internship—even an unconventional one—that exposes you to the actual operations and genuine problems you'd face in more advanced settings. And I don't mean unpaid internships. There's nothing wrong with negotiating a fair wage for a short-term assignment.

Career Counsel

In discussions with prospective employers, try to convey that you can be an interpreter of or bridge between generational values. (It also wouldn't hurt to suggest, if you can honestly do so, that you have good networks of other qualified employees your age—in great many fields, these are in a short supply.)

Who's the Boss?

It may be human nature to want to gravitate to the top of the organizational chart within your target industry, but the cold, hard fact is this: In today's economy, you shouldn't expect to climb up the managerial ladder at any overwhelming speed. As you've seen, those jobs are getting pretty scarce in many organizations.

But that doesn't mean you can't advance. If you can effectively refine your skills in, say information technology or graphic arts, you could eventually find yourself self-employed, very profitably, and at a much younger age than you could if you depended on an outside organization to throw an opening your way.

Keep the Package Complete

Perspective employers tend to be very suspicious about young applicants who've already found some reason to leave a significant portion of their work history unexplained or otherwise inaccessible. It's not a good idea for anyone to leave big gaps on a targeted resume, but applicants in their early or mid-20s who seem reticent to offer any meaningful information about a two- or three-year stretch will turn off hiring officials.

Keep the Package Up-to-Date

In your discussions with contacts and prospective employers, emphasize current skills—skills that directly relate to tasks that need doing and problems that need solving right now.

Is everyone in your target field using a particular brand of graphics software? Does everyone in your target field keep up with late-breaking industry news by reading *Widgets Monthly*? Does everyone in the position you've targeted have strong personal selling skills?

Sometimes, a skill set only takes a few months to become outdated. Popular software programs in word processing, spreadsheet work, or graphics applications come to mind. Don't let a commitment to an outdated software (such as my infatuation with WordStar) make your resume less competitive than it ought to be.

Be True to Yourself

Above all, be who you are. Celebrate your age, and don't be ashamed to emphasize the new perspectives and energy you bring to the professional opportunities that come your way.

The Least You Need to Know

➤ You should highlight your strong suits: adaptability and energy.

➤ Be aware that older workers may be likely to believe you aren't willing to commit for the long haul.

➤ You'll want to develop compelling, accurate anecdotes that undercut these stereotypes of your generation and your ability to contribute on the job.

➤ Position yourself as a bridge to other people (perhaps other customers) in your age group.

SO, WHAT DID YOU USED TO DO?

Chapter 24

When You're New to the Field

In This Chapter

➤ Making the big jump

➤ Questions you should ask

➤ Winning allies

Think of it as the ultimate career shift. You have your sights set on a great new job—a new position in an exciting field that really motivates you. But there's one problem. You have no background in that industry. Absolutely zero. Nada. Zilch. What can you do to make connections?

In this chapter, you'll learn some strategies that can help you resolve this dilemma.

Can It Be Done?

Talk with career counselors, and they'll tell you stories of people who have broken into totally foreign fields. But they'll also offer a warning. They'll tell you that a 180-degree career shift is not the norm; it's the exception.

"Most career changers find themselves moving along something like a sundial," says career counselor Sandra Hagevik. "Usually you move from 12 o'clock to 1:00 and then to 2:00. You don't leap from noon over to 7:00 in the evening. I tell my clients that your

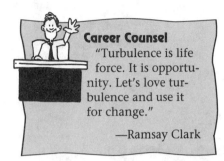

Career Counsel

"Turbulence is life force. It is opportunity. Let's love turbulence and use it for change."

—Ramsay Clark

Career Counsel

"Change is inevitable. Except from a vending machine."

—Walter Buchmann

Job Jargon
Trailing spouse is a term usually employed to describe the half of a two-income couple who *didn't* receive the job offer across the country, but is nevertheless moving to accompany a husband or wife who did.

next job will be more like your last job." Glennda Alcaraz, another counselor, puts it this way. "Think of your employment as having three or four components. There's the industry where you're working, the organization, your job title, and your geographical location. When you change career direction, you can modify any one of those factors at a time but seldom two or more."

Alcarez tells of an acquaintance who spent the first years of his career as an accountant. He tired of that work, so he started taking classes in accounting software—just some evening classes at a local computer store. Now he's working for the same employer, as an accounting software specialist. But he's recently enrolled in a full-fledged computer science degree program, and is moving toward a full-time job as an in-house programmer—and still with the same employer.

A Step at a Time

That's the most common pattern one sees among career changers. Change comes incrementally, gradually. It's like a sundial. It's especially difficult to change more than one component if one is changing geographic locale. Of course, if you're someone affected by a move that is already a foregone conclusion—a *trailing spouse*, say—you may not have much choice in the matter. But try to maintain some career constants.

A Career Changer Who Came Out on Top

Clay moved to Denver from Massachusetts when his wife took a teaching job in the new city. He'd spent several years in the parish ministry, but was tired of the long hours and decided to take this opportunity to change careers.

I took him through a line-down-the-legal-pad process of separating the wheat from the chaff in his career. What had he liked about the work he'd done? What was it he'd rather not encounter again? He listed his previous job functions in the left column, starred the parts he'd liked, and drew a line through the stuff that felt like chaff.

As is usually the case, there were few starred highlights. Clay had been a youth minister and he felt he was getting a little up in his years to do that much longer. But he had enjoyed working with the parents of the kids in his youth group. Many of them were

234

struggling with various kinds of mid-life transitions. As a result of his counseling, some had gone back to school, and that felt exciting. He gave his work with the parents two stars.

In the right column, I asked Clay to make some notes and do some research into places where that kind of work with adults went on. It didn't take him long to turn up a local college that operated a number of programs for mid-career adults. That was 10 years ago. He got a job there as an administrator three months later and is still happily employed there today.

Branching and Transplanting

I think of the process Clay underwent as *branching*—sending out a tendril into a new field, the way some bushes and trees take root.

But, now and then, you come across cases of absolute *transplanting*. Sometimes the work that people have been doing leaves them in a position where they have no points of contact with a new field.

It's not that there are no transferable skills when transplanting takes place. But the connection between the transferable skills and the problems to be solved in the new field are probably going to require some explaining.

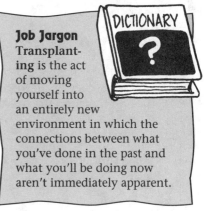

Job Jargon
Branching is the act of taking some aspect of what you used to do and finding a way to connect it to what you'd like to do in a new field.

Job Jargon
Transplanting is the act of moving yourself into an entirely new environment in which the connections between what you've done in the past and what you'll be doing now aren't immediately apparent.

Fishing for Leads

Sven works on a fishing boat in the north Pacific Ocean. He's been in that field for a few years now and has begun to move upward. Currently, he's a ship's mate and supervises a large crew. He's paid well—something like $80,000 a year—and he earns it. The work is sometimes dangerous, and he's away from home for weeks at a time. Now he and his wife are talking about starting a family, and he's giving thought to a career change. He'd rather not be an absentee father. But what to do? All his contacts are (quite literally) out at sea.

What's the solution if you find yourself in a situation like Sven's? You probably already know. Begin with the line down the legal pad. Left-hand column: what you've been doing. Right-hand column: markets where that's happening.

What You've Been Doing	Markets Where That's Happening
_____	_____
_____	_____
_____	_____
_____	_____
_____	_____
_____	_____

Job Jargon

Sourcing is specifying the kinds of skills a job requires, identifying how those skills are generally acquired, and where one would look for individuals who have them.

One of Sven's transferable skills might turn out to be personnel management. That's a skill that could be grafted onto another industry that appealed to him—something on-shore.

This brings us back to the bottom line: How do you investigate and make contact with a truly and totally foreign field? My advice, you'll recall, is to think like a recruiter, especially when it comes to turning up new leads.

Back to the Source

That means making a commitment to do some *sourcing*. Take the approach headhunters use when they begin to look for job candidates. They ask the same kinds of questions I do when I look into the workforce needs of a given industry—they focus on the three Ws.

To get somewhere else, start by asking yourself questions about where you are now:

1. *What* do you do now?
   What product or service are you turning out? Is there a particular reason you're in this industry or occupation? Do you have special skills in this work?

2. *Who* does the work you're trying to move into?
   What kinds of skills and experience do they have? Do they have other traits in common? (Are they primarily one gender or another? Are they all from the same ethnic group? Are they all about the same age? Did they all pledge the same sorority or fraternity?)

---

3. *Where* would you typically find those people?
   Do they all have degrees in the same field (for instance, engineering)? Are the degrees from the same institution? Or did most of the people you're focusing on get their training, say, in the military? (That's typical of positions in some industries, such as cellular phones.) Is there a typical path in the line of work you're focusing on—a job in which more or less everybody starts out?

Start this way. Find your way to a professional association or trade group. Interview admissions people at a nearby school. Ask to speak to graduates of their program who have made the same kind of radical career shift you have in mind. Talk with friends and relatives.

Think like a recruiter. Think about sourcing.

How Inventive Do You Want to Get?

It's an especially good idea to make a habit of attending relevant industry events, such as trade shows and professional meetings. That's certainly not the only way to go, though. The following list outlines a few of the inventive strategies that delivered results for some career seekers—one or more of them may inspire you and help to broaden your contact network.

Making New Contacts in a New Field

➤ Develop a written plan of action for your career-shifting campaign, one that mirrors the type of activity you'd pursue in the position you desire. Circulate it by mail to industry contacts and follow up afterward.

➤ Research and compose a speech of interest to people in your target audience— and deliver it at a local business or chamber of commerce function they're likely to attend. Pass out plenty of business cards afterward.

➤ Appear as a guest on a local radio talk-show program your audience is likely to listen to. This strategy is worth considering if you have a confident vocal delivery. (It's easier to get bookings than you might think, as long as the subject is one you know well. A few well-targeted faxes to producers whose formats you know well may yield some interest when you follow up by phone.)

➤ Find out which high-ranking members of a target organization in your field of specialty have some connection—even a tangential one—to your own alma

continues

> *continued*
>
> mater. Develop written and phone appeals based on the common link, and ask for help in figuring out the ins and outs of employment in the new employment field you've targeted.
>
> ➤ Develop a compelling written "advertisement" (not a resume, but something with graphic appeal) that highlights your strong suits. Send it to key decision-makers, then follow up by phone. Warning: If you're trying to enter a highly competitive field populated by lots and lots of creative people (such as advertising or public relations), you'd better make sure what you send along is not perceived as amateurish or uninformed! When in doubt, ask the competition.

These are just a few examples of some innovative techniques that you may want to use or adapt to your own situation. But you don't have to get fancy. A letter and a follow-up phone call is still a very effective way to get information on a field of interest to you.

Play It Straight

I once met with someone who's an aspiring writer. She'd sent me a letter with a few samples of her writing, and posed a few questions she said she'd like to ask me. She also expressed interest in the organization where I had my office and suggested that she might like to find work there too. That was helpful. I knew up front that she was looking for a bit more than just information.

"I'm running a bicycle shop to make a living," she told me, "but I live and breathe writing. Right now, I'm just writing letters to the editor of the local newspaper, but some day I want to make my living as a writer. I want to write about serious issues, such as school reform and the relationship between poverty and crime. So, what can you tell me about the field?"

I liked her approach She had a goal—something that excited her. Her attitude was positive, intelligent, and open. So it was second nature for me to respond in essentially the same way to her request. I think you'll find that principle will hold true with most of the people you talk to in a field where you have no direct experience. Remember: While most of us are inclined to cringe when approached for a job, we're likely to respond positively to a well-focused request for help.

How Did You Get Started?

I told her what I could about how my own career as a writer has evolved, and how almost every book writer I know has another source of income. (Estimates are that no more than 200 people in the U.S. earn their living solely from royalties on books.) "So, don't quit your day job," I told her in effect.

What about writing for my organization? I told her that most people here were at a more senior level. They're ex-college professors and the like. Then I went on to tell her what I saw in her samples. Unless she wanted to get a job writing for policy-makers—say, as an analyst for a state legislature—she needed to write more graphically.

"What do you mean when you say that?" she asked. I said, "I mean, writing in pictures. Using more examples. One way to learn to do that is to take some good journalism courses, the kind where they make you come up with 12 different images for something dark other than, 'as night.'"

What Should You Do Next?

Then I gave her some specific suggestions. I suggested that she try submitting some "op-ed" pieces to the editorial section of the local newspapers. Or ask a reference librarian to help her find some of the directories that indicate which publications in her field of interest use a lot of freelancers. Finally, I suggested a good local journalism program.

That's the process. Write letters; make calls; schedule interviews. Do just as that aspiring writer did. Not just one, but dozens of letters and calls if need be. In the end, that's probably the most reliable way to learn your way around a new field. Keep your efforts focused but also keep 'em coming. There's an old saying in basketball: "100 percent of the shots you don't take don't go in."

Ask the basic questions. Then see if you can get a referral or suggestion for the next step along your way. You certainly can ask if there are opportunities in the organization of the person you're interviewing. Just be explicit about what you're trying to find out. Remember, sending a letter in advance, and then following up by phone, is always a good way to set up an information interview.

Work Alert!
Don't turn new contacts off in the first five seconds! The way you phrase questions with new contacts can make all the difference. Calling to ask, "Do you know of a job for me?" is one of the worst ways to look into a new field.

The Least You Need to Know

➤ You should be prepared for gradual, incremental change when you seek a career change. Leaping into a totally foreign field is the exception rather than the rule.

➤ Sourcing skills will help you identify the questions you need to ask about the relevance of what you're doing now, who does the work you're trying to move into, and where employers would typically find those people.

➤ Make a habit of attending relevant industry events.

Chapter 25

Overcoming Problems in Your Background

In This Chapter

➤ What to say on an application

➤ How to handle the interview

➤ Broadcasting what you've learned from challenges

Sometimes, events in your past can cause employers to look aghast when you approach them during a career-change campaign. How do you get decision-makers to look beyond the problems (if, indeed, there ever were problems) and evaluate your candidacy on its merits?

That's one of the most challenging questions that can confront any job seeker. In this chapter, you learn some important strategies for helping prospective employers develop an appropriate sense of perspective on your background and experience.

Bad Breaks

It was the night before your best friend's wedding five years ago, in the wake of the bachelor party—about midnight, to be exact. That's when you and a few of your buddies came up with the brilliant scheme. You'd break into your friend's rented limousine and put an obscene disc in his CD player, then crank up the volume full blast. Imagine the look on his face when he turned it on, with his wife in the car, the next day!

But the prank backfired when the neighbors spotted you using a coat hanger to get into the limo. They called the cops. The company that owned the limousine wasn't amused. You and your buddies were arrested, and you spent three abhorrent days in the county jail. What was even worse was that you acquired a criminal record. That's why, nowadays, if someone looks you up on the NCIC, the National Crime Information Clearinghouse computer system, they'll find you. You have a record.

Sometimes a few beers can make you think you're a little more brilliant than you actually are at the time. But should you really have to pay for an incident like that for the rest of your working life?

Take It Easy

There's no shortage of problems that can befall job applicants and career changers. What if you've been fired, or been convicted of an offense of some kind—serious or not-so-serious? What do you tell a prospective employer?

The first rule is, don't panic. Freezing up or becoming aggressive when the issue comes up isn't likely to score you any points with prospective employers. (In fact, this sort of response will probably only serve to reinforce their fears.)

Career Counsel
The *way* you discuss the problems that may be in your background may well have a greater effect on the response you receive from prospective employers than the events themselves.

Don't assume the worst, either. Career counselors confront questions of this kind all the time, and they've developed some fairly effective strategies for dealing with them.

I called a few of my colleagues and asked them to pool their experience with mine. What follows is in part the result of my own experience in the employment field, and in part the input of my good friends Sandra Hagevik, Glennda Alcarez, and Gene Spanarella, all of whom have helped plenty of people with significant "background hurdles" find jobs and careers that made sense for them.

What to Do?

Here, then, are some guidelines to follow if you've had a difficult problem in your life outside work, or have been fired from a job, or have had an unusually high number of jobs for your field.

Resume Rewrites

When it comes to your resume, if you've had "too many jobs," draft your resume in a "functional" format. That is, organize your work history by job title. Instead of putting down:

Wonder Widget. Senior Widget Designer. 1992–1993. Winning Widgets. Senior Widget Consultant. 1991.

Write your work history this way:

Widget Designer/Consultant. Wonder Widget, 1992–1993. Winning Widgets, 1991, etc.

(You can clump quite a number of jobs under the same heading. If your job titles varied, invent a broader category—say, Real Estate Professional for some jobs in real estate sales and others in property management.)

Application Blues

On the application form, which may be your next hurdle in the hiring process, your aim is always to get past the form to an interview. Remember that, for an employer, an application form is basically a screening and defense mechanism. It's an attempt to get all the facts out on the table. No one gets a job based on the quality of their answers on a form. So there's nothing wrong with taking a few intelligent risks—risks that stay on the right side of the honesty line—in order to win attention and interest with the prospective employer.

So if you're filling out an application, and a question related to your problem comes up on the form, here's what you do. Simply put down, "will discuss with interviewer." That will flag the attention of the person doing the interview—and perhaps even slightly increase the chance of your winning that face-to-face meeting.

The question then arises: How do you prepare for that discussion you've suggested on the form?

Face to Face

During the interview, take the initiative in discussing the problem. Bring it up yourself—after the customary exchange of pleasantries.

The idea is to get the negative data out of the way as soon as possible so that you can move on to more positive points. A friend of mine who's an attorney taught me this lesson years ago. It's a basic principle in conflict resolution. "In a trial, I always concede the points where my client was clearly at fault right off the bat," he told me. That way, the problem doesn't get magnified, and the opposing lawyer can't get any mileage out of springing it on the jury."

Work Alert!
Never, ever supply a prospective employer with false information on an application, a resume, or any other document. That kind of stunt could come back to haunt you once you're hired.

For example, if your new job requires that you be bonded (insured in the event of loss or theft), it's important that your employer know about a criminal record. Otherwise, the bond coverage could be invalidated. The company could get into serious trouble—and so could you.

Career Counsel
The "concede-the-negative" strategy has worked for countless attorneys dealing with clients facing very serious charges—so why not let it work for you?

Several years ago, I agreed to teach a graduate course for a friend who was going off on a consulting assignment. The consulting job had come up at the last minute, so none of the students were prepared to be greeted by a substitute instructor. They were not over-joyed. To make matters worse, the class was huge and the course was required; most of the students resented having to be there in the first place. As the class went on, some did so poorly that I gave them low grades.

The students protested—not just the grades they'd received, but the fact that I'd not taken time to write critical comments on their final papers. There were hints of legal action! When I met up with the department chair, I was sweating, but I followed my friend's advice. I 'fessed up that I'd been wrong not to have written comments on the papers. But I affirmed that my grades had been fair. The strategy worked. The department head said he appreciated my honesty, and he supported me. That's a lesson I've never forgotten—in the teaching work I've done since, or in any other setting!

No Cover-Ups!

Gene Spanarella is a career counselor who works with former prison inmates. He told me of a client who got a job with a supermarket chain by following the same advice—being honest up front. He'd been convicted of a crime and jailed, and he told the human resource manager so. Later, the HR manager called up Spanarella. "If they all would just tell us the truth from the beginning, we could work through a lot of problems," she said.

Spanarella adds, "Most employers understand human nature. They're people, too. They know that everybody makes mistakes. So, get your problem out on the table. Say some-thing like, 'I know I've made some bad choices in my life. My conviction was for _____. I take full responsibility for what happened, but since that time I've learned a lot. These are the ways I've changed _____.'"

If appropriate, use some humor. "I used to act before thinking when I was young. 'Ready-fire-aim'—that was my motto. I realize now that that's why I was dismissed from my job as a _____. But this is how I've changed since that time…"

Be Prepared!

Of course, it goes without saying, you should outline and rehearse this part of your interview, complete with stories of recent successes and good-faith efforts, until you can recite it from a coma.

One great reason to rehearse your explanation is that you'll want to get the time alloca-tions right. Don't spend the whole interview talking about how sorry you are for having refused to take appropriate instruction and guidance on your last job!

A one-minute summary of any sin is sufficient. Then, launch into a two-minute spiel to tell 'em what's good about you. If you can, supply the names and phone numbers of people who are prepared to vouch for your character, diligence, and professionalism.

If It Was (at Least Partly) Your Fault

If a problem on a previous job was clearly your fault, focus on exactly what you learned from the experience. Here's what a client of Sandra Hagevik, one of my career-counselor friends, told her recently:

"I got fired for a very good reason. You see, early in my career, I was taught to micro-manage employees. That was the way my first boss supervised me. But since then I've taken some courses in personnel management, and I've cleaned up my act. That approach doesn't work. Now I've got a much better idea of what does."

Or, you might convert an apparent failure into a shining virtue—again if it seems appropriate. "Why did I lose my job as a steel salesman? My liver couldn't handle it. The job just involved too much late-night entertaining, and there was no way I could restructure it. I had to go out drinking with clients, and I got reprimanded by my sales manager if I tried to order soda water. It was an unhealthy lifestyle, and while I regret the experience of having been separated from the company, I really believe I'm much better off now."

Prospective employers will want to hear about how you've matured as a result of the dismissal. So far as you can honestly do so, point the spotlight on the ways you've grown, changed, and benefited from the experience you've had. Following is a list of possibilities.

Bear in mind, too, that turnover and *downsizing* in some fields—such as advertising, book publishing, and banking—is extremely high. If you were on the job for four years, and the industry average is three, you should consider pointing that out.

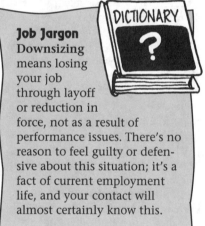

Work Alert!
There's a lot a good interviewer will be able to look past, but claiming you were completely right, and the employer who fired you was completely wrong, won't win you any points. Someone who claims to have learned absolutely nothing from a bad experience with a supervisor will almost certainly be seen as a poor risk for employment.

Job Jargon
Downsizing means losing your job through layoff or reduction in force, not as a result of performance issues. There's no reason to feel guilty or defensive about this situation; it's a fact of current employment life, and your contact will almost certainly know this.

Fill in the blank:

It was certainly no fun getting fired, but as a result of that experience, I've…

➤ Learned to delegate effectively

continues

---

continued

➤ Dramatically improved my listening skills; learned how to prioritize my work

➤ Become a much better team player

➤ Learned how to deal with colleagues of a different generation

➤ Found out how important it is to pay attention to details

➤ Learned how to issue suggestions that motivate subordinates

---

Career Counsel
Timing can make a big difference when you're dealing with prospective employers about your loss of a job. If you've just been fired or forced to quit a bad job, make every effort to work through your anger or grief before you begin going on information or employment interviews. Find someone you trust—a career counselor, a friend, a relative—and talk the problem through. Whatever pain you feel, take the time to get it out of your system. Find some objective way of framing that problem. Put some boundaries around that problem. Try to put it behind you. Then, when it finally comes time to go out on interviews, summarize the problem as succinctly and constructively as you can.

The list of possible positive lessons from bad employment experiences could probably go on forever. Just be sure the response you give is one that honestly reflects your own situation, experience, and current outlook.

If It Really Wasn't Your Fault

If you've lost a job for reasons that you believe are not your fault, be prepared to discuss that problem in the interview as well. Show how or why you were not the whole problem. But do not, under any circumstances, demean a previous colleague or employer. Nothing will turn off an interviewer more quickly than that.

As anyone who's done any amount of professional interviewing can attest, applicants who talk at length of dark schemes and elaborate vendettas in previous jobs represent the very poorest chance of working out. Don't fall into that trap. The aim is to send the message that there was a communication problem, perhaps even one that would have left Mother Teresa feeling a bit stressed. But that was then, and this is now. You don't harbor any bitterness about past events, and you certainly aren't out to use this job to settle any scores with people who remind you of your past supervisor.

If the problem was outside you, just say something neutral. Maybe, "It was a bad fit." In a sentence or two, describe why you feel this way and close by acknowledging that no one is perfect. *Do not* recite a laundry list of grievances about the former employer even if the interviewer invites you to do so.

Some Parting Thoughts

As simplistic as this statement sounds, it's worth repeating to yourself regularly: Everybody makes mistakes. Even employers—without exception. Everybody screws up, including the people you'll be talking to.

Common Ground

It's true. There is not a personnel interviewer on this planet whose own work background doesn't include a project or two that didn't work out as well as it might have. There's no decision-maker you'll ever run into whose own career doesn't harbor a few unpleasant episodes. Appeal to your contacts as one human being to another, and you'll find that people aren't altogether heartless about your problems.

And don't exclude the possibility that the experience of having overcome a serious problem in your life may qualify you to appeal to an entirely new audience of prospective employers. Over the years, I've counseled recovering drug addicts who went on to head drug treatment centers and reformed professional thieves who became well-paid security consultants.

There Are Problems and Then There Are Problems

Every veteran career counselor has seen people who've had a major problem that has inspired a new career direction based on helping others with the same difficulty. These people typically go through a cycle of 1) recovering from the problem in their own lives, 2) getting some training in the recovery process, and then 3) going to work to help others. The one cardinal rule is: Be sure you're past the problem in your own life.

If you have friends who are recovering alcoholics, you're probably familiar with the extended healing process I'm talking about. But there are countless other areas where this model applies. I know of a young man who came back from death's door as a teenager when he came down with a form of childhood leukemia. As he recovered and the leukemia went into remission, he found a new sense of direction in his life. Last month he graduated from medical school.

One career counselor in Denver tells of having been rushed to the hospital, not once but twice, with apparent heart attacks on the job. That's how much stress she was under. Now she tries to help others avoid the kinds of problems she had. The keys, of course, are to get good training, and to first resolve your own problems.

The Least You Need to Know

➤ You can reduce the "shocking revelation" quotient by admitting background problems early on in your contacts with prospective employers.

➤ By approaching decision-makers as fellow human beings, you can talk through some daunting obstacles in your past history.

➤ You should never lie to prospective employers about your background.

➤ Sometimes the experience of overcoming personal difficulties can form the groundwork for helping others who are facing similar problems.

Chapter 26

So You're Not a "Computer Person"

In This Chapter

➤ Hope for the "technopeasant"

➤ Touting your current skills

➤ Expanding your skills painlessly

Bits. Bytes. Hard drives. Dialog boxes. Operating systems. Usenet newsgroups. The Web. "Push" technology. Not only do you not understand what these terms refer to, you're not so sure you *want* to know.

Worry not. In this chapter, you learn how to make the world of technology a little less intimidating—and come to a successful, if somewhat reluctant, accommodation with the often-bewildering world of information technology. As you'll see, I'm not without my biases on this subject.

"I'm Not Getting All This..."

You say you're feeling like a "technopeasant?" You can't keep up with all the technological changes that keep coming down the pike? Well, if it's any comfort, you're not alone.

There are days when I wonder if I'm not turning into a serf in some newfangled feudal system. Here I am writing this book in WordStar (a prehistoric word processing program that isn't even manufactured anymore) while using a version of Windows that's been out of date since the dawn of creation. At least, that's how it seems.

> **Bet You Didn't Know**
>
> If you're old enough to remember Ronald Reagan's first inauguration as President of the United States, you're old enough to remember an entirely different technological era. Reagan, who was elected in 1980 and sworn in in January of 1981, came to the presidency at a time when:
>
> Personal computers did not exist as a significant consumer product category.
>
> The word "Macintosh" referred, first and foremost, to a variety of fruit.
>
> Vinyl LPs were the primary means of listening to prerecorded music.
>
> Nobody had ever visited a Web site.

A Different World

America in the early '80s was a very different (or at least less thoroughly wired) nation than today. Nowadays, somewhere in that cloudbank that surrounds Seattle, sits the lord of the manor in his recently completed, megabucks mansion. King Bill Gates is worth $36 billion at last count. If you're keeping score at home, that means he's roughly 60 times richer than Paul McCartney. That might not be so bad except that for someone who's redesigning the world, Gates has a mighty odd way of looking at it sometimes. Take this reminiscence from Gates's 1995 book, *The Road Ahead*:

"I used to date a woman who lived in a different city. We spent a lot of time together on e-mail. And we figured out a way we could sort of go to the movies together. We'd find a film that was playing at about the same time in both our cities. We'd drive to our respective theaters, chatting on our cellular phones. We'd watch the movie, and on the way home we'd use our cellular phones again to discuss the show."

"In the future," Gates assures us, "this sort of 'virtual dating' will be better because the movie watching could be combined with a videoconference."

It's enough to make you proud to be a technopeasant.

Clinging to Low-Tech

Lots of us are non-computer-people for a variety of reasons. Many of us fail to find excitement in electronic technology. We don't enjoy being plugged into the world in the same way someone such as Gates does. (Notice how consistently I have avoided epithets such as "propeller-head," "geek," and "nerd.")

Others may have an interest in computers, but have given it up with those unintelligible manuals of instructions that came with the machines. This approach carries both pluses and minuses.

I once had a colleague who didn't get into word processing for the very good reason that she couldn't type. She'd refused to take typing classes as a matter of principle: She'd never be a secretary! So she hired others as secretaries instead. One day her organization eliminated the position of her secretary and put a computer on her desk so she could do her own correspondence. I never saw anyone learn to type so fast. For her, as for so many of us, the rules had changed at halftime.

Today, more and more mid-career professionals find themselves in that sort of position. And many people are terrified in the process. I believe that one of the major contributing factors to technophobia—basic computer fright—is that many people have been introduced to computers in the context of downsizing. Suppose the automobile had turned up in the same way—not as a vehicle of social freedom but as something that threw huge numbers of managers and workers out of their jobs. The history of the automobile might be very different indeed.

What Will You Do?

There may be some good reasons you're not particularly enamored of electronic technology. Maybe there are some understandable incompatibilities between you and that one-eyed, humming monster on your desk. The question is: What will you do about the fact that you're not a "computer person?"

Will you try to tout your other skills in the job market? Or will you break down, bite the bullet, and upgrade your computer skills? The strategy I'll suggest is: all of the above.

Techniques for Technopeasants

You read right. You're going to highlight the skills you already have and find a way to upgrade your computer abilities in a way that makes sense for you. Let's take a look at each approach briefly right now.

Touting Your Current Skills

Have you ever found yourself wondering what people did at work before they had computers? The answer is pretty basic: They did the same kind of work everybody does today, only in different ways. Sure, it took more people to do the same amount of work, and they probably did it less efficiently. (Although sometimes, when I stare for long periods of time at a program that has stopped responding to human input, that seems debatable.)

But the industries in which people were working and the kinds of needs they were attempting to meet were pretty much the same. People worked in the garment industry, the wholesale food industry, the entertainment industry, and so on. Just as they do today.

251

That's a point worth bearing in mind if you consider the skill sets found in a particular job.

Back to Basics

If you think of a job you want to explore in the same way an employer or a recruiter would, you're likely to see it as a set or linkage of skills. Typically, one of the skills has to do with an industry; another skill relates to serving customers; and only the third concerns technology—the "how" of the equation.

Skill sets, revisited

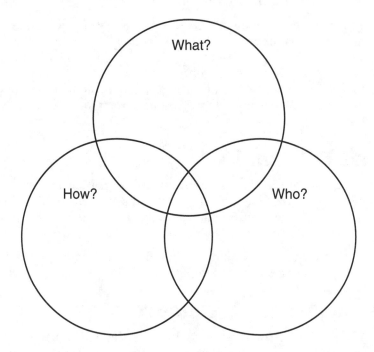

Suppose you're a hardware store owner who needs to hire a new employee. What'll you look for? Well, probably the first requirement is to find somebody who understands the merchandise. Since a large percentage of customers who venture into a hardware store have no clue how to find what they need, you'll want to employ people who have worked with the various tools and supplies. In recent years we've seen a trend toward hiring retirees from the building trades because they know the stock. It's the same reason a bookstore may recruit retired elementary school teachers for their children's department. They've read a lot of kid-lit.

But back to the hardware store. This second circle in our skill set has to do with many aspects of customer service. You don't want a surly individual snarling at customers who are already feeling pretty insecure. Nor do you want someone who's not detail-oriented enough to match paint colors or recognize different screw sizes.

And, finally, in the third circle in the cluster, you'd probably like to recruit someone who's conversant with the technology you're using to manage the affairs of the store—someone who can operate a cash register and record stock in a computer. But technology is only one part of the skill set.

So, the bottom line is, don't be afraid to play up your other strengths if technology is not your strong suit. Do your homework when it comes to the skill set that's needed in a given job. In your resume and interviewing, emphasize the skills that you do have, recognizing that industry knowledge and customer service skills are valuable in their own right.

Career Counsel
Most prospective employers want to interview people who are skilled in their industry and *willing to learn* about technological tools. (Relax. These tools change so fast that they're used to teaching new people how to use them.)

However, having said all that, consider the second of my strategies for technopeasants.

Boot Up!

Yes, you will need to expand your computer skills and make it clear you're ready, willing, and eager to do so to anyone who asks. Fortunately, today's graphically driven operating systems make the task of stumbling around in a new program a lot less complex and intimidating than it was, say, seven or eight years ago.

Why do you need to make the effort? Because you want to stay competitive. Peoples' skill set is the first to lose its shelf life. And that's their technical skills.

I've seen many an individual with a good foundation in a certain profession jump-start his career by picking up some new technology in the field. Take the librarian who learns how to do electronic database searching. Or the MBA in marketing who finds that her degree has outlived its time. In recent years, there's been an explosion in the application of geographic information systems (*GIS*)—translating computer data files to maps—to strategic market analysis. Courses in GIS are widely available and it's an exciting technology to work with.

Author! Author!

To cite a third example, consider "authoring" technology in the field of education. Authoring is the process of creating one's own courses in a multimedia format, so that students can study the material independently on CD-ROMs. Dr. Vicky Seehusen, a computer specialist at Red Rocks Community College outside Denver, told me that authoring courses are growing by leaps and bounds. She said, "It used to be that on a typical campus, only one or two instructors knew anything

Career Counsel
Sometimes universities and professional associations will offer cut-rate courses in new technology that turns up in their fields to help mid-career professionals upgrade their skills.

253

about authoring. Those were the 'campus geeks.' But, nowadays, more and more people are learning to do it."

Turn, Turn, Turn

In other instances, I've seen individuals transfer a core competency from one industry to another—while learning the technology of the new field.

Career Counsel
"A man only understands what is akin to something already existing in himself."

—Henri Frederic Amiel

Clara graduated from college with a degree in elementary education, and then was dismayed to discover that spending eight hours a day in the company of little kids was not her cup of tea. So, what to do? At age 25 and feeling adventurous, she packed up her duds and moved to Aspen, Colorado.

Once out West, Clara filled out an application for the Aspen Ski Company and quickly found herself in an interview. "Have you ever thought about becoming a ski instructor?" the interviewer asked.

"Sounds all right," said Clara, "except for one thing." She paused in embarrassment. "You see, I've just moved here from the flat Midwest. And, the fact is, I'm not great at skiing."

To her astonishment, the instructor replied, "No problem. We've found that we can convert a teacher to a ski instructor far easier than the reverse."

And so, the next morning, Clara found herself halfway up a slope in a beginner's ski class. And, sure enough, the next month she was teaching the same class. She became a ski bum for the next several years, and it was a good chapter in her career.

Mix and Match!

The trick is to combine technical skills with other kinds of knowledge in an integrated skill set. To return to the subject of computers, that's where most of the job growth is taking place—in the applications of computer technology to specific industries, not in pure computer science such as software development.

Suppose you're not even at the applications level. Forget about learning the latest software—you're starting from square one. Is there any hope for the rank novice in mid-career?

There is. People such as Vicky Seehusen who teach in community colleges deal with technopeasants all the time. Most of these instructors teach in special departments labeled something like "learning development centers."

What Works?

What are the latest trends in teaching novices?

"Playing games, for one thing," Vicky told me. "Time was, we used to delete the games that came with our computers—solitaire, minesweeper. Then we came to realize that playing games is a great way to learn the basic mechanics of computer operations, such as clicking a mouse. So that's one of the first places I'd encourage beginners to start."

Sue Knepley, one of Vicky's colleagues at Red Rocks College, adds, "We also recommend taking a class at the outset if you don't know anything about computers. For a while, we were starting people out with some of the self-paced books that are coming out for learning software like Word for Windows (word processing program), Excel (spreadsheet program for managing finances and databases), and PowerPoint (a program for slides and visual presentations).

Career Counsel

Something you already know can serve as your entry to new technological competence. If you doubt it, buy a snazzy CD-ROM game on a subject that's interesting to you and enlist the aid of a friend who knows how to install the program and get it running for you. See how long it takes you to become "computer literate!"

"These books come with a CD right inside the back cover, so people can go through the course at their own pace. But we found that, if someone has no knowledge of computers, it's hard for them to figure out the logistics of playing a CD. Plus, there's no substitute for a live instructor who can give encouragement and correct errors on the spot."

So, there you have it. There are all sorts of resources for learning about computers at any stage of life these days. The best resource is probably your local community college. Look for a department called something like a "learning development center."

And, as your first step, enroll in a beginning class. Red Rocks offers courses at all hours—Friday nights, weekends, whatever. You'll likely find that your local college does, too.

Whatever trail you choose, get on that slope!

The Least You Need to Know

➤ Expand your current skills to embrace computer technology.

➤ Typically, skills you already have will relate directly to problems the prospective employer would like to see solved.

➤ Plenty of prospective employers are interested in interviewing people who are skilled in key areas and willing to learn about technological tools.

➤ Playing computer games and taking advantage of training resources your community college may offer can help you get computer-savvy in a hurry.

Chapter 27

Call It a Comeback!

In This Chapter

➤ Overcoming obstacles to re-entry

➤ Finding meaning on your own terms

➤ Revisiting the key questions: Where are you? Where is the market?

Have you ever gone back to visit someplace you lived as a child? It can be an eerie experience if you've been gone a while. When I was about 35, I tracked down the neighborhood where I'd spent first grade in a suburb of Pittsburgh. I hadn't been there since age six, but managed to find the very intersection where my family had lived. The buildings had all changed, but I was just able to recognize the contours of the streets and hills.

Returning to the workplace after a long absence is like that. You may think you know the territory of an institution or a profession where you once worked, but in reality it's new. If you take time to look around and listen to the people who are working there now, you may find that only the contours are the same—and that many of the details are different.

In this chapter, I'll show you some strategies for reconnecting with the workplace and making sense of the changes after you've been away for a while.

Asking Questions (Again!)

The best way to begin is to pull out that dog-eared legal pad you've been marking up while working through this book. Draw a line down the middle of the page once again, and label the left side "Where am I?" At the top of the right column, write the heading "Where's the Market?" What you want to do is examine the fit between what you offer and what's "out there."

Bet You Didn't Know

If at first you don't come up with the perfect career, be ready to try and try again. Here are the original, working titles of the following famous bestselling novels.

Of Mice and Men—Something That Happened

Roots—Before This Anger

Pride and Prejudice—First Impressions

East of Eden—The Salinas Valley

The Blackboard Jungle—To Climb the Wall

War and Peace—All's Well That Ends Well

(Source: *Now All We Need Is a Title: Famous Book Titles and How They Got That Way* by Andre Bernard, W.W. Norton & Co., 1996)

The Biggie: Where Am I?

You may have some good questions to ask yourself when it comes to going back to work. Why did you leave in the first place? Was it to raise your family? That's a common scenario. Or, perhaps something happened to throw your career off course—a lack of perspective or a problem with career balance. I saw a television feature on Dick Vermeil, who at age 60 came back to pro football as head coach of the St. Louis Rams. Vermeil had been out of the NFL for 11 years, the victim of overstress. In his previous life as a head coach, he'd worked around the clock and virtually lived in his office. Vermeil claimed he'd learned his lesson. He's hired a staff of assistant coaches to share the workload and keep him in line. They're all reconstructed ex-head coaches as well, and all are in their 60s.

How Much to Give?

Here's another good question to ask under the "Where am I?" column, and it's one I've posed before. What kind of work are you looking for? I don't mean what type of industry or occupation. I mean how much of yourself do you want to devote to paid employment?

Are you simply looking for a job—something to help you make ends meet and become reacquainted with the regimen of work? If so, that's fine. One of the best employees I've ever had was just returning to the workplace when I was lucky enough to find her for a college administrative assistant job. Dorothy's kids were growing up and leaving home at the time. Although she had a college degree, the electronic revolution had struck the workplace while she was an at-home mom, and she'd never laid hands on a computer.

> **Career Counsel**
> Sometimes a job in an academic or other non-profit organization is a good bridge to a resumed career if it offers a low-pressure work environment and some good mentors.

But Dorothy learned so quickly and performed so well that it wasn't long before my boss hired her. She became a full-fledged administrator a few years after that. Dorothy's back-to-work strategy—getting her feet wet in a college setting, then ratcheting up her goals—may be one that makes sense for you.

Some people are happy holding "just a job." Perhaps their "real life" takes place after hours. If they're interested in a modest job and are returning to the workplace, they're in a seller's market. With the downturn in numbers of Generation X young adult workers, many employers are desperate to fill jobs in retail sales, for example. I know of a department store that's hiring clerks with no experience for close to $20,000 per year.

Granted, these positions many not be where you want to spend the rest of your working life. But they may make sense as a transitional strategy. So, how long will this labor shortage last? Well, at least until those born since 1978—the Echo Generation—begin turning up for work in significant numbers. (Remember, that group is expected to become very large.)

What's Next?

Another facet of the "Where Am I?" question is: Do you want a career? About 20 years ago, there was a well-publicized study of men at the age of retirement. The researchers asked their subjects if the jobs they'd held had followed some sort of logical progression—an "orderly career." Only one-third of the subjects reported they'd compiled "orderly careers." The other two-thirds confessed to "disorderly careers," somewhat random work experiences. What the researchers failed to ask, however was whether anybody cared.

Career Counsel
If you want to limit your work life to certain areas—keep it, in other words, from invading every corner of your life—then don't be afraid to scale down and take a lower-level job.

Of course, many people do care about the meaningfulness of their working lives. In fact, they have such a sense of vocation that the meaning is almost all that matters. I know a retired teacher who's still volunteering as a tutor at his old school. "I couldn't live without teaching," he told me.

The important thing is to know how much work means to you and at what level you want to be. If it's logical for you, that's probably enough whether or not your career follows industry (or social) norms.

Not long ago I had breakfast with a man who used to run a janitorial service. "I had Ph.D.s on my staff," he told me. "They needed some extra income, so they'd come in and clean buildings late at night. It was a great job from their perspective." "Why's that?" I asked. "Because nobody'd see 'em!" But think of the other opportunities these people might have had—as retail clerks in a store that sold products they enjoyed, for example, or teleservice representatives for a business within their specialty—had they been less sensitive to the reactions of others.

Finding Your Phoenix

Sometimes, career problems can't be hidden. Here's one last anecdote from the world of sports:

Last month, I spent some time with Mike Veeck, a celebrated minor-league baseball owner who is the son of the legendary Bill Veeck, one of major-league baseball's great innovators. Mike is riding high these days, operating the St. Paul Saints of the Class A Northern League. (That's the lowest—and, some would say, most entertaining—level of the minor leagues.) One of his partners is the comedian Bill Murray. The night I interviewed Veeck, his team had drawn a million fans in just over four years, which is pretty remarkable for a minor-league team at this level.

Veeck has received all kinds of accolades and national media coverage for his efforts. His team was the subject of a television special, *Baseball Minnesota*, and a new book is reportedly in the offing. It was Mike Veeck who helped Darryl Strawberry recover his baseball career after a long battle with drug and alcohol addiction threatened to end his career.

"Darryl Strawberry rose from his ashes," Veeck said with some feeling. "He started with the lowly St. Paul Saints—hit 18 home runs in 29 games—and ended up with the New York Yankees in a World Series. We get a ticker-tape parade and a World Series ring. They don't come any more Biblical than that!"

"Where Am I?": Overcoming Obstacles

As I spoke with Veeck, I found that his own story wasn't much different. In 1981, at age 29, he'd left major league baseball when his father sold the Chicago White Sox. Mike had been through a volatile time as a minority partner in the team. In 1979, he'd come up with a unique promotion—Disco Demolition Night—when fans were encouraged to bring disco records and burn them in a bonfire after a ball game. It was a fine idea, except that, lubricated with liquid refreshments, a group of rowdy fans began flinging the records onto the field, threatening to decapitate the umpires and the opposition. The game was called and forfeited, and the promotion became a black mark in big-league baseball history.

To make matters worse, the following year, Mike got in a fight with an ex-ballplayer on-camera, during a TV broadcast. By then, others could recognize what he could not. Mike Veeck had a serious drinking problem. "I could not get a job," he recalls. "And I wrote letters—a lot of which I'd like to have back—to people who never even accorded me the decency of a response…"

Mike spent a lot of time away from the game he loved. He's still angry about it.

"Where Am I?": Beyond the "Bone Heap"

Part of Mike's problem was that while his father, Bill, had been popular with the media, he'd aggravated some other major league franchise owners with his promotional stunts. (The most famous of the elder Veeck's ploys was hiring a midget to pinch hit for the St. Louis Browns, but there were dozens more just as outlandish.) Yet, the larger part of Mike's problem was his own. "I kept drinking, kept drinking… And about a year later I went down the sewer—lost everything. My marriage fell apart, my wife took my son… I'd look in the mirror, and I'd look away. And, um, I dunno, six months later or eight months later, I went to Alcoholics Anonymous…" That was Mike's life only eight years ago.

"In 1989, the end of the year, Marv Goldklang (a partner in the Yankees) called… Picked up the phone, he goes, 'I think there oughta be a Veeck in baseball.' And I said to him, 'If you think I've never heard that line before!' and I hung up. And he called back and he said, 'Well, you're as rude as they said you were. What do you have to recommend you?'

I said, 'I work hard. I'm honest. I used to be pretty good. I lost 10 years of my professional career right now, though, so—I don't know…'

And he said, 'Can we get together and meet?' I said, 'Sure, why not?' He's kinda pushy. He didn't care about my reputation. All he cared about was had I really stopped drinking and was I not in fights all the time. I said, 'Well, I'm old now.' Three or four meetings and he and Bill Murray [and another partner] hired me to run the Miami Miracle.

They rescued me from the bone heap. [I] took a 70 percent cut in pay and was thrilled! Was introduced to minor league baseball seven years ago, and I fell in love all over again…"

"Where Am I?": The Bottom Line

Career Counsel

"Security is mostly a superstition. It does not exist in nature... Avoiding danger is no safer in the long run than outright exposure. Life is either a daring adventure or nothing."

—Helen Keller

"So," Veeck says now, "I sleep real well at night. I love these [fans] out here for what they've done—not only for the Saints but for me personally. It was a tremendous validation when I needed it desperately..."

"It's like Darryl Strawberry," says Veeck. The point is, "There's a chance. There's death and rebirth. Darryl Strawberry represents the phoenix in all of us. He rose from his ashes."

Isn't that the bottom line in this business of changing careers? We can change our lives. And sometimes we have to.

The Other Side of the Page

On the right side of your legal pad—the "Where's the Market?" section—I'll propose a set of well-known questions. They're the same questions journalists use to frame a news story: What? How? Who? Where? Why?

If you've been paying attention to the earlier chapters of this book, the approach I'm about to outline will look pretty familiar to you. That's good, because if your goal is to reconnect with the workplace after a significant time away, these questions should be second nature to you.

Say you've been out of the workplace for a while and are addressing a new field, or even a familiar field that doesn't quite feel familiar. Try asking the following questions as you interview people who can help you get your bearings.

"Where's the Market?": The "What" Factor

The first word to write down on the right side of your legal pad is "What?"

What are these people doing in this organization? What's the product or service they're providing? Has the industry in which they're working changed?

My father was in the transatlantic steamship business back in the 1930s. He booked passengers on trips to Europe aboard such stately vessels as the Queen Elizabeth and the Queen Mary. Those ships were virtually floating luxury hotels and the company's advertising slogan was, "Getting There Is Half the Fun." But with the outbreak of World War II, the transatlantic steamship business closed down in four days. After the war, my Dad returned to work for the same firm...but it was clear that their business would never be the same. Airlines were burgeoning; the first thing people looked for now in crossing the Atlantic was speed. "Getting There Is Half the Fun?" Not anymore, it wasn't.

Yet, my father still made a living in the travel industry, even as the steamship business shrank. And many of his skills transferred to related areas of the travel industry. He used his organizational skills to help a large group of independent travel agents throughout the Upper Midwest band together in a trade association. And all that time, as the steamship business waned, the travel industry thrived. Today, it is the world's largest industry. Fortunately, my father was able to look to the larger trend.

That's the kind of scenario that may await you in a field where you once worked—say, newspaper publishing in an age of interactive electronic communication. You'll want to find the basic business that has not gone out of date and try to connect some of your core competencies to it.

"Where's the Market?": The "How" Factor

This is a question we've come back to again and again. How is the work being done today?

If you don't find an appropriate program, and if it seems that others are in the same boat, don't be afraid to take the lead and organize the kind of course you need. Buttonhole the dean of the local community college, and make it clear to him or her how many people need the kind of training you're looking for.

Career Counsel
If your technical skills could use some fast-forwarding, a professional association may be the best place to turn. It may be that the association has made arrangements with a local community college to offer fast-track courses to people such as you.

"Where's the Market?": The "Who" Factor

Who are the people working in your field these days? Ask this question not just in terms of skills and training, but workplace culture as well. Tory, a fellow I know in Portland, Oregon came across a newspaper ad for a position in tenant relations. It was with a company that rented houseboats on the Willamette and Columbia Rivers. They were trying to hire somebody who could write up policies and provide good customer service. But at the bottom of the ad, he came across this line: "Must be a good cook."

"Huh?" Tory muttered. "What's that have to do with it?"

Tory did a little background research and found this company had a close-knit staff that thrived on monthly potluck lunches. These were no mere salad-and-casserole affairs. There were some real gourmets in the crowd. In addition, they closed the office several times a year for an all-day yacht cruise where all they did was chow down on delicacies.

At this point, Tory's eyes lit up. What a workplace! So he retargeted his resume, enrolled in a gourmet cooking class, and exuded enthusiasm in his interview. Today, he's happily employed with the rest of the food fans, swilling mimosas and forking down lobster thermador on the back deck of a yacht. See? Research pays off!

"Where's the Market?": The "Where" Factor

Is there a particular locale where the industry in which you're interested is based? The research group DRI McGraw Hill has done some interesting studies on *industry clusters*. These industries may have common needs for personnel or technology. Or they may be close to an important natural resource. Suppliers tend to put down roots in the same seedbed. That's where "supplier networks" take hold.

In Appendix B, you'll find a list of industry clusters based on the DRI McGraw Hill research. It's not an exhaustive list, but it will suggest a pattern that appears in most

Job Jargon
Industry clusters refer to locations where businesses in the same industry tend to gather.

industries. Each of them has a "home base" where most of their activity goes on. Notice how often New York City appears on these lists. So does Los Angeles. Those may not be the leading entries in the latest best-places-to-live survey—and, remember, this list is not complete—but the truth is, if you want to carve out a career in, say, the film industry, chances are you'd better make tracks for L.A. That may not be where your career will wind up, but that's probably the place where it had better begin.

Where Lone Eagles Soar

But what if you're no longer a novice? Suppose you're about to resume a career in which you have considerable expertise. Is it possible that you could hang out a shingle and do your thing in a locale of your own choosing?

Job Jargon
A **lone eagle** is a self-employed professional who handles all or nearly all aspects of a one-person business. They can work wherever they like.

According to some research I've been conducting, the answer is, decidedly, yes. For the past few years, I've been tracking patterns of the U.S. Department of Commerce, which keeps track of people who file Schedule C income tax forms, designating self-employment. These are sole proprietors: the kind of people my colleague, Phil Burgess, calls *lone eagles*.

Both Phil and I have met many of these individuals. Often, they're corporate refugees who've used today's technology to set up an entrepreneurial home-office environment. In many instances, they've sold consulting services back to their original employers sometimes doing essentially the same work they did before.

Tracking the Flocks Further

About two-thirds of the counties where lone eagles are multiplying at the fastest rates are in the suburbs of large cities. That's no surprise if we assume that many of these people are continuing to do business with former employers. The employers are nearby and that's where the eagles own their houses. A few years ago, an economic development agency in one of the suburbs south of Denver took a survey of local software development companies. They found 91 of them! And they were astonished. Their area hardly qualified as a second Silicon Valley.

So they took a closer look at the software firms. Almost all of them, it turned out, were one-person operations housed in home offices. The software developers were doing contract work for the same large aerospace firm that had originally let them go.

> ## Bet You Didn't Know
>
> If you decide to go it alone, you'll be part of one of the most dramatic shifts in the modern American economy. Between 1969 and 1994, the number of sole proprietors filing Schedule C forms—tax forms associated with self-employment—grew by an astonishing 86 percent.

That's typical of the majority of counties where lone eagles are nesting. But the other third of the cases are very different. What's distinctive about these places is that they lie a fair distance beyond the commuting range of major cities.

The Death of the Daily Commute

McHenry County in Illinois is one example. While I'm told some people commute from there every day on the train into Chicago, I'm here to tell you that I'd hate to try it. Yet McHenry County shows high rates of growth among lone eagles.

Now take a look at Whatcom County, Washington, which lies within hailing distance of Seattle to the south and Vancouver, British Columbia northward. But are those cities within daily commuting range? Not really. Yet that's where a lot of lone eagles are setting up shop.

The trend is clear—lone eagles are establilshing themselves within driving distance but not regular commuting distance of major cities. They're letting modems do the commuting work for them. And they're saving business trips to the city for relatively rare occasions.

Take a look at the other counties on the following table, which identifies the top 20 counties with the fastest growth rates in proprietorships for the period 1989–1994. (Minimum 10,000 proprietorships in 1989.)

*McHenry County,
Illinois*

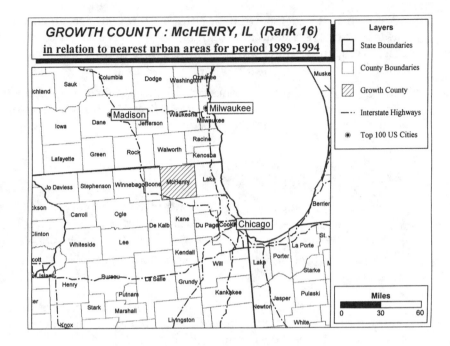

*Whatcom County,
Washington*

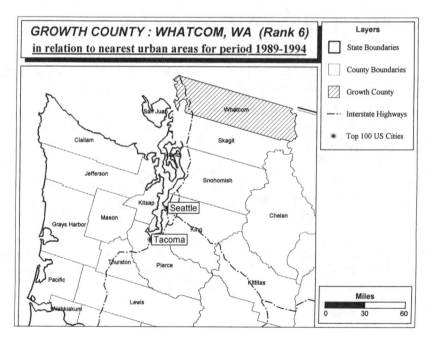

Top 20 Fastest-Growth Proprietorships by County

Rank	State	County or Area Name	Growth Rate 1989–1994
1	Texas	Fort Bend	40.89%
2	Idaho	Ada	33.75%
3	Texas	Randall	33.58%
4	Florida	Seminole	33.41%
5	Washington	Kitsap	33.31%
6	Washington	Whatcom	32.79%
7	Nevada	Clark	32.72%
8	Indiana	Hamilton	32.08%
9	Georgia	Gwinnett	31.67%
10	New Mexico	Santa Fe	31.40%
11	Washington	Thurston	30.40%
12	Texas	Montgomery	30.02%
13	Texas	Collin	29.59%
14	Washington	Snohomish	29.09%
15	Washington	Clark	29.49%
16	Illinois	McHenry	27.73%
17	Florida	Orange	26.67%
18	Minnesota	Anoka	26.45%
19	Florida	Collier	26.40%
20	Oregon	Deschutes	26.32%

(Minimum 10,000 proprietorships in 1989.)

Some of these counties are far from cities. They're mighty nice places to live if you don't need a city every day, which many of these folks don't. And that's my theory when it comes to lone eagles. Most of these people need access to a city the way middle-aged people need sex. It's still a requirement, but not every day!

If you are in a position to market your career skills on an independent basis, consider whether you can do so in a setting of your own choosing. (Perhaps a move to a new area will ease some of the financial demands you face.) Today's telecommunications hookups are so efficient that it may be possible for you to work in ways you never dreamed possible—perhaps making a once-a-week, or even a once-a-month trek into The Big City as needed.

"Where's the Market?": The "Why" Factor

Finally, I'll add the question "Why?" to the right column because in the last analysis, I don't think anyone returning to the workplace after a long absence can get around it. Why does the work going on in this field interest you? Spend as much time as you can addressing that fundamental question.

The Fateful Question

I'll never forget the experience of writing a news article some years ago, when I was just breaking into journalism. I was doing so, not as a fresh-faced young recent grad, but as a mature worker who'd made a choice to explore something new.

My editor warned me about the subject I was taking on when she assigned me the story. It was on glitches in the health care system—something called "the Utah gap" that could leave people destitute if they had just a bit too much money to qualify for Medicaid.

I called an elderly woman who was confined to a wheel chair and now had to change nursing homes because she'd fallen into the Utah gap. She had just a little bit too much income for the government to pay for where she was—the home where all her friends were. I spent hours researching that story, and I did a pretty good job of making a very complex issue accessible.

Finally, I called the nursing home resident and told her when the story would appear. She thanked me for all the work I'd done, and then she paused for a moment. Then, she asked an unexpected, and unsettling, question. "Bill, does this subject mean anything to you? The substance of it?"

The honest answer, I realized, had to be "no." I was trying to learn how to break into newspaper reporting, and to me this health care story, in and of itself, had simply represented a new challenge to me as part of that career goal. I didn't want to hear anything more about the logistics of medical insurance.

But today, I could tell her about a good friend, a psychotherapist, who's trying so hard to enter the field of health care policy that he's driving a bus while he studies on his own and applies for jobs in his new field. That's what it means to follow your own leadings, to pursue a vocation.

Career Counsel

"To be nobody but yourself—in a world which is doing its best, night and day, to make you everybody else—means to fight the hardest battle which any human being can fight, and never stop fighting."

— e. e. cummings

Toward "Hey! This Matters!"

So ask yourself, does the subject you're taking on really mean anything to you? The substance of it? And if the answer you get back is "no," ask yourself, is there something else you should be devoting your day to?

In the long run, answering such questions honestly is what changing careers comes down to. It's about finding your way to a place where someone needs what you can do, and where you feel your energies are truly well invested.

The Least You Need to Know

➤ Ask yourself: Where am I?

➤ Ask yourself: Where's the market?

➤ If the career re-entry strategy you pick is logical for *you*, that's probably enough—whether or not your career follows industry (or social) norms.

➤ Consider the "lone eagle" working mode—it may make sense for you.

➤ Always ask yourself, does the direction you're taking really mean something to you?

Online Resources

Here's a listing of some popular career-related Web sites. Check them out to get a feel for this new mode of hiring.

The Riley Guide (Employment Opportunities and Job Resources on the Internet). Compiled by Margaret Riley, author of *The Guide to Internet Job Searching*. Internet columnist, *National Business Employment Weekly*.
http://www.jobtrak.com/jobguide/

Career Mosaic. Job listings can be searched by keyword or you can choose a listed company and view its available positions. Information about each company is included. There is also an index by geographical locale.
http://www.careermosaic.com/cm/

JobBank USA. A good site for jobs in many kinds of fields. Can be searched by keyword, company name, or a specific field.
http://www.jobbankusa.com

The Monster Board. Sponsored by a large recruitment agancy in New England. Offers an overview of major employers and several interfaces for job hunting.
http://www.monster.com/

Online Career Center. Enormous database of job listings that can be searched by geographic regions or keywords. Includes a resume bank for submission by e-mail. **http://www.occ.com/occ**

E-Span (The Interactive Employment Network). Provides a searchable database of job openings as well as a wide variety of resources for the job seeker. Accepts resumes and transmits job postings via e-mail. **http://www.espan.com/**

The Current Hot Employment Industries

As I've written before in this book, the idea of isolating a single, growing job category—and then placing all of one's career "eggs" in that basket—is not recommended. The problem with that approach is that we live in a very fast-moving economy. Job titles are constantly shifting, as are the skills necessary to perform them.

My advice—familiar, no doubt, from the main chapters in this book—is to focus on the problems associated with the target industry you've selected, rather than on job titles that may change from month to month (or, let's face it, week to week). That said, it's worthwhile to share the following information from the U.S. Department of Labor on projected growth by occupation.

I've adapted the growth data from "Employment by Occupation," a table compiled by the Bureau of Labor Statistics, and focused on job categories that the Labor Department predicts will grow significantly between the middle '90s and the middle of the first decade of the 21st century. The highest-growth occupations are listed at the top. I've excluded some categories predicted to grow dramatically because the labels attached to them (i.e., "All Other Professional Workers") seemed too broad to be very helpful.

What follows, then, is a snapshot of select, broadly defined jobs now experiencing robust growth. Both total projected job openings due to growth and net replacement and projected percentage increase are between 1994 and 2005. Included (following this listing) is an overview of where the growth potential is for certain industries. This information may be helpful to you as you develop your career goals and develop a sense of the kinds of job-creation patterns today's economy is producing.

For more specific information (such as earnings and typical training prerequisites), see the *Occupational Outlook Handbook*, published by the Bureau of Labor Statistics and available at most public libraries. (My thanks to Dave McDermott and Virginia Guzman of BLS for their assistance with this section.)

Occupation: Computer engineers and scientists
Total projected job openings due to growth and net replacement: 819,000
Projected percentage increase: 90 percent

Occupation: Homemakers/home health aides
Total projected job openings due to growth and net replacement: 747,000
Projected percentage increase: 107 percent

Occupation: Systems analysts
Total projected job openings due to growth and net replacement: 481,000
Projected percentage increase: 92 percent

Occupation: Teacher's aides and educational assistants
Total projected job openings due to growth and net replacement: 480,000
Projected percentage increase: 39 percent

Occupation: Police officers/detectives
Total projected job openings due to growth and net replacement: 416,000
Projected percentage increase: 24 percent

Occupation: Social workers
Total projected job openings due to growth and net replacement: 288,000
Projected percentage increase: 34 percent

Occupation: Special education teachers
Total projected job openings due to growth and net replacement: 262,000
Projected percentage increase: 53 percent

Occupation: Human services workers
Total projected job openings due to growth and net replacement: 170,000
Projected percentage increase: 75 percent

Occupation: Medical assistants
Total projected job openings due to growth and net replacement: 155,000
Projected percentage increase: 59 percent

Occupation: Dental assistants
Total projected job openings due to growth and net replacement: 137,000
Projected percentage increase: 42 percent

Occupation: Physical therapists
Total projected job openings due to growth and net replacement: 96,000
Projected percentage increase: 80 percent

Occupation: Physical and corrective therapy assistants and aides
Total projected job openings due to growth and net replacement: 87,000
Projected percentage increase: 83 percent

Occupation: Medical records technicians
Total projected job openings due to growth and net replacement: 59,000
Projected percentage increase: 56 percent

Occupation: Occupational therapists
Total projected job openings due to growth and net replacement: 47,000
Projected percentage increase: 72 percent

On the Decline

It may be just as helpful, in developing a sense of how the current economy affects employment patterns, to take a look at a few representative categories tracked by the Department of Labor that are projected to *decline* during the same period.

Industrial production managers: down 7 percent

Communication, transportation, and utilities operations managers: down 12 percent

Directory assistance operators: down 70 percent

Computer operators and peripheral equipment operators: down 39 percent

(That is to say, people whose *primary role* is to operate computers and peripheral equipment. The increasing accessibility of technology means that more and more of us operate computers without having to be experts.)

Typists and word processors: down 33 percent (much the same phenomenon)

File clerks: down 15 percent

Billing, posting, and calculating machine operators: down 67 percent

Precision structural metal fitters: down 35 percent

Regional Growth Industries

Particular regions are strongly associated with growth in certain industries. If you're interested in entering one of the following fields, you should know that your odds of initiating a successful career change will go up if you live in one of the metropolitan areas listed after that industry. The areas are listed in order of industry leadership.

Aerospace/Defense

1. Seattle/Tacoma/Bremerton, Washington
2. Wichita, Kansas
3. Biloxi, Mississippi

Agriculture/Food Processing

1. Los Angeles/Riverside/Orange County, California
2. Chicago, Illinois/Gary, Indiana/Kenosha, Wisconsin
3. Fayetteville, Arkansas

Automotive Products

1. Detroit/Ann Arbor/Flint, Michigan
2. Kokomo, Indiana
3. Elkhart, Indiana

Biomedical Products

1. New York City metropolitan area
2. Greenville, South Carolina
3. Philadelphia, Pennsylvania/Wilmington, Delaware/Atlantic City, New Jersey

Business Services

1. New York City metropolitan area
2. Washington, D.C./Baltimore, Maryland
3. Los Angeles/Riverside/Orange County, California

Construction Products

1. Los Angeles/Riverside/Orange County, California
2. Lakeland, Florida
3. Columbus, Georgia

Educational Services

1. New York City metropolitan area
2. Boston, Massachusetts and outlying areas
3. Provo, Utah

Electronic Machinery and Systems

1. San Francisco Bay Area metropolitan area
2. Binghamton, New York
3. Boston, Massachusetts and outlying areas

Energy and Processed Materials

1. Houston/Galveston/Brazoria, Texas
2. Odessa, Texas
3. Los Angeles/Riverside/Orange County, California

Fashion, Apparel, and Textile Products

1. Greenville, South Carolina
2. Hickory, North Carolina
3. Danville, Virginia

Financial Services

1. New York City/New Jersey/Long Island
2. Bloomington, Illinois
3. Hartford, Conneticut

Forest Products

1. Appleton, Wisconsin
2. Wausau, Wisconsin
3. New York City/New Jersey/Long Island

Health Services

1. New York City/New Jersey/Long Island
2. Rochester, Minnesota
3. Los Angeles/Riverside/Orange County, California

Home and Lifestyle Products

1. Hickory, North Carolina
2. Greensboro, North Carolina
3. Los Angeles/Riverside/Orange County, California

Industrial Machinery

1. Rochester, New York
2. Chicago, Illinois/Gary, Indiana/Kenosha, Wisconsin
3. Rockford, Illinois

Info/Media/Entertainment Services

1. New York City/New Jersey/Long Island
2. Los Angeles/Riverside/Orange County, California
3. Washington, D.C./Baltimore, Maryland

Metals

1. Steubenville, Ohio
2. Chicago, Illinois/Gary, Indiana/Kenosha, Wisconsin
3. Los Angeles/Riverside/Orange County, California

Tourism and Recreation

1. Las Vegas, Nevada
2. Orlando, Florida
3. Reno, Nevada

Transportation, Trade, and Distribution

1. New York City/New Jersey/Long Island
2. Los Angeles/Riverside/Orange County, California
3. Laredo, Texas

(Source: Economic Competitiveness Group, DRI McGraw Hill)

Associations and Advocacy Groups

One of the best ways to gain information about a new industry or career field is to take advantage of the resources offered by an association or advocacy group. Here's a brief sampling of some of the most prominent organizations. A fuller list can be found at your local library. If you don't find information here for a group that reflects activity in an industry of interest to you, ask the reference librarian for help identifying an organization that fits your profile.

Many of the following organizations have local or regional chapters that may be helpful to you. Ask about local affiliates.

AARP (American Association of
Retired Persons)
601 E Street
Washington DC 20049
202/434-2277

Actors Equity Association
165 W. 46th Street
New York, NY 10036
212/869-8530

Air Line Pilots Association
535 Herndon Parkway
Herndon, VA 20170
703/689-2270

American Bar Association
750 N. Lake Shore Drive
Chicago, IL 60611-4497
312/988-5000

American Business Women's Association
9100 Ward Parkway
P.O. Box 8728
Kansas City, MO 64114
816/361-6621

American Counseling Association
5999 Stevenson Avenue
Alexandria, VA 22304
703/823-9800

American Hospital Association
1 North Franklin
Chicago, IL 60606
312/422-3000

American Institute of Architects
1735 New York Avenue NW
Washington DC 20006
202/626-7300

American Institute of Certified Public
Accountants
1211 Avenue of the Americas
New York, NY 10036
212/596-6200

American Institute of Mining,
Metallurgical and Petroleum Engineers
345 East 47th Street
New York, NY 10017
212/705-7695

American Library Association
50 East Huron Street
Chicago, IL 60611
312/944-6780

American Management Association
1601 Broadway
New York, NY 10019
212/586-8100

American Nurses Association
600 Maryland Avenue SW
Suite 100
Washington DC 20024-2571
202/554-4444

American Physical Therapy Association
1111 N. Fairfax Street
Alexandria, VA 22314
703/684-2782

American Society for Quality Control
611 East Wisconsin Avenue
Milwaukee, WI 53201
414/272-8575

American Society of Appraisers
P.O. Box 17265
Washington DC 20041
703/478-2228

American Society of Civil Engineers
1801 Alexander Bell Drive
Reston, VA 20191-4400

American Society of Clinical Pathologists
2100 West Harrison Street
Chicago, IL 60612-3798
312/738-1336

American Society of Heating, Refrigeration
and Air-Conditioning Engineers
1791 Tullie Circle NE
Atlanta, GA 30329
404/636-8400

American Society of Interior Designers
608 Massachusetts Avenue NE
Washington DC 20002
202/546-3480

American Society of Journalists and
Authors
1501 Broadway
Suite 302
New York, NY 10036
212/997-0947

American Society of Magazine Editors
919 Third Avenue, 22nd Floor
New York, NY 10022
212/752-0055

American Society of Mechanical Engineers
c/o Dr. Dean Mook
Dept. of Engineering, Science, and
Mechanics
Virginia Tech
Blacksburg, VA 24801-1176
540/231-4175

American Society of Newspaper Editors
11690-B Sunrise Valley Drive
Reston, VA 20191
703/453-1122

American Veterans Committee
6309 Bannockburn Drive
Bethesda, MD 20817
301/320-6490

Association for Investment Management
and Research
5 Boar's Head Lane
P.O. Box 3668
Charlottesville, VA 22903
804/977-6600

Association of Conservation Engineers
Alabama Department of Conservation
and Natural Resources
Engineering Section
64 North Union Street
Montgomery, AL 36310
334/242-3476

Association of Consulting Chemists and
Chemical Engineers
The Chemists Club
P.O. Box 297
Sparta, NJ 07871
212/983-3160

Association of General Contractors of
America
1957 E Street NW
Washington DC 20008
202/393-2040

Association of Legal Administrators
175 East Hawthorn Parkway #325
Vernon Hills, IL 60061
847/816-1212

Authors League of America
330 W. 42nd Street, 29th Floor
New York, NY 10036-6902
212/564-8350

Bibliographical Society of America
P.O. Box 397, Grand Central Station
New York, NY 10163
212/452-2710

Digital Printing and Imaging Association
10015 Main Street
Fairfax, VA 22031
703/385-1335

Direct Marketing Association, Inc.
1120 Avenue of the Americas
New York, NY 10036
212/768-7277

Drug, Chemical, and Allied Trades
Association
2 Roosevelt Avenue
Syosset, NY 11791
516/496-3317

Exec-U-Net (employment networking
organization aimed at needs of
executives)
25 Van Zant Street
Norwalk, CT 06855
203/851-5180

Federal Career Opportunities (newsletter)
c/o Federal Research Opportunities
Box 1059
243 Church Street NW
Vienna, VA 22183
703/281-0200

Forty Plus Club of New York
(objective: assist job-seekers over 40)
15 Park Row, Suite 810
New York, NY 10038

Gray Panthers Project Fund
2025 Pennsylvania Avenue NW
Suite 821
Washington DC 20006
202/466-3132

Information Industry Association
1625 Massachusetts Avenue NW
Suite 700
Washington DC 20036
202/986-0280

Institute of Food Technologists
221 N. Lasalle
Suite 300
Chicago, IL 60601
312/782-8424

Institute of Industrial Engineers
25 Technology Park
Norcross, GA 30092
770/449-0461

Institute of Management Consultants
521 Fifth Avenue, 35th Floor
New York, NY 10175-3598
212/697-8262

International Association of Business
Communicators
One Hallidie Plaza
Suite 600
San Francisco, CA 94102
415/433-3400

International Circulation Managers
Association
11600 Sunrise Valley Drive
Reston, VA 22091
703/648-1150

National Aeronautic Association
1815 N. Fort Myer Drive
Suite 700
Arlington, VA 22209
703/527-0226

National Association for Female
Executives
135 W. 50th Street
New York, NY 10003
212/445-6235

National Association of Broadcasters
1771 N Street NW
Washington DC 20036
202/429-5300

National Association of Legal Secretaries
314 East Third Street, Suite 210
Tulsa, OK 74120
918/582-5188

National Association of Life Underwriters
1922 F Street NW
Washington DC 20006
202/331-6000

National Association of the Physically
Handicapped
Bethesda Scarlet Oaks
440 Lafayette Avenue #GA4
Cincinnati, OH 45220
513/861-0400

National Business Education Association
1914 Association Drive
Reston, VA 22091
703/860-8300

National Cartoonists Society
2676 Gerritsen Avenue
Brooklyn, NY 11229
718/627-1550

National Educational Association
1201 16th Street NW
Washington DC 20036
202/833-4000

National Environmental Health
Association
720 South Colorado Boulevard
Suite 970
Denver, CO 80222
303/756-9090

National Federation of Federal Employees
1016 16th Street NW
Washington DC 20036
202/862-4400

National Institute of Graphic Arts
164 Fifth Avenue
New York, NY 10021
212/255-4004

National Society of Professional Engineers
1420 King Street
Alexandria, VA 22314
703/684-2800

Professional Secretaries International/
The Association for Office Professionals
P.O. Box 20404
Kansas City, MO 64195
816/891-6600

Professional Photographers of America
57 Forsyth Street NW
Suite 1600
Atlanta, GA 30303
404/522-8600

Screen Actors Guild
5757 Wilshire Boulevard
Los Angeles, CA 90036
213/954-1600

Society for Human Resource Management
606 North Washington Street
Alexandria, VA 22314
703/548-3440

Society of Exploration Geophysicists
Box 702740
Tulsa, OK 74170-2740
918/493-3516

Society of Illustrators
128 East 63rd Street
New York, NY 10021
212/838-2560

Society of Motion Picture and Television
Engineers
595 West Hartsdale Avenue
White Plains, NY 10607
914/761-1100

Society of Plastics Engineers
14 Fairfield Drive
Brookfield, CT 06804
203/775-0471

Society of Professional Journalists
16 South Jackson Street
Greencastle, IN 46135
765/653-3333

Society of Women Engineers
120 Wall Street, 11th Floor
New York, NY 10005
212/509-9577

Writer's Guild of America
7000 West Third Street
Los Angeles, CA 90048
213/951-4000

Employment Letters for Career Changers

In this appendix, you'll find outlines and complete samples for a number of effective employment letters. Whether you're trying to take advantage of an existing contact, upgrading a new one, or creating a new relationship by means of a written appeal and a follow-up phone call, you'll find some helpful strategies here.

This basic letter—which needs some phone research on your part—may be one of the most effective tools available to you if you're most comfortable making initial contact via a letter. But don't make the mistake of assuming that simply writing and sending letters is enough to develop a list of hot prospects. As you'll see in the following examples, these letters have a built-in "I'll plan to call you" postscript. Use it! Once you do, I think you'll find the follow-up process relatively easy.

The letter is strongest when it's used in combination with a contact you develop within the target industry. That person's name should lead the main text of your letter: "Jane Smith of the Widget Development Department suggested I contact you..."

This is a classic, powerful appeal that's hard to forget after it's been scanned even once. Keep it to a single page! Don't go off on tangents—keep the reader's attention riveted on precise matches between what you have to offer and the requirements of the position, as you've been able to determine them. Save your detailed employment information for the interview...and don't make the mistake of beginning the letter with those dreaded words "Please consider this my application for the position of..."

Remember, don't call these letters—or any of the others that appear in this book—"cover letters." You are better off using letters like the ones in this appendix to develop an initial meeting—or at least a contact—and then finding some other way to deliver a customized resume in person. As I mentioned earlier in the book, you will increase the odds of your developing a meaningful connection if you do your level best to hand over a customized resume, rather than mail one with a cover letter.

Your Name
Your Address
Your City, State, and Zip

(Insert today's date)

Your Contact's Name
Your Contact's Organization
Organization Address
City, State, and Zip

Dear Mr./Ms. (contact's last name):

The very first words of the body text should probably be the name of the person who referred you and a brief explanation of your relationship to that person; follow up by explaining the nature of the opportunity you understand to be available. Move directly into an aggressive, well-researched, two-column summary of what makes your candidacy a perfect fit.

HEADLINE READING "REQUIREMENTS" OR "QUALIFICATIONS"	HEADLINE READING "(YOUR NAME'S) EXPERIENCE"
List the first job requirement here.	List experience that directly and specifically fulfills or exceeds the first requirement here.
List the second job requirement here.	List experience that directly and specifically fulfills or exceeds the second requirement here.
List the third job requirement here.	List experience that directly and specifically fulfills or exceeds the third requirement here.
List the fourth job requirement here.	List experience that directly and specifically fulfills or exceeds the fourth requirement here.

In your closing paragraph, suggest that you and the contact discuss the possibility of your making a contribution to the organization.

Use a salutation like "Sincerely," or "Yours truly,"

(Your signature here)

Your name
Your daytime and evening telephone numbers

P.S.: Include a tactful but persistent update here about the specific time and date you plan to follow up with a phone call.

Vera Jones
321 Elm Street
Boston, MA 02134

March 1, 1998

Jake Bossman
EFI Corporation
321 Maple Street
Boston, MA 02134

Dear Mr. Bossman:

Frank Rodriguez, of the Widget Reconstruction Department, suggested during a break in one of his recent seminars that I get in touch with you about the opening in your department for a Senior Widget Process Analyst. Here's why you should interview me for this job:

EFI'S REQUIREMENTS:	VERA JONES'S EXPERIENCE:
Three years of process analysis experience in large-scale systems.	Four years of process analysis experience in large-scale systems.
Familiarity with WidgetGauge software.	Familiarity with WidgetGauge software.
Two years experience in supervisory role.	Two and a half years' experience in supervisory role.
American Council of Engineers Certification.	American Council of Engineers Certification.

Let's talk soon about the contributions I could make to EFI!

Sincerely,

(Signature here)

Vera Jones
617/555-1212 (h) 617/555-1213, ext. 111 (w)

P.S.: I will plan to call you on Monday, March 5, at 8:00 a.m. to discuss this opening.

Here's an example of a letter that catches the reader just a little off-guard. That's probably a good approach if you're writing someone "cold," because starting your letter with a timeworn opening will make the reader assume that you look, sound, and act just like every other applicant on the block. Opening the letter with a well-researched, responsibly cited analysis, on the other hand, is likely to win you a measure of recognition when you call to follow up.

Your Name
Your Address
Your City, State, and Zip

(Insert today's date)

Your Contact's Name
Your Contact's Organization
Organization Address
City, State, and Zip

Dear Mr./Ms. (contact's last name):

Launch the main text without any attempt at self-introduction by citing a recent industry development from a respected source. Develop a preliminary conclusion, based on the trend you've identified, that is of direct and immediate interest to your reader. In other words, pretend you're a consultant offering a one-paragraph free sample: Your objective in the first paragraph is to make the reader just a little edgy—"Who is this person…and where did he track down this information?"

In the second paragraph, introduce yourself briefly and explain that you've been following the industry closely. Tell why you have been impressed by the target organization. Show off a little more of your research by demonstrating your familiarity with an important organizational objective—perhaps one elucidated by the president, director, or other high official within the target organization. Conclude by explaining that you're in a good position to help the organization attain key objectives in that area by virtue of your experience, background, accomplishments, skills, etc.

* Specific skill/experience (first bullet)

* Specific skill/experience (second bullet)

* Specific skill/experience (third and final bullet)

Close the body text of the letter by suggesting that both you and the contact could benefit from an in-person meeting about the savings, efficiency, or new income opportunity you've examined in the letter.

Use a salutation like "Sincerely," or "Yours truly,"

(Your signature here)

Your name
Your daytime and evening telephone numbers

P.S.: Include a tactful but persistent update here about the specific time and date you plan to follow up with a phone call.

Vera Jones
321 Elm Street
Boston, MA 02134

March 1, 1998

Jake Bossman
EFI Corporation
321 Maple Street
Boston, MA 02134

Dear Mr. Bossman:

According to a recent article in *Widgets Today*, significant changes are forecast in the way consumers purchase and replace home widget units: "Thanks to new electronic purchasing tools, a thorough review of consumer-based widget pricing structures may be in order for industry leaders." (*Widgets Today*, January 1, 1998, page 178.) EFI's dominant position in this industry leads me to believe you may be conducting just such a review in the near future.

I'm an experienced design and data-management professional with a thorough understanding of both engineering and pricing issues. I've been impressed by EFI's record of achievement for a long time, especially your firm's dedication to tapping the home widget market. I feel sure that your company goal of "serving the customer first" will, in the coming months and years, require a seasoned analyst who knows how to obtain cost reductions through redesign and reengineering. My background:

* Four years of process analysis experience in large-scale systems.
* Familiarity with WidgetGauge software.
* Two and a half years of experience in supervisory role.
* American Council of Engineers Certification.

Let's talk soon about the contributions I could make to EFI's efforts to maintain competitive consumer price structures!

Sincerely,

(Your signature here)

Vera Jones
617/555-1212 (h) 617/555-1213, ext. 111 (w)

P.S.: I plan to call you on Monday, March 5, at 8:00 a.m. to discuss the possibility of a mutually beneficial business relationship.

The following model employment letter wins attention, interest, and curiosity by highlighting a single "superstar" achievement of direct relevance to the problems the decision maker faces on any given day. The more your miracle resembles ones your contact would like to see happen on a regular basis, the more likely you are to hear a positive response when you call, as promised, to follow up by phone.

Remember—the idea is to isolate one and only one accomplishment that concisely appeals to the reader's desire to get through the day with (relative) ease.

Your Name
Your Address
Your City, State, and Zip

(Insert today's date)

Your Contact's Name
Your Contact's Organization
Organization Address
City, State, and Zip

Dear Mr./Ms. (contact's last name):

In a single sentence, probably one that begins with "I" and follows with an action verb or a phrase like "was awarded" or "was named," cite a single extraordinary accomplishment that measurably increased productivity, saved time, saved money, raised revenue, or did all four.

In your second paragraph, go into more detail. Describe yourself in confident, unapologetic terms, stressing industry-related competence and your commitment to being a team player. Explain in a single sentence the source that led you to contact the reader and the reason you believe the target organization represents a dynamic, positive working environment where you can make a significant contribution.

Close the body of the letter with a straightforward, enthusiastic request for a personal meeting—but save the specifics of "what will happen next" for the postscript!

Use a salutation like "Sincerely," or "Yours truly,"

(Your signature here)

Your name
Your daytime and evening telephone numbers

P.S.: Include a tactful but persistent update here about the specific time and date you plan to follow up with a phone call.

Vera Jones
321 Elm Street
Boston, MA 02134

March 1, 1998

Jake Bossman
EFI Corporation
321 Maple Street
Boston, MA 02134

Dear Mr. Bossman:

I reconfigured an important database system so that it was accessible to all 45 people in our division, rather than the four or five people who used it most often. This project represented only a weekend's work, but it significantly increased our division's overall effectiveness, and it won me the annual Eagle award for "Best New Initiative" at ABC Accounting in 1996.

After leaving ABC voluntarily in 1997 to take a sabbatical, I have returned to the workforce. I'm eager to learn more about the contributions I could make to those who use complex data and design systems within the widget industry. I'm an experienced design and data management professional with a thorough understanding of both engineering and pricing issues and a team-first attitude. I'm writing you because Frank Rodriguez, in Widget Design, suggested I drop you a line. I was eager to do so, because I've been impressed for some years by your company's achievements within the widget industry.

I think we should meet soon so we can discuss where EFI is going—and what kind of team players you're looking for.

Sincerely,

(Your signature here)

Vera Jones
617/555-1212 (h) 617/555-1213, ext. 111 (w)

P.S.: I will plan to call you on Monday, March 5, at 8:00 a.m. to discuss the possibility of a meeting.

Here you'll find a letter you can use or adapt if you have been able to develop little or no information about the opportunity in question and your contacts within the organization are few. I wouldn't suggest that you spend too much of your time or energy on "low-information" appeals such as this one, but the truth is that, every once in a while, a letter is worth developing for a company about which you don't have a great many facts. This is a straightforward appeal based on existing skills that you feel are likely to resonate with an employer in a specific industry.

Your Name
Your Address
Your City, State, and Zip

(Insert today's date)

Your Contact's Name
Your Contact's Organization
Organization Address
City, State, and Zip

Dear Mr./Ms. (contact's last name):

Mention the name of a front-line administrative person with whom you've spoken within the target organization. Explain that you believe you've determined three of the most important elements for success in the target organization's next hire:

* List your first relevant skill, and an example to back it up in one to two sentences.

* List your second relevant skill, and an example to back it up in one to two sentences.

* List your third relevant skill, and an example to back it up in one to two sentences.

Concisely outline why this organization, as opposed to any other, is of deep interest to you. Express your interest in discussing the possibility of your making a contribution to the firm on a part-time, contract, or full-time basis. Leaving the door open in this way will take a great deal of pressure off the contact, and make it more likely that you'll be well-received when you follow up by phone.

Use a salutation like "Sincerely," or "Yours truly,"

(Your signature here)

Your name
Your daytime and evening telephone numbers

P.S.: Include a tactful but persistent update here about the specific time and date you plan to follow up with a phone call.

Vera Jones
321 Elm Street
Boston, MA 02134

March 1, 1998

Jake Bossman
EFI Corporation
321 Maple Street
Boston, MA 02134

Dear Mr. Bossman:

Yesterday, I had a brief discussion with Eloise, at your reception desk, concerning hiring patterns at EFI. Based on her comments and my own research, I believe I've determined three of the most important elements for a successful new hire in your Redesign department:

* Four years of process analysis experience in large-scale systems; ability to pursue aggressive redesign schedules.
* Deep familiarity with WidgetGauge software.
* Two and a half years of experience in managing and motivating others.

I've been following EFI since it launched the ProWidget model back in 1991; that was truly a breakthrough product, one that was noticed well beyond the reaches of widget industry. I've been similarly struck by your more recent releases. I'd like very much to discuss the possibility of making a contribution to your firm on a part-time, contract, or full-time basis. Can we get together to discuss this?

Sincerely,

(Signature here)

Vera Jones
617/555-1212 (h) 617/555-1213, ext. 111 (w)

P.S.: I will plan to call you on Monday, March 5, at 8:00 a.m. to discuss the possibility of a meeting.

Finally, here's an example of a letter format that you can use after a meeting with a new contact has gone well. So well, in fact, that your suggestion that you develop "some ideas" about independent contractor work within the target organization was greeted with interest. If the idea wasn't shot down, that means there's some level of interest. If the possibility of contract work still exists after your meeting, even on a "that might be interesting to look at" basis, consider taking the initiative with a letter like the following one.

Your Name
Your Address
Your City, State, and Zip

(Insert today's date)

Your Contact's Name
Your Contact's Organization
Organization Address
City, State, and Zip

Dear Mr./Ms. (contact's last name—if your experience within the meeting suggests that the contact is more comfortable conducting business on a first-name basis, you should probably use that):

In a single-sentence paragraph, express your satisfaction about how well the recent meeting went.

Explain what you found most interesting about the meeting, taking care to emphasize those elements of your background that appeared to resonate most positively with your contact. Focus, if possible, on an upcoming project that is subject to some time pressure. Mention that you'd like, with your contact's permission, to assemble an outline of a work agreement that would permit you to help the contact meet a key goal on a temporary, "independent contract" basis. Explain that you'll be assembling both a project outline and a draft of a formal agreement.

Say when you plan to fax or forward this material. Indicate that you'll be following up by phone on a specific date to get your contact's reactions.

Thank your contact for the time he or she has spent with you. Mention a non-business-related topic of mutual interest as the body text of the letter closes.

Use a salutation like "Sincerely," or "Yours truly,"

(Your signature here)

Your name
Your daytime and evening telephone numbers

P.S.: Use the postscript to refocus the reader's attention on your upcoming call.

Vera Jones
321 Elm Street
Boston, MA 02134

March 5, 1998

Jake Bossman
EFI Corporation
321 Maple Street
Boston, MA 02134

Dear Mr. Bossman:

Thanks so much for taking time for our meeting that I thought went quite well.

I was particularly excited about the widget redesigning programs you're implementing at EFI. The Peters 2000 model seemed to me to be the highest item on your priority list. With your permission, I'd like to assemble an outline of a work agreement that would permit me to help EFI meet its goals on this project on a temporary, "independent contract" basis. Today and tomorrow, I'll be assembling both a project outline and a draft of a formal agreement we can review together.

I plan to fax this material to you by the end of the week, and then follow up by phone no later than Monday, March 12, to get your feedback and reactions.

Thank you once again for your time. It was great talking to you about widgets—and, of course, about baseball! (Go Red Sox!)

Sincerely,

(Signature here)

Vera Jones
617/555-1212 (h) 617/555-1213, ext. 111 (w)

P.S.: Look forward to speaking with you on the 12th!

Sample Resumes for the Career Changer

The following models offer a wide variety of formats from which to choose when developing your resume. These are by no means the only acceptable outlines for resume development, but they are among the most reliable and successful. Each appears with a formatting template on the left and a fully developed resume example on the right. Follow one model, or combine elements to develop a resume that's right for you.

Please bear in mind the advice that appears earlier in the book. If you pass along a resume, find some way to do so in person! Mailing a resume and a cover letter is often a waste of time. Get the best information you possibly can, customize your resume to the position under discussion, then find some way to hand it over in a face-to-face meeting. If you must send something before the meeting, see the separate appendix on letters.

Career changers often find that a resume that emphasizes skills, rather than a providing a simple recitation of past employment, is the most effective. Most of the resumes that follow take advantage of this principle.

A final word of caution—think twice, and perhaps three times, before extending your resume beyond a single page. Many hiring officials these days are so snowed under with work that a multi-page resume is considered something of a turnoff.

*The following is a sample **Three Skills Resume**. You will notice that is stresses the skills you have acquired and any glowing reviews of them from a supervisor or coworker that would make you, the prospective candidate, an excellent match for the organization you want to join. Chronological work history is secondary. You are highlighting your skills and "employee-of-the-month-type" experiences relevant to the position you want.*

Your Name / Address

Home and work phone numbers and other relevant contact information

SUMMARY — Lead off with a thumbnail sketch that highlights your fitness for the position for which you're applying. Emphasize duration of experience and specific skills. If you can, work in a verbatim quote from a supervisor or an excerpt from a written reference that bears directly on your application.

FIRST SKILL — Highlight the strongest match in your skill/experience base for the position. Use **bold text** to emphasize particularly important connections.

> ➤ First supporting bullet item.
>
> ➤ Second supporting bullet item.
>
> ➤ Third supporting bullet item.

SECOND SKILL — Highlight the next strongest match in your skill/experience base for the position. Use **bold text** to emphasize particularly important connections.

> ➤ First supporting bullet item.
>
> ➤ Second supporting bullet item.
>
> ➤ Third supporting bullet item.

THIRD SKILL — Highlight the third strongest match in your skill/experience base for the position. Use **bold text** to emphasize particularly important connections.

> ➤ First supporting bullet item.
>
> ➤ Second supporting bullet item.
>
> ➤ Third supporting bullet item.

EDUCATION — List all the pertinent details.

WORK HISTORY — Briefly list the essentials for each of the employers in your recent work history.

Melanie Deacon   /   123 Elm Street, Boston, MA 02134
617/555-1212 (w) 617/555-1213 (w) * melanie@deeworld.com

SUMMARY   A highly organized, results-driven professional who would make a great **Sales Representative for Allenway Transport**. Ten years of experience in business, including three with heavy customer contact. Significant contact with vendors and other outsiders. Solid interpersonal and negotiating skills. Praised by a former supervisor as "personable, optimistic, persistent, and goal-oriented."

PRESENTATION   Skilled at developing and delivering persuasive presentations. As Office Manager for BC Consulting, I was called on, during weekly meetings, to **summarize and persuade others to accept** recommendations for new expenditures. As Service Representative for Rightway Engineering, I summoned extensive problem-solving abilities, **developed original summaries of service options**, and **outlined proposed maintenance programs** to existing customers who made final purchase decisions.

➤ Comfortable in front of groups

➤ Skilled public speaker (member of Toastmasters)

➤ Dealt with many of Allenway's potential customers during stint as Service Engineer

CLIENT SERVICE   Committed to delivering **positive results** for customers and clients.

➤ Cited as "Representative of the Month" for July, 1993, at Rightway Engineering.

➤ Promoted "good neighbor policy" at BC Consulting, ensuring that all departments had access to most recent customer data.

➤ Praised by supervisor at BC Consulting as "our **last, best hope** when customers need the very best on-the-spot summaries of where their projects stand." (Personnel review, August, 1995.)

ORGANIZATION   **Highly organized**; proficient in ACT! and PalmPilot software systems, as well as all Microsoft Office applications.

➤ Manage own time aggressively and tactfully.

➤ Personally responsible for maintenance of schedule and day-to-day administrative assignment allocations at BC Consulting.

➤ Praised for "superior organizational ability and interpersonal skills." (Personnel review, August, 1995.)

EDUCATION   B.A., Theater Arts, Vessey University, Tempe, Arizona, 1993. (Performed in lead or supporting roles in eleven campus productions.)

WORK HISTORY   BC Consulting (Boston, MA): Office Manager, 1994–present.

Rightway Engineering (Boston, MA): Service Representative, 1993–1994.

*The following is a **Two Skills Resume**. You are bringing attention to your most recent work experience that makes you a valuable asset to have around. Of course, this recent work experience should be relevant to the position you are applying for.*

Your Name / Address
Home and work phone numbers and other relevant contact information

SUMMARY

Offer a succinct overview of the recent experience that makes you a good candidate for the job in question. Provide all the relevant technical details that may be required. Lead directly into:

➤ First relevant area of expertise

➤ Second relevant area of expertise

➤ Third relevant area of expertise

➤ Fourth relevant area of expertise

➤ Fifth relevant area of expertise

FIRST SKILL

Isolate the strongest match in your skill/experience base for the position. Use **bold text** to emphasize particularly important connections.

➤ First supporting bullet item.

➤ Second supporting bullet item.

➤ Third supporting bullet item.

SECOND SKILL

Isolate the next strongest match in your skill/experience base for the position. Use **bold text** to emphasize particularly important connections. You may want to omit bullets in this section to save space.

OTHER EXPERIENCE

Briefly list the essentials for each of the employers in your recent work history.

EDUCATION

List all the pertinent details.

Jane Wallace / 123 Freedom Street, Hartford, CT 00000

617/555-1212 (business) and 617/555-1213 (home)

SUMMARY
An energetic, innovative Radio Production Professional with more than two years of exposure within public broadcasting at a variety of levels. Skilled in production, research, copy development, and programming. Capable of taking challenging projects from initial idea to successful conclusion. Skilled in Microsoft Word, SoundShape, and Photoshop. Areas of experience include:

- ➤ Concept development
- ➤ Project management
- ➤ Meeting tough deadlines
- ➤ Budgeting and financial analysis
- ➤ Documentary and feature production on WXMP's weekly *Street Talk* program

PLANNING
Developed preliminary budgets, scripts, and time estimates for over a dozen radio pieces at WXMP, where I serve as a part-time Production Assistant. My planning work was praised by supervisor Cheryl Naroni as **"consistently reliable and virtually always on-target."**

- ➤ Developed new checklist system for studio use.
- ➤ Installed and customized database software, resulting in dramatic increases in efficiency.
- ➤ Served as interim producer during two nights of WXMP fundraiser.

TRAINING
Selected to train public television volunteers in quarterly radio fundraising drive; developed policy manual for production crew interacting with volunteers. Helped to streamline efforts between development and production personnel.

OTHER EXPERIENCE
Previous professional experience includes:

➤ <u>MasterWay</u>, New York, NY **CONSUMER LOAN ANALYST**	1994–1997
➤ <u>Consumer Loan</u>, New York, NY **COLLECTIONS REPRESENTATIVE**	1993–1994

EDUCATION
Ongoing night coursework in Radio Arts at Wallace Community College (Wallace, Oregon)
B.A. in English from Brentwell University (Ocean Cliff, New York), 1992

301

*The following is a **Career Highlights Resume**. You will identify, right up front, which position you are applying for within your prospective new employer's organization. The rest of the resume simply highlights your experiences that closely resemble the new position you want.*

Your Name

Address   /   Phone Number

OBJECTIVE: List the specific position within the target organization you are seeking. Identify the target organization by name.

CAREER HIGHLIGHTS: Use two or three sentences to emphasize those aspects of your background that present the best "fit" with the position.

MAJOR SKILLS: Use *italics* and **bold type** to emphasize major skills as employed in relevant freelance or volunteer work that directly correlates with your employment objective. (That is, of course, if full-time experience in your background is lacking!)

SUPPORTING SKILLS: Own Macintosh SE; proficient in Adobe Photoshop; also familiar with IBM environments. Familiar with CorelDRAW! in Windows 95 environment.

ORAL AND WRITTEN COMMUNICATIONS: Offer details on how your communication skills support your employment objective. Give real-world examples; buttress this, if you can, with a personal endorsement or compelling quote.

EMPLOYMENT HISTORY: Briefly list the essentials for each of the employers in your recent work history.

First employer

- ➤ Relevant experience in stand-alone bullets
- ➤ Relevant experience in stand-alone bullets

Second employer

- ➤ Relevant experience in stand-alone bullets
- ➤ Relevant experience in stand-alone bullets

(And so on.)

EDUCATION: List all the pertinent details.

You may wish to close with a personalized statement featuring appropriate professional information.

Art Benton

35 Shutterbug Way, Boise, ID 83707   /   208/555-1212

OBJECTIVE: A position as a Staff Photographer with the *Boise News and Herald.*

CAREER HIGHLIGHTS: Excellent foundation of experience in commercial photography, supported by general knowledge of business operations and procedures. Strong news orientation from college onward.

PHOTOGRAPHIC SKILLS: *Experienced freelance photographer* with record of sound planning, careful execution, and superior final output. Clients include **ABC Industries**, New York, NY (front cover of 1997 Annual Report), **Universal News Service**, Cincinnati, OH (provided shots of homeless shelters for nationally praised series of articles), and **WGJU-Boston** (provided shots of production facilities used in *5, the Member Magazine*).

COMPUTER SKILLS: Own Macintosh SE; proficient in Adobe Photoshop; also familiar with IBM environments. Familiar with CorelDRAW! in Windows 95 environment.

ORAL AND WRITTEN COMMUNICATIONS: Provide regular written reports on status of projects. Capable of developing face-to-face working plans via discussions with clients, and developing accurate written summaries as a preliminary to beginning field work. Praised by Mel Bentley, of WGJU, as "the best organized freelancer we've worked with in a very long time."

EMPLOYMENT HISTORY: Other employment includes:

Mel's Stores * Floor Manager, Evening Shift * Boise, ID * (1996–Present)

- ➤ Hire, train, and oversee staff of six
- ➤ Maintain accurate accounting and operational records
- ➤ Develop advertising strategy for approval by owner
- ➤ Establish merchandise layout procedures and graphic displays

ABC Technologies * Data Entry Professional * Somerville, Massachusetts * (1995–1996)

- ➤ Named "Employee of the Month," December, 1995

EDUCATION: B.A., Politics, Louis University (Arlington, Massachusetts), 1995. Named "Journalist to Watch" in campus yearbook. **Staff Photographer** on school paper, the *Call*; named head photographer senior year.

I am skilled in developing and printing both color and black-and-white photographs. My portfolio is available on request.

*The following is a **Career Objective Resume**. You state your career objective and the organiza-tion you are contacting. The resume will then go into a bullet point format of experiences that will support your career objective relevant to your new prospective position.*

Your name   /   contact information

Career Objective: List the job and the target organization here.

Summary of Qualifications:

➤ Offer your first and best experience/skill match in concise bullet format.

➤ Offer your next best experience/skill match in concise bullet format.

➤ Offer your next best experience/skill match in concise bullet format.

➤ Offer your next best experience/skill match in concise bullet format.

Achievements: Emphasize, if appropriate, the totality and length of your relevant work experience, and introduce your record of performance in...

FIRST KEY SKILL AREA

Give appropriate background information.

➤ Outline your accomplishments with fairly detailed bullet points.

➤ Outline your accomplishments with fairly detailed bullet points.

➤ Outline your accomplishments with fairly detailed bullet points.

SECOND KEY SKILL AREA

Give appropriate background information.

➤ Outline your accomplishments with fairly detailed bullet points.

➤ Outline your accomplishments with fairly detailed bullet points.

➤ Outline your accomplishments with fairly detailed bullet points.

THIRD KEY SKILL AREA

Give appropriate background information.

➤ Outline your accomplishments with fairly detailed bullet points.

➤ Outline your accomplishments with fairly detailed bullet points.

➤ Outline your accomplishments with fairly detailed bullet points.

Employment:
List your most recent employers, supplying all appropriate information.

Education:
Provide all the pertinent details.

Mel Cruz / **45 Smith Street, Providence, RI 01111** / 413-555-1213

Career Objective: To become a recruiter for Wilson Associates.

Summary of Qualifications:

- ➤ Seven years of experience in one-on-one career counseling.
- ➤ Four years of experience in face-to-face sales.
- ➤ Able to develop workable plans and strategies for organizations and individuals.
- ➤ Skilled at negotiation, mediation, written and oral communication, and conflict resolution.

Achievements: Fifteen years of experience as a salesperson, writer, and counselor with a record of superior performance in such areas as...

HIRING

Over a period of seven years, I was personally responsible for the hiring and motivation of administrative and support staff at The Career Counseling Center at Evergreen University.

- ➤ Between six and nine staff members have reported directly to me at all times; since 1986, I have made the final decision on all new hires and enjoyed an average 3.5 year incumbency rate. None of my hires has ever been subject to disciplinary action or termination.
- ➤ Developed superior interviewing technique (and can coach both applicants and hiring managers).
- ➤ Skilled at performance evaluation and individual motivation.

COUNSELING

As the head of The Career Counseling Center, I meet regularly with university undergraduates and graduate students in search of career guidance.

- ➤ 116 of my clients were offered positions within Fortune 1000 organizations.
- ➤ User surveys indicate that 81% of clients are "satisfied" or "extremely satisfied" with the counseling they received from me at the Center.
- ➤ Launched an innovative online referral service that allowed major employers to review student resumes via the World Wide Web.
- ➤ Developed resume guidelines, catalog copy, and brochure material.

REVENUE GENERATION

Before signing on as Director of the Career Counseling Center, I served as regional sales manager for Educational Learning Tools, Incorporated, and...

- ➤ Brought territory from 16% below quota to 24% above quota in only six months.
- ➤ Coached underperforming sales people to meet or exceed sales goals.
- ➤ Assumed personal responsibility for territories on three different occasions; delivered pro-rated results equal to or superior to the reps who had handled them before.

Employment:

Director, The Career Counseling Center at Evergreen University (Portland, OR) 1985–present
Regional Sales Manager, Educational Learning Tools (Verona, NJ) 1981–1985
Sales Associate, Educational Learning Tools (Verona NJ) 1981

Education:

B.A., Sociology, Wellstone College, Provide details of higher education, listing degree, university, and year of graduation.

*The following is called a **Qualifications Summary Resume**. You immediately start off by highlighting relevant career accomplishments that will make you a perfect fit in the new organization you want to join. Give details, but do not present the reader with staggering amounts of information that will smother the rest of your resume.*

Your Name
Street address
City State Zip
Phone number, etc.

QUALIFICATIONS

Use **bold type** to offer a summary of relevant career highlights. Provide as many relevant details as seems appropriate, but don't allow the opening section to overwhelm the resume. Provide dates, names, titles, and other relevant information on key projects.

WORK HISTORY

Dates   Provide information about the organization and your position. Explain key accomplishments in sufficient detail.

Dates   Provide information about the organization and your position. Explain key accomplishments in sufficient detail.

Dates   Provide information about the organization and your position. Explain key accomplishments in sufficient detail.

Dates   Provide information about the organization and your position. Explain key accomplishments in sufficient detail.

EDUCATION

List all the relevant details.

Mike Cleary
107 Taylor Street
San Rafael, CA 94901
Phone/fax: 415/555-1212
e-mail: mcleary@dataway.com

QUALIFICATIONS

Accomplished writer who conducted initial research and interviews for a wide variety of business publishing projects as a freelance consultant. These include Dirk Melvin's *Management by Innovation*, Myron Halliway's *The New Era Dawns*, and Mike Cooper's *Straight to the Top* (all titles ABC Press, Whitcomb, NJ, 1994–1997) Since 1986, I have written nine seminar manuals for sales trainer Don Denning, with an in-print total of approximately 300,000 copies. Author of three books: *Flea Markets of California*, *Flea Markets of New York*, and *Flea Markets of Illinois* (Collector's Press, 1994–1997).

WORK HISTORY

1994–present   *President, Storygate Productions, San Rafael, CA (Freelance Writing)*

Developed business and career proposals/manuscripts for new titles, and for projects requiring speechwriting services.

1988–1994   *VP/Editorial, Crestway, Inc., San Francisco, CA*

Oversaw and helped to revise a broad range of career and business titles, including Denson and Denson's *Lifetime Weight Manager* and books in Melvin Harrison's *You Can Do It* series. (*You Can Do It* eventually appeared on the **New York Times bestseller list**.) There are now over **3.5 million** *You Can Do It* books in print.

Contributed new book ideas to weekly editorial meetings, one of which (*Mr. Sloppy's Guide to Life*) reached the **#1 position** on the *San Francisco Chronicle* local bestseller list. Four sequels followed; the series sold over **150,000 copies**. **Ghostwrote or supplied substantial rewrites** for such successful titles as *What Not to Say in Iraq* (over 75,000 copies in print) and *What Zen Buddhists Eat* (over 100,000 copies in print).

1985–1988   *Editor, Dateline Series, Crestway, Inc., San Francisco, CA*

Coordinated these local bestselling directories of major local dating services. **Oversaw annual editorial work** on time-sensitive national database project, *The National Dating Service Directory*, which was marketed to public libraries. Edited and updated introductory material for each book.

1982   *Intern, office of Senator Mike Riley (D-CA)*

Provided initial drafts of correspondence as part of the Senator's constituent response team.

EDUCATION

1979–1983   B.A., Spotsworth University, Lompoc, CA; dual concentrations in Theater and Sociology; awarded Highest Honors in Theater.

*The following is a **Selective Chronological Order Resume**. The flow of the resume begins your objective followed by most recent experience, your next previous work experience, and so on. Of course, if there are large gaps in employment, you may want to leave dates out or combine work experiences into a overall heading. It's an extremely flexible format that will allow you to emphasize strong suits based on specific past work experience.*

Your Name

Your contact information

OBJECTIVE: Identify the position and the target organization at which the resume is directed.

PROFESSIONAL EXPERIENCE

List your most relevant work experience and offer supporting details. In cases where there are large, difficult-to-explain gaps in your employment background, your best bet may be to leave dates out of the picture entirely and account for everything at an appropriate point during your in-person interview. Alternatively, you may decide to combine employment periods under large "umbrella" subheadings and account for longer stretches of time that way.

➤ Offer a supporting anecdote or key achievement.

List your next most relevant work experience and offer supporting details.

➤ Offer a supporting anecdote or key achievement.

List your next most relevant work experience and offer supporting details.

➤ Offer a supporting anecdote or key achievement.

List your next most relevant work experience and offer supporting details.

➤ Offer a supporting anecdote or key achievement.

VOLUNTEER EXPERIENCE

List appropriate unpaid experience here.

EDUCATION

Provide all the relevant details.

HONORS AND AWARDS

These may be helpful in placing an "exclamation point" at the conclusion of your resume.

Matthew J. Wilson

27 'S' Street, Bradford, Massachusetts 01835 (508.555.9020)

OBJECTIVE: A position as a Conferencing Manager at Hartford Hospital.

PROFESSIONAL EXPERIENCE

Administrative Director, New England Opera Alliance. Responsible for all negotiating, scheduling, accounting, and marketing initiatives at this not-for-profit professional arts management firm. Contracted to manage all technical aspects of the operettas Patience and Gondoliers at A.J. Vessey Memorial Chapel (Dedham, Massachusetts).

> ➤ In one twelve-month period, coordinated and scheduled 32 separate workshops involving local schools and arts organizations. Peter Waldron of Bradford College: "Beautifully organized. You make it so easy!"

Program Assistant, Red Hill Arts & Symphony. Coordinated volunteer staff of eight; handled setup, ticketing, and logistical duties for ongoing series of chamber music performances. Reported to Director of the Symphony.

> ➤ Handled all marketing, public relations, and ticketing work for annual theatrical production.

Technical Director, Bay State Ballet. Coordinated volunteer staff of 35 for this New Hampshire dance company. Assisted in selection and scheduling of performance spaces. Helped organization expand repertoire from three productions a year to five productions a year. Reported directly to Artistic Director, and helped her determine feasibility of stage designs. Responsible for execution of all technical components of the organization's seasons.

> ➤ Responsibilities increased every year.

Company Manager, Volk Opera Theater. Handled all contract negotiations and booking arrangements related to touring efforts of this, the first educational touring opera company in the United States. Oversaw all administrative operations of the Touring Group.

> ➤ Personally handled all transportation logistics related to performers, sets, and costumes.

VOLUNTEER EXPERIENCE

Handicapped Student Volunteer Coordinator, University of Springfield. Coordinated lectures for students in greater Springfield area. Acted as liaison between university and state and federal agencies focusing on handicapped awareness and rights for physically and emotionally challenged people.

EDUCATION

Bachelor of Arts/Management, Crestview College. Crestview, Massachusetts—Accelerated night-course program.

HONORS AND AWARDS

Received Volk Opera Guild Scholarship

Named Massachusetts Gilbert and Sullivan Society Student of the Year

Described as "Exceptional in every way" by Brook Carlos, Chair, Department of Music, Centerway College

Glossary

Ageism is discrimination based on a person's chronological age.

Aptitude means an innate ability to learn something.

Baby Boomers are a huge, exceptionally well-educated, and immensely powerful generation: the people born between 1946 and 1964. There's been a lot written about this group. The value that comes to the fore here is self-expression (both in terms of idealism and personal ambition). One writer has observed that the Boomers "sometimes seem to see themselves as walking works of art." In addition to the elaboration of self, this group has focused intently on the value of the immediate. (The savings rates among Boomers are quite low.) At work, self-sufficiency and independence are key values for Boomers. *See also:* Generation X; Echo Generation; Organization Group; Silent Generation.

Branching is the act of taking some aspect of what you used to do and finding a way to connect it to what you'd like to do in a new field.

Career comes from the Latin word *carraria*, "the way of the cart." A career is a path that, like a set of cart tracks, generally follows a straight line. Many people think of their work as a series of jobs that lead somewhere, that fall in line. *See also:* job.

A **career audit** is an account of your current skills and objectives, as well as any important changes in the market. You should conduct one, at least informally, at least once a year.

Co-creation is the process of working with an employer to define the parameters of a job. One good category for older workers to explore on this score: temporary employment services. Some of these operations now specialize in placing older workers.

Contingency hiring is the practice of employing workers on a temporary or as-needed basis.

Core competencies are the underlying skills you use to solve problems and develop income. As a rule, they're what you do best in the field you know best. Another way of looking at core competencies is to think of them as the basic abilities that help you generate marketable products and job-specific skills.

The **Echo Generation** includes "post-X" people (born 1978 or later). For the most part, they're workers whose influence and outlook has yet to be fully felt. One thing is certain: We can expect this group to significantly outnumber the Gen-Xers, leaving that group with imposingly large demographic groups both in front of it and behind it. *See also:* Baby Boomers; Generation X; Organization Group; Silent Generation.

An **entrepreneur** is a person who creates and manages an enterprise or business.

Family profile means the identity you cultivate and reinforce during interactions with family members. *See also:* professional profile, social profile.

Flow is a word for those moments in your life when time seems to come to a standstill because you're so taken up in what you're doing.

Freelancing is pursuing a profession without a long-term commitment to a single employer.

Generation X is the group of individuals born between 1965 and 1977. This group is worthy of note primarily because its dominant work values are so striking: skepticism (sometimes bordering on cynicism), a search for family-like work communities (to replace actual family structures that may have left something to be desired), and an ongoing search for sensory stimulation (perhaps guided by an attention span profoundly influenced by commercial television). Detachment and alienation figure prominently in Generation X music and culture. *See also:* Baby Boomers; Echo Generation; Organization Group; Silent Generation.

A **hard skill** comes from training in a certain discipline, experience in a related industry, or knowledge of technical tools.

An **independent contractor** is a person who is responsible for his or her own livelihood, and who works "by the assignment" (as opposed to being kept on indefinitely).

An **industry** is an organized effort to meet some human need. As such, it doesn't generally disappear into thin air. It's far more likely to take on (or inspire) a new form, a form that creates new kinds of related jobs—or, at the very least, the same job in a different setting.

Industry clusters refer to locations where businesses in the same industry tend to gather.

An **informed interview** is an employment interview in which you participate effectively and completely, and ask questions yourself of the prospective employer.

Job is a word of distant origin; it's derived from the same root as *gob*, or the middle English term *gobbe*, which translates to lump, or piece. Some people in England still speak of "a job of work." In our culture, we tend to use this word when we view work as a unit of activity or a means to an end: "It's just a job." *See also:* career.

A **job club** is a group for unemployed workers in a certain field in which job briefings and leads are passed out.

Job obsolescence is the elimination of a position in which the skills and objectives associated with it often live on.

Kinesthetic learning is a way of taking on new facts or procedures that involves physical action. A kinesthetic learner is one who easily uses some form of movement or physical activity (such as writing) to assimilate new information.

Learning projects are any attempts to grow or change in a significant way.

A **lone eagle** is a self-employed professional who handles all or nearly all aspects of a one-person business. They can work wherever they like.

Marketing is the process of promoting, selling, and distributing a product or service.

Mismanagement means that you are working in a job that presents a good match for your skills and interests, but you have to perform under excruciating conditions.

Networking means taking action to expand your current contact network to benefit both you and the people to whom you're reaching out.

The **Organization Group**, also known as the "Organization Man," or "GI Bill" group, includes people born between 1909 and 1929. These are people for whom the Great Depression and World War II were formative experiences. Strong work values include: leadership, loyalty, self-sacrifice, and conformity to organizations—and, last but not least, strong gender-related work roles. Eric Hoffer called their success in World War II "the triumph of the squares." Many, but not all, of these workers are now retired. *See also:* Baby Boomers; Echo Generation; Generation X; Silent Generation.

Overspecialization means to limit oneself or to concentrate too much in an activity, field, or practice.

Peak experiences are activities that gave you a sense of personal accomplishment, where you contributed something that felt valuable, while making good use of your abilities.

Proactive means anticipatory, or serving to prepare ahead of time for potentially challenging circumstances. Taking a proactive approach on the job search front means taking the initiative to make suggestions and follow through on your own.

Professional profile means the identity you cultivate and reinforce at work. It is not necessarily your social or family profile, but neither is it a façade or false identity. It's who you naturally are at work.

Professional recycling is the process of building new skills from the base of what you already know.

A **public company** is one that sells stock and is publicly traded.

Reorganized labor is a movement toward the organization of people based on a craft or trade.

Reserve skills are the basic principles behind the skills you use that enable you to learn new ones.

The **Silent Generation** is the group that followed the "Organization Group" workers, people born between 1925 and 1945. Their work focus has typically been on mediation, sensitivity, and, to a certain degree, an instinct for reform and improvement. This group has produced more psychotherapists, and more service-oriented professionals, than has any other group in American history. It also had to come to terms with gender rules that began to change dramatically on both the personal and professional fronts in the 1960s and 1970s. *See also:* Baby Boomers; Echo Generation; Generation X; Organization Group.

A **skill** is some knowledge or technique you use to perform a task. Generally speaking, a skill can be acquired, while a trait is innate. Skills are the bridge between the jobs of today and the workplace of tomorrow. The mix of skills required in a given position depends on the problems to be solved on the job. *See also:* traits.

Skills obsolescence refers to skills that generally are no longer in use.

Social profile means the identity you cultivate and reinforce in social situations. *See also:* professional profile, family profile.

Sourcing is specifying the kinds of skills a job requires, identifying how those skills are generally acquired, and where one would look for individuals who have them.

A **stopgap job** is a position that serves as a temporary measure while you're re-evaluating long-term career direction.

Strong suits are the areas in which you excel; your strong suits represent your forte.

Title fixation is the attempt to cling to a single, narrowly defined job, typically one with a familiar label, despite important changes that have taken place in the industry in which you are looking for work.

Trailing spouse is a term usually employed to describe the half of a two-income couple who didn't receive the job offer across the country, but is nevertheless moving to accompany a husband or wife who did.

Traits are personal qualities that enable one to use a skill. For example, it's a good idea to be extroverted if you aspire to have a career in door-to-door or cold-calling sales.

Transplanting is the act of moving yourself into an entirely new environment in which the connections between what you've done in the past and what you'll be doing now aren't immediately apparent.

Value means positive results. Adding value is (or at least should be) the basis of all work.

Vocation is a word that carries many meanings these days, and encompasses everything from a religious occupation to a course of study. The root is found in Hebrew and Greek words meaning "to call out" or "summon." A vocation is meaningful work that we feel called to do.

"X-ers"—*see:* Generation X.

Index

A

A-frame-structured
  companies, 97
ABI/INFORM database, 174
accomplishments
  answering questions, 196
  employment letters, samples,
    290-291
  resumes, 183
actors' associations, 279, 283
ads, classifieds, 59-61, 160
advocacy groups/associations,
  279-283
aerospace industry, 282
  regional growth rate, 276
age discrimination, 311
  overcoming, 216-217
agriculture industry regional
  growth rate, 276
airline industry, 106
analyses of markets,
  resources, 171
answering questions
  former employers, 245
  tips, 195-196, 198
apparel industry regional
  growth rate, 277
appearance,
  professionalism, 162
aptitude tests, 36-37
arts, graphic artists'
  associations, 282
associations, 279-283
audits, career audits, 75, 311

authors' associations, 280-281
automotive products industry
  regional growth rate, 276

B

Baby Boomers, 220-221
background summaries, 197
  preparing for interviews,
    196-197
    obstacles, overcoming,
      244
  sample, 87-88
banking industry changes,
  28-29
benefit package, considerations,
  210
biomedical products industry
  regional growth rate, 276
books
  Accounting and Tax Index, 170
  American Statistics Index
    (ASI), 171
  Change at Work, 73
  Complete Idiot's Guide to
    Microsoft Excel 97, The, 98
  Complete Idiot's Guide to
    Microsoft Word 97, The, 98
  Complete Idiot's Guide to
    Windows 95, Second Edition,
    The, 98
  Complete Idiot's Guide to
    WordPerfect for Windows,
    Second Edition, The, 98
  Contacts Influential, 169

  County Business Patterns, 172
  Demographics USA, 171
  Direct Marketing Market Place,
    171
  Directory of Corporate
    Affiliations, 169
  Directory of Executive
    Recruiters, 61
  Dun's Directory of Service
    Companies, 169
  Editor and Publisher Market
    Guide, 171
  Employment Opportunities and
    Job Resources on the
    Internet, 175
  Encyclopedia of Associations,
    The, 64, 172
  Encyclopedia of Careers and
    Vocational Guidance, 172
  Generations, 221
  Index of Majors and Graduate
    Degrees, The, 129, 173
  International Directory of
    Company Histories, 169
  International Statistics, 170
  Internet Business 500, data-
    base guide, 173
  Learning to Learn, 54
  Leo Burnett Worldwide
    Advertising and Media Fact
    Book, 172
  Million Dollar Directory, 169
  Moody's Manuals, 170
  Occupational Outlook
    Handbook, 172, 274

Prentice Hall Directory of Online Business Information, 173
Professional Careers, 172
Reader's Guide to Periodical Literature, 148
Registry of Interim College and University Presidents, The, 67
S&P Corporation Records, 170
Service Industries USA, 172
Simmons Study of Media and Markets, 171
Sourcebook of ZIP Code Demographics, 172
Specialty Occupational Outlook: Professions, 172
Standard & Poor's Industry Surveys, 172
Standard & Poor's Register of Corporations, Directors, and Executives, 169
Standard Directory of Advertisers, 169
Standard Industrial Classification Manual, 169
Statistical Abstract of the United States, 171
Statistical Reference Index (SRI), 170
Thomas Registry of American Manufacturers, 169
Twenty-Something, 221
Value Line Investment Survey and Expanded Edition, 170
borrowing money, 16
branching, 311
    changing fields, 235
broadcasters' associations, 282
Bureau of Labor Statistics, 273
Business Information: How to Find It, How to Use It, 171
businesses
    directories, 169
    communication associations, 282
    self-employment, 76
        reentering the workforce, 264
        regional growth rates, 264-265, 267

services industry regional growth rate, 276
starting, 16

C

calls
    follow-up action, 205
    job searches
        changes in methods, 75-76
        samples, 164-165
    networking, 84-85
        guidelines, 85
        note-taking, 85-86
    professionalism, 162
    samples, job searches, 164-165
career audits, 75, 311
Career Highlights Resume sample, 302-303
Career Mosaic Web site, 271
Career Objective Resume sample, 304-305
career planning, 21-23
    aptitude tests, 36-37
    considerations, 23
    goals in life, 24-25
    interpersonal relationships, 24
    markets, 23-24
        banking industry, 28-29
        opportunities, 27-28
        seismic data brokers, 29-30
        unmet needs, 30-31
    retraining, 31
    skills/market gaps, 25
    vocational tests, 13-14, 36
    workplace changes, 22
career outlooks, 274-275
cartoonists' associations, 282
CD-ROM databases, 174
Change at Work, 73
changes
    fields, 233-234
        branching, 235
        considerations, 234-237
        exercises, 234-236
        goal-setting, 238
        guidelines, 239

networking, 237-239
past experiences, 235-237
sourcing skills, 236
spouses, 234
tips, 238-239
transferable skills, 236
job markets
    banking industry, 28-29
    financial planners, 28-29
    frequency, 242
    opportunities, 27-28
    retraining, 31
    seismic data brokers, 29-30
    unmet needs, 30-31
job search process, 74-75
workplace, 22
    younger workers, 225-227
chemical engineers' associations, 281
Chronological Order Resume sample, 308-309
civil engineers' associations, 280
classified ads, 59-61
    benefits, 59
    guidelines, 60-61
    job search techniques, 160
    rejections, 60
climbing corporate ladders
    diamond-structured companies, 95
    economy and workplace, 102
    pyramid-structured companies, 94
    younger workers, 230
college education, 123
    continuing education, 129
        advantages, 131-132
        necessity, 130
        tips, 132
        two-year degrees, 130-131
Colorado Alliance of Research Libraries (CARL) database, 173
companies
    culture, 137-139
        diamond-structured companies, 96-97, 194
        pyramid-structured companies, 194
        questions to ask, 138-139
        resumes, 181
    large companies, needs/desires, 140

318

organizational structures,
managers, 141-142
profiles, 140-141
public companies, 170
researching, 61-62, 174,
194-195
company research, 177
considerations, 139
culture, questions to ask,
138-139
profiles, 140-141
resources, 170
small companies, needs/
desires, 141
see also diamond-structured
companies; pyramid-
structured companies
CompuSkills short-course
school, continuing education,
133
computer-related careers,
employment outlooks,
274-275
computers
apprehension, 250-251
increase, 249-250
response strategies, 251
basic knowledge, focusing
on, 252-253
continuing education,
253-254
current skill, stressing,
251-252
transferable skills, 254
software, 134
teaching trends, 255
conservation engineers'
associations, 281
construction products industry,
276
contacts, 58
fields, changing, 237-239
friends, 58-59
Contacts Influential, job search
resources, 169
contingency hiring, 65-66, 312
continuing education, 63
college courses, 123
considerations, academic
credentials, 127
company culture, 139
essentials, 126
knowledge level neces-
sary, 126

Council for Adult and
Experiential Education, 132
learning styles, 53-55
MBA programs, 95
methods, 127
college education,
129-132
Internet, 133
learning projects, 127
product vendors, 128-129
professional organiza-
tions, 128
self-managed learning,
127
teaching part-time, 63
TV courses, 133
volunteering, 134
tuition reimbursement
programs, 103
see also skills
contractors' associations, 281
contributions
determining, informal
interviews, 114
employee contributions,
112-114
employers' needs/desires,
115-118
initiative, 116
interest in industry,
116-117
production level, 115
coping strategies, unemployment, 16-17
core competencies, *see* transferable skills
Council for Adult and Experiential Education, 132
counseling services, careers,
67-68
cover letters, resumes, 189-190
creative networking, 162-163
criminal records, overcoming
obstacles, 241-242
falsifying information, 244
culture, companies, 137-139
diamond-structured compa-
nies, 96-97, 194
pyramid-structured compa-
nies, 194
questions to ask, 138-139
resumes, 181
customizing resumes, 182

D

databases, 173-174
decline rate, careers, 275
defense industry, 276
degrees/titles
self-promotion, 35
younger workers, 229
dental assistants, employment
outlook, 274
desires/needs
employees
career planning, 23-25
identifying, 11-15
offers, jobs, 209
older workers, 217
reentering the workforce,
258-259
employers, 34-35
filling, 142-143
interviews, 200
large companies, 140
skills/market gap, 139
small companies, 141
offers, jobs, 209
reentering the workforce,
258-259
desperation, job search
obstacles, 163
detectives, employment
outlook, 274
diamond-structured companies,
95-97
Comfertech, 96
culture, 96-97, 194
management styles, 99
managerial positions, 116
misconceptions, 99
researching companies,
195-196
stability, 97
transferable skills, 96
Direct Marketing Market Place,
171
directory assistance operators,
employment outlook, 275
disabled, National Association
of the Physically Handi-
capped, 282
discrimination, age discrimination, 216-217
displaced workers, 67
unemployment rate, 77

dissatisfaction, 3-9
    mismanagement, 7-9
    reasons, 5
    unemployment, 6-7
distribution industry, 278
downsizing, 103, 245
downturns, industries, 106-107

E

E-Span (The Interactive Employ-
    ment Network) Web site, 272
Echo Generation, 222, 312
economy
    economic trends, 149
    workplace, effects on, 102
editors' associations. 280
education
    associations, 282
    background
        resumes, 182
        transferable skills, 50
    continuing, 46, 63
        academic credentials, 127
        broadening skills, 46-47
        college courses, 123
        CompuSkills short-course
            school, 133
        Council for Adult and
            Experiential Education,
            132
        essentials, 126
        Internet, 133
        knowledge level neces-
            sary, 126
        learning projects, 127
        learning styles, 53-55
        MBA programs, 95
        teaching part-time, 63
        transferable skills, 47-48
        tuition reimbursement
            programs, 103
        TV courses, 133
        volunteering, 134
    younger workers, degrees,
        229
    see also skills
educational assistants, employ-
    ment outlook, 274
educational services industry,
    regional growth rate, 277

elderly workers
    Access Coordinators for the
        Elderly (ACE), 218
    age discrimination, 216-217,
        311
    appropriate positions,
        219-220
    internships, 229
    needs/desires, 217
    opportunities, 218-219
    overcoming obstacles,
        216-217
    reasons to work, 215-216
    Silver Fox Computer Club,
        219
    strategies, 223
electronic machinery and
    systems industry regional
    growth rate, 277
employees
    benefit packages, 210
    federal, 282
    needs/desires
        career planning, 23-25
        identifying, 11-15
        offers, jobs, 209
        older workers, 217
        reentering the workforce,
            258-259
    older workers
        Access Coordinators for
            the Elderly (ACE), 218
        age discrimination,
            216-217, 311
        appropriate positions,
            219-220
        Forty Plus Club of New
            York, 281
        needs/desires, 217
        opportunities, 218-219
        reasons to work, 215-216
        strategies, 223
    younger workers
        changes in workplace,
            225-226
        climbing corporate
            ladders, 230
        educational background,
            229
        flexibility, 226
        gaps in employment, 230
        internships, 229
        productivity, 228

skills, updating, 230
    stereotypes, 226-228
    strategies, 228-229
    temporary services, 228
    white-collar jobs, 226
employers
    annoying perspective
        employers, 163
    answering questions about,
        245
    interviewing skills, 198-199
    large companies, needs/
        desires, 140
    needs/desires, 34-35, 114-118
        employee contributions,
            112-114
        filling, 142-143
        initiative, 116
        interest in industry,
            116-117
        interviews, 200
        large companies, 140
        productivity, 115
        skills/market gaps, 139
        small companies, 141
    profiles, 140-141
    questions to ask, company
        culture, 138-139
    small companies, needs/
        desires, 141
    unmet needs, 209
employment, letter samples
    accomplishments/
        requirements, 287
    little company informa-
        tion, 292-293
    new contacts, 294-295
    single accomplishments,
        290-291
    well-researched company,
        288-289
    outlook, careers, 274-275
    see also job searches
energy industry regional growth
    rate, 277
engineers, professional organi-
    zations, 280-283
entertainment services industry,
    278
executive search firms, *see*
    search firms
executives' organizations,
    281-282

experiences
  answering questions, 196
  peak experiences, 38
    identifying, 53
    learning styles, 53-55
  resumes, 182
extroverts vs. introverts,
  networking, 86-87

F

fairs, virtual job fairs, 177
falsifying information
  hiring obstacles, overcoming,
    243
    criminal records, 244
  resumes, 183-184
fashion industry regional
  growth rate, 277
federal jobs, 281-282
  employee associations, 282
  employment programs, 67
fields
  changing, 103
    branching, 235
    career counselors, 233-234
    considerations, 234-237
    exercises, 234-236
    goal-setting, 238
    guidelines, 239
    networking, 237-239
    past experiences, 235-237
    related fields, changing,
      104
    sourcing skills, 236
    spouses, 234
    tips, 238-239
    transferable skills, 236
file clerks, employment outlook,
  275
financial
  aspects, 15-16
  planners, 16
    industry changes, 28-29
  products industry regional
    growth rate, 277
FirstSearch database, 173
flexibility, younger workers, 226
flow-experiencing learning,
  120-121
    vs. necessity-based learning,
      123-124

follow-up action
  interview guidelines, 203-205
  letter samples, 205-206
  network contacts, calling,
    206-207
  offers, 208-209
  phone calls, 205
  recalling interviews, 203-204
  rejections, 207
  short-term project proposal
    samples, 207-208
food processing industry, 282
  regional growth rate, 276
foreign language skills, 144
forest products industry
  regional growth rate, 277
formatting
  letters, employment
    accomplishments/
      requirements, 287
    little company informa-
      tion, 292-293
    new contacts, 294-295
    single accomplishments,
      290-291
    well-researched company,
      288-289
  resumes
    Career Highlights Resume,
      302-303
    Career Objective Resume,
      304-305
    Chronological Order
      Resume, 308-309
    Qualifications Summary
      Resume, 306-307
    Selective Chronological
      Order Resume, 308-309
    Three Skills Resume,
      298-299
    Two Skills Resume,
      300-301
Forty Plus Club of New York,
  281
freelancing, 25, 29

G

gaps
  employment
    resumes, 182
    younger workers, 230

skills/market gap, reentering
  the workforce, 262-263
Generation X, 220, 222, 312
geophysicists' organizations,
  283
goals
  career planning, 24-25
  defining, 147-148
    career matches, 154-155
    industry research, 148
    market needs, 149-150
    market/skills gap, 152-153
    skills, 151-152
  fields, changing, 238
  reentering the workforce,
    259-260
graphic artists' organizations,
  282
Gray Panthers Project Fund, 281
growth rate
  careers, 274-275
  industries, 276-278
  self-employment, 264-265
    chart, 267

H

*Handbook of Business Informa-
tion: A Guide for Librarians,
Students, and Researchers*, job
search resources, 171
handicapped, National Association of the Physically Handicapped, 282
hard skills, 23, 40-41, 312
  vs. soft skills, 40
  see also skills
headhunters, *see* search firms
health care, 274-275, 280
  health aides, employment
    outlook, 274
  health services industry,
    regional growth rate, 277
  insurance, 15
  nurses' associations, 280
home products industry
  regional growth rate, 278
human resources organizations,
  283
human services workers,
  employment outlook, 274

I-J-K

illustrators' organizations, 283

independent contractors, 76-77

indexes, job search resources, 170-171

individual retirement accounts (IRAs), 15

industrial engineers' organizations, 282

industrial machinery industry, 278

industrial production managers, employment outlook, 275

industries
banking, 28-29
clusters, 264, 312
downturns, 106-108
financial planners, 28-29
growth rates, 276-278
interest, employers' needs/desires, 116-117
regional growth rates
reentering the workforce, 264
researching, 148
Standard & Poor's Industry Surveys, 172
stereotypes, 105-106
telecommunications, 104-105
U.S. Industrial Outlook, 172

Information Industry Association, 281

information services industry, 278

information technology, 144-145

informed interviews, 114

initiative, employers' needs/desires, 116

Institute of Certified Financial Planners, 16

Institute of Food Technologists, 282

Institute of Industrial Engineers, 282

Institute of Management Consultants, 282

insurance, unemployment, 16

Interior Designers' Associations, 280

Internet
continuing education, 133
Employment Opportunities and Job Resources on the Internet, 175
hiring via Internet, 175
industry research, 148
job searches
advantages/disadvantages, 176
appropriate situations, 175-176
company research, 177
narrowing searches, 176-177
newsgroups, 177
resources, 168
virtual job fairs, 177

Internet Business 500, database guide, 173

internships
project internships, 100
younger workers, 229

interviews
answering questions, 195-196
employers' needs/desires, 200
initiative, 116
production levels, 115
follow-up action
guidelines, 204-205
letters, 205-206
network contacts, calling, 206-207
phone calls, 205
recalling interviews, 203-204
short-term project proposals, 207-208
guidelines, follow-up action, 204-205
informed interviews, 114
letters, 205-206
note-taking, 198-201
essentials, 203-204
phone calls, follow-up action, 205
preparing
advantages, 195
answering questions, 195-196

background summaries, 196-197
self-promotion, 195
solutions to problems, 196
rapport, establishing, 199
rejections, 207
short-term project proposal sample, 207-208
tips, 195-196, 200-201

introverts vs. extroverts, networking, 86-87

inventories, learning styles, 54

investments, 15

job changes, younger workers, 227

job clubs, 62-63

job fairs, virtual job fairs, 177

job obsolescence, 7

job searches, 71-73
career counseling services, 67-68
benefits, 68
guidelines, 68
tips, 68
changes in guidelines, 73-75
federal programs, 67
guidelines, points to address, 78-79
managing change, 77
methods
classified ads, 59-61, 160
Internet, 175-177
phone calls, 85, 164-165
search firms, 61, 209
temporary services, 65-67
Web sites, 271-272
offers, 208-210
preparing for interviews, 195-196
rejections, 60, 165, 207
project proposals, 207-208
responsibilities, 72
self-promotion
preparing for interviews, 195
strategies, 34-36
short-term projects, 160
skills
broadening, 42
guidelines, 40-41
overspecialization, 41-42

strategies
  elderly workers, 223
  younger workers, 228-229
strengths, determining,
  37-39
timing, 7, 82
tips, 165-166, 193-194
titles/degrees, 35
transferable skills, 50-53
Web sites, 175, 271-272
workforce changes, 77-78
job titles
  job search changes, 74
  looking beyond, 105
JobBank USA Web site, 271
journalists' associations, 280,
  283

L

large companies, needs/desires,
  140
lay-offs, 103
learning projects
  continuing education, 127
  proposals, job searches,
    207-208
learning strategies, 127
  college education, 129
    advantages, 131-132
    necessity, 130-132
    tips, 132
    two-year degrees, 130-131
  flow-experiencing learning,
    120-121
  internal vs. external motiva-
    tion, 123-124
  necessity of skills, 122-123
  on-the-job training, 124
  product vendors, 128-129
  professional organizations,
    128
  self-managed learning, 127
  three-cycle learning process,
    121-122
  TV courses, 133
  volunteering, 134-135
learning styles, 53-55
Learning to Learn, 54
legal administrators' associations, 281

legal secretaries' associations,
  282
letters
  cover letter samples, 189-190
  employment, samples
    accomplishments/
      requirements, 287
    little company informa-
      tion, 292-293
    new contacts, 294-295
    single accomplishments,
      290-291
    well-researched company,
      288-289
  follow-up action, interviews,
    205-206
  networking, sample, 82-84
  samples
    accomplishments/
      requirements, 287
    follow-up action, inter-
      views, 205-206
    little company informa-
      tion, 292-293
    new contacts, 294-295
    single accomplishments,
      290-291
    well-researched company,
      288-289
librarians, job search resources,
  168-170
life insurance, 15
lifestyle products industry, 278
lower-level jobs, 260

M-N-O

machine operators, employment outlook, 275
management
  associations, 280-283
  company structure, 141-142
  positions, 116, 275
  styles, diamond-structured
    companies, 99
managing change, 77
markets
  advancements, reentering
    workforce, 263
  analyses, 171
  career planning, 23-24
  changes, 111

banking industry, 28-29
  financial planners, 28-29
  opportunities, 27-28
  retraining, necessity, 31
  seismic data brokers,
    29-30
  unmet needs, 30-31
  skills, 107-108
  skills/market gaps, 25, 108,
    142-143
    employers' needs/desires,
      139
    goals, defining, 149-150,
      152-153
    reentering the workforce,
      262-263
Matchpoint software, 134
MBA programs, 95
McBer & Company Training
  Resources Group, 54
mechanical engineers' associations, 280
media services industry
  regional growth rate, 278
medical issues
  employment outlooks,
    274-275
  health care, 280
    health aides, employment
      outlook, 274
    health services industry,
      regional growth rate,
      277
    insurance, 15
  nurses' associations, 280
meetings, networking, 88-89
metal fitters, employment
  outlook, 275
metals industry regional growth
  rate, 278
Million Dollar Directory, 169
misemployment, 5-6
mismanagement, 5, 7-9
money issues, 15-16
Monster Board Web site, 271
Myers-Briggs Type Indicator, 14,
  36

National Trade Data Bank
  database, 174
natural abilities, transferable
  skills, 49-50

needs/desires
   career planning, 23-25
   employers, 34-35
      filling, 142-143
      interviews, 200
      large companies, 140
      skills/market gaps, 139
      small companies, 141
   identifying, 11-14
      alternatives, 14-15
   offers, jobs, 209
   older workers, 217
   reentering the workforce,
      258-259
network interviewing, 13
networking, 58, 71-73
   background summaries,
      87-88
   creativity, 162-163
   federal employment pro-
      grams, 67
   fields, changing, 237-239
   friends, 58-59
   identifying key people, 82
   interview follow-up action,
      206-207
   job clubs, 62-63
   job search changes, 74
   letter samples, 82-84
   organizations, 64-65, 281
   persistence, 86
   personality types, 86-87
   phone calls, 84-86
      guidelines, 85
      note-taking, 85-86
   rejections, 84
   temporary services, 65-67
newsgroups, 177
newsletters, *Federal Career
   Opportunities*, 281
newspaper editors' associations,
   280
NEXIS database, 173
note-taking, job search techniques, 198
nurses associations', 280

obsolescence
   jobs, 7
   skills, 6, 45-46
obstacles
   bad breaks, overcoming
      in interviews, 243-244

background summaries,
   preparing, 244
phrasing on applications,
   243
rewriting resumes,
   242-243
criminal records, 241-242
   falsifying information,
      244
employers' needs/desires,
   200
job searches
   annoying perspective
      employers, 163
   company structure,
      98-100
   creative networking,
      162-163
   desperation, 163
   focus, 161
   professionalism, lack of,
      161-162
   threatening perspective
      employers, 163
overcoming
   bad breaks, 242-246
   criminal record, 241-242,
      244
   falsifying information,
      243-244
   guidelines, 242
   in interviews, 243-244
   older workers, 216-217
   phrasing on applications,
      243
   preparing bios, 244
   quitting jobs, 246
   rewriting resumes,
      242-243
   terminations, 245-246
   tips, 247
quitting jobs, 246
terminations, 245-246
Occupational Outlook Handbook,
   job search resources, 174, 274
offers, 208-210
older workers
   Access Coordinators for the
      Elderly (ACE), 218
   age discriminations, 216-217,
      311
   appropriate positions,
      219-220

Forty Plus Club of New York,
   281
needs/desires, 217
obstacles, overcoming,
   216-217
opportunities, 218-219
reasons to work, 215-216
Silver Fox Computer Club,
   219
strategies, 223
on-the-job training, 22-23
   broadening skills, 124
Online Career Center Web site,
   272
operations managers, employment outlook, 275
Organization Group (generational group), 220-221, 313
organizational structure
   managers, 141-142
   see also diamond-structured
      companies; pyramid-
      structured companies
organizations, professional
   organizations, 64-65
   see also associations
overspecialization, 41-42
overworking, 8

P

part-time jobs, 18
   job searches, 17
   reentering the workforce,
      259
pathologists' associations, 280
peak learning experiences, 38
   identifying, 53
   learning styles, 53-55
      present-oriented, 54-55
      project-oriented, 54-55
      tips, 55
   personal satisfaction,
      120-121
perception skills, transferable
   skills, 48-49
peripheral equipment operators,
   employment outlook, 275
personal satisfaction, peak
   learning experiences, 120-121
personality traits, 39, 73

personnnel departments, job search changes, 74-75
phone calls
    follow-up action, interviews, 205
    job searches, 75, 85
        samples, 164-165
    networking, 84-86
    professionalism, 162
    samples, job searches, 164-165
photographers' associations, 283
physical therapists
    associations, 280
    employment outlook, 275
planning careers, 21-23
    aptitude tests, 36-37
    considerations, 23
    goals in life, 24-25
    interpersonal relationships, 24
    markets, 23-24
    offers, 210
    professional careers, 172
    resources, 172
    skills/market gap, 25
    vocational tests, 36
    workplace changes, 22
plastics engineers' associations, 283
police officers, employment outlook, 274
precision structural metal fitters, employment outlook, 275
Predicasts F & S Index database, 174
preparing for interviews
    advantages, 195
    answering questions, 195-196
        tips, 198
    background summaries, 196-197
    self-promotion, 195
    solutions to problems, 196
priorities, 139
processed materials industry, regional growth rate, 277
product vendors, continuing education, 128-129

productivity
    employers' needs/desires, 115
    younger workers, 228
professional organizations, 64-65
    continuing education, 128
    see also associations
professional recycling, learning strategies
    flow-experiencing learning, 120-121
    internal vs. external motivation, 123-124
    necessity of skills, 122-123
    on-the-job training, 124
    three-cycle learning process, 121-122
professionalism, lack of, 161-162
profiles, 140-141
projects
    internships, 100
    project-oriented learning styles, 54-55
    proposal samples, 207-208
promoting yourself, 33
    defining yourself, 34-35
    strategies, 34-36
    strengths, determining, 37-39
public companies, 170
pyramid-structured companies, 94-95, 97
    culture, 194
    researching companies, 195

Q

Qualifications Summary
Resume sample, 306-307
questions
    answering
        former employers, 245
        tips, 195-196, 198
    asking, 198
quitting vs. terminations, 6

R

radical changes, 103
rapport, interviews, 199
rate of unemployment, displaced workers, 77
recreation industry, regional growth rate, 278
reentering the workforce
    considerations, 258
    demographics, 263
    desires, 258-259, 268
    goals, 259-260, 268
    industry growth, 264
    lower-level jobs, 260
    part-time jobs, 259
    reasons, 268
    self-employment, 264
        regional growth rate, 264-265, 267
    skills/market gaps, 262-263
    technical skills, 263
    volunteering, 259
regional growth
    industries, 276-278
    self-employment, 264-265
    table, 267
rehirings, 76
rejections
    classified ads, 60
    follow-up action, 207
        project proposals, 207-208
    networking, 84
reorganized labor, 64
researching
    companies, 61-62, 174
        considerations, 139
        culture, questions to ask, 138-139
        diamond-structured companies, 195
        Internet, 177
        large companies, 140
        profiles, 140-141
        pyramid-structured companies, 195
        resources, 170
        small companies, 141
    industries, 148
reserve skills, 131

resumes
  accomplishments, 183
  changing jobs frequently,
    rewriting resumes, 242
  company culture, 181
  cover letters, 189-190
  customizing, 182
  distributing, 180, 189
  educational background, 182
  effectiveness, 180, 188
  electronic versions, 190
  experience, 182
  falsifying information,
    183-184
  feedback, 181
  gaps in employment, 182
    younger workers, 230
  hobbies, 183
  job search changes, 74
  layout, 181
  length, 181
  personal knowledge, 180-181
  purpose, 188-190
  rewriting, 242-243
  samples, 184-188
    Career Highlights Resume,
      302-303
    Career Objective Resume,
      304-305
    chronological format, 186
    Chronological Order
      Resume, 308-309
    functional/chronological
      format, 185
    Qualifications Summary
      Resume, 306-307
    Selective Chronological
      Order Resume, 308-309
    Three Skills Resume,
      298-299
    Two Skills Resume,
      300-301
  Summary statement, 181-182
  templates, 188
retraining, 31
Riley Guide (Employment
  Opportunities and Resources
  on the Internet) Web site, 271

S

salary, industry research, 148
samples, background summaries, 87-88
  calls, job searches, 164-165
  cover letters, 189-190
  employment letters
    accomplishments/
      requirements, 287
    little company informa-
      tion, 292-293
    new contacts, 294-295
    single accomplishments,
      290-291
    well-researched company,
      288-289
  follow-up action, interviews,
    205-206
    networking letters, 82-84
  resumes, 184-188
    Career Highlights Resume,
      302-303
    Career Objective Resume,
      304-305
    Chronological Order
      Resume, 185-186,
      308-309
    Qualifications Summary
      Resume, 306-307
    Selective Chronological
      Order Resume, 308-309
    Three Skills Resume,
      298-299
    Two Skills Resume,
      300-301
satisfaction
  dissatisfaction, 3-4
    mismanagement, 7-9
    reasons, 5
    unemployment, 6-7
  misemployment, 5-6
  personal satisfaction
    flow-experiencing
      learning, 120-121
    three-cycle learning,
      121-122
scheduling meetings, networking, 88-89
search firms, 61, 209

searching for jobs, *see* job
  searches
secretaries' associations,
  282-283
Selective Chronological Order
  Resume sample, 308-309
self-assessments, identifying
  needs/values, 11-15
self-employment, 76
  growth rates, regions,
    264-265, 267
  reentering the workforce,
    264
self-managed learning, 127
self-promotion, 33
  defining yourself, 34
    employers' expectations,
      34-35
    titles/degrees, 35
  preparing for interviews, 195
  strategies, 34-36
  strengths, determining, 37
    exercises, 37-39
Service Industries USA, 172
severance packages, 16
short-term projects
  job search techniques, 160
  proposal samples, 207-208
Silent Generation, 220-221, 314
Silver Fox Computer Club, 219
skills, 39
  broadening, 42, 101, 108,
    119-120
    academic credentials, 127
    CompuSkills short-course
      school, 133
    computer skills, 253-254
    Council for Adult and
      Experiential Education,
      132
    essentials, 126
    flow-experiencing
      learning, 120-121
    internal vs. external
      learning, 123-124
    Internet, 133
    knowledge, level neces-
      sary, 126
    learning projects, 127
    necessity of learning,
      122-123
    on-the-job training, 124

professional organizations, 253
project-oriented, 54-55
three-cycle process, 121-122
TV courses, 133
volunteering, 134
younger workers, 230
career planning, 23
continuing education, 46-47
diamond-structured companies, misconceptions, 99
essentials, 126
foreign languages, 144
goals, defining, 151-152
guidelines, 40-41
hard skills, 23, 312
vs. soft skills, 40
interviewing skills, interviewers, 198-199
market/skills gaps, 25, 107-108
employers' needs/desires, 139
goals, defining, 152-153
reentering workforce, 262-263
necessity of skills, 122-123
obsolescence, 6, 45-46
overspecialization, 41-42
peak experiences, 53-55
pyramid-structured companies, misconceptions, 98
reserve skills, 131
sets, 42
sourcing, 236
strengths, determining, 37-39
technical skills, reentering the workforce, 263
testing, 36-37
three-cycle learning process, 121-122
tips, 55
transferable skills, 47-48
changing fields, 236
computer skills, 254
diamond-structured companies, 96-97
educational background, 50
employers' needs/desires, 142-143

examples, 48
exercises, 51-53
goals, defining, 151-152
job searches, 50-51
market/skills gap, 108
natural abilities, 49-50
perception skills, 48-49
vs. jobs, 107-108
see also technology
small companies, needs/desires, 141
social interaction, 24
needs/values, 13
social workers, employment outlook, 274
soft skills, 40-41
software, 134
sourcing, 236
special education teachers, employment outlook, 274
Specialty Occupational Outlook, 172
spouses, changing careers, 234
stereotypes
industries, 105-106
younger workers, 226-228
stopgap jobs, 18, 314
strengths, 40-41
aptitude tests, 36-37
determining, 37-39
overspecialization, 41-42
vocational tests, 36
Strong-Campbell Vocational Interest Inventory, 13, 36
Summary statement, resumes, 181-182

T-U-V

teaching, 274, 282
part-time, 63
technical skills, reentering the workforce, 263
technology
apprehension, 250-251
effects on industry, 107
increase, 249-250
response strategies, 251
basic knowledge, focusing on, 252-253
continuing education, 253-254

current skills, stressing, 251-252
transferable skills, 254
teaching trends, 255
telecommunications industry, 104-105
temporary services, 65-67
benefits, 66-67
federal programs, 67
growth rate, 65-66
National Association of Temporary Services, 228
terminations
overcoming obstacles, 245-246
vs. quitting, 6
tests
aptitude tests, 36-37
learning styles, 54
vocational tests, 13-14, 36
textile products industry, 277
therapy assistants, employment outlook, 275
three-cycle learning process, 121-122
Three Skills Resume sample, 298-299
timing job searches, 7, 82
titles/degrees
changes in guidelines, 74
looking beyond, 105
self-promotion, 35
younger workers, 229
tourism industry, regional growth rate, 278
trade industry, regional growth rate, 278
trailing spouse, 234
training, on-the-job, 22-23
traits, 39
transferable skills, 47-48, 109
changing fields, 236
employers' needs/desires, 142-143
examples, 48
exercises, 51-53
goals, defining, 151-152
job searches, 50-51
market/skills gap, 108
sources
educational background, 50

natural abilities, 49-50
perception skills, 48-49
technology, 254
transportation industry,
regional growth rate, 278
tuition reimbursement programs, 103
TV courses, continuing education, 133
Twenty-Something, 221
Two Skills Resume sample,
300-301
two-year degrees, 130-131
typists, employment outlook,
275

U.S. Industrial Outlook, 172
underemployment, 8
underwriters' association, 282
unemployment, 5, 6-7
coping strategies, 16-17
displaced workers, 67, 77
insurance, 16
rate, 77
*Using Government Information
Sources: Print and Electronic,
Second Edition*, 171

value
employee contributions,
112-114
employers' perceptions, 115,
117-118
initiative, 116
interest in industry,
116-117
production lever, 115
*Value Line Investment Survey and
Expanded Edition*, job search
resources, 170
values/needs
career planning, 23-24
goals in life, 24-25
identifying, 11-14
alternatives, 14-15
skills/market gaps, 25
virtual job fairs, 177
vocational tests, 13
aptitude tests, 36-37

Myers-Briggs Type Indicator,
14, 36
Strong Campbell Interest
Inventory, 36
Strong-Campbell Vocational
Interest Inventory, 13
volunteering
continuing education, 134
reentering the workforce,
259
unemployment, 17

W-X-Y-Z

Web sites, 175, 271-272
white-collar jobs, 226
women, professional organizations, 282-283
word processors, employment
outlook, 275
work groups, 13
Work Related Abstracts, job
search resources, 171
workforce
changes, 77-78
lower-level jobs, 260
part-time jobs, 259
reentering
considerations, 258
demographics, 263
desires, 258-259
goals, 259-260, 268
industry growth, 264
skill/market gaps, 262-263
technical skills, 263
self-employment, 264-265,
267
volunteering, 259
workplace
changes, 22
younger workers, 225-226
economic effects on, 102
stability, diamond-structured
companies, 97
technology
apprehension, 250-251
continuing education,
253-254
increase, 249-250
response strategies,
251-253
teaching trends, 255

Yellow Pages, 169
younger workers
changes in workplace,
225-226
climbing corporate ladders,
230
educational background, 229
flexibility, 226
gaps in employment, 230
internships, 229
productivity, 228
skills, updating, 230
stereotypes, 226-228
commitment, lack of, 227
job changes, 227
productivity, 228
strategies, 228-229
temporary services, 228
white-collar jobs, 226